THE COMMONWEALTH AND INTERNATIONAL LIBRARY

ELECTRICAL ENGINEERING DIVISION

General Editor: N. HILLER

Analog and Hybrid Computing

Analog and Hybrid Computing

BY

D. E. HYNDMAN, M.Sc.

Lecturer in Analog and Hybrid Computing
Cranfield Institute of Technology

PERGAMON PRESS

OXFORD · NEW YORK · TORONTO
SYDNEY · BRAUNSCHWEIG

Pergamon Press Ltd., Headington Hill Hall, Oxford
Pergamon Press Inc., Maxwell House, Fairview Park, Elmsford, New York 10523
Pergamon of Canada Ltd., 207 Queen's Quay West, Toronto 1
Pergamon Press (Aust.) Pty. Ltd., 19a Boundary Street, Rushcutters Bay, N.S.W. 2011, Australia
Vieweg & Sohn GmbH, Burgplatz 1, Braunschweig

First edition 1970
Library of Congress Catalog Card No. 75-120691

Printed in Great Britain by Bell & Bain Ltd., Glasgow

08 015572 3 (flexicover)
08 015573 1 (hard cover)

Contents

Preface

THE purpose of this book is to introduce students to analog and hybrid computing. As the space available is limited, the author has decided to treat in detail those parts of the subject which he feels are basic knowledge for the newcomer, and to leave the more sophisticated aspects for further study. For those students who want to probe the subject deeper, an extensive Bibliography is given at the end of the book.

It is possible to use analog computers knowing nothing about the basic principles of the computing units, but the author considers that this is a dangerous practice. It could lead to assumptions being made which would result in computational errors. This is particularly true when complex simulations involving large numbers of nonlinear computing units are carried out. It is not, however, necessary to be an expert in electronics. This book is aimed at those students who want to use analog and hybrid computers, so the description of hardware is limited to basic theory and operation, and does not include detailed circuitry.

There is a large body of opinion which has over the years been saying that analog computers can be scrapped. Claims are made that they are difficult to use and not very accurate. The author is convinced that people holding these opinions have either never used a modern analog computer, or have tried to use it to solve the wrong types of problems. The analog computer is one of the tools available to help with our scientific investigations and when a problem arises we want to use the best tool available for solving it. It is necessary to know the capabilities of the different types of computing tools and as problems arise to be able to select the best one for the job on hand.

In Chapter 1, the author has described briefly the history of computing devices leading to the present generation of analog and digital computers. With the aid of a simple example, a generalized flow diagram of computation is developed and considering how the computations could be done brings out the fundamental differences between analog and digital computers. In the last section mathematical models of some simple mechanical and electrical systems are developed. Chapter 2 gives the theory and describes the operation of the basic units found in electronic analog computers. It shows how errors can be introduced into computations and some of the ways by which they can be minimized. Practical information about typical computer hardware is also included. Problem preparation is considered in detail in Chapter 3, and methods of scaling problems for the computer are looked at, and applied to a number of examples. A large part of Chapter 4 is devoted to a description of how the computer is organized and operated. This is of necessity very generalized, and students will need to consult the manufacturer's handbook for details of how to operate a particular computer. There is a section which shows how the computer set up can be checked and a section describing output equipment. Chapter 5 continues from Chapter 3 and shows with the aid of examples how time-varying and nonlinear differential equations are solved. There are also sections describing the generation of functions of time and special nonlinear circuits. The simulation of transfer functions is an important aspect of analog computation, so the author felt that it was necessary to include Chapter 6 to cover this subject. For those readers unfamiliar with the Laplace transform, this chapter can be omitted. In Chapter 7 there is a description of some of the additional hardware available in modern computers. This gives the ability to compare voltages, make logical decisions, and hence change the problem parameters automatically. Using these units, fast iterative solutions of some boundary value and optimization problems are possible. Chapter 8 gives a brief review of hybrid computing. By comparing analog and digital computers the author has tried to show how the idea of linking them into a hybrid system originated. Some of the problems which arise in interfacing the two types of machine are considered, and there is a discussion of the types of problems which could be solved using a hybrid computer.

The author is indebted to Professor G. A. Whitfield of the Cranfield Institute of Technology for the use of computer time for setting up and plotting the results of some of the examples. He would also like to thank his wife for her patient work in typing the manuscript. Without her help, the book would never have been completed.

D.E.H.

CHAPTER 1

Introduction

THROUGHOUT the centuries man has developed many types of computing devices to help him to carry out calculations. Perhaps the earliest form of calculator was the abacus, which is still widely used. With the total acceptance of the Arabic numbering system in Europe by about the seventeenth century, the abacus became less important as the knowledge of arithmetic spread. The discovery of logarithms by John Napier at the beginning of the century was a major breakthrough, simplifying the operations of multiplication and division. This was followed by the invention of the slide rule, on which the logarithms of numbers are represented by lengths of wood which slide past each other, allowing multiplication and division to be carried out by adding and subtracting the lengths of wood. Further inventions soon followed, the first mechanical calculating machines based on the use of gear wheels appearing in the latter half of the seventeenth century, the names associated with them being Pascal and Leibnitz. These have been developed into the familiar sophisticated desk calculators of today.

The first suggestions for an automatic calculating machine were put forward by Charles Babbage in the early part of the nineteenth century. Unfortunately, he was too far ahead of his time and none of his efforts to develop an analytical engine proved successful. Many of the ideas which he put forward are, however, incorporated in the present-day digital computers. Towards the end of the century Herman Hollerith conceived the idea of using punched cards for storing and sorting information, and the type of machines developed from this idea are still in use, although rapidly being replaced by digital computers. About the same time Lord Kelvin constructed a harmonic analyser, using the ball-and-disk integrator which had been developed by his brother James Thomson. In this field the next step was by Vannevar Bush, who started work in 1927 on a differential analyser. Later models of his machine were in use until about twenty years ago.

During the Second World War many special purpose computers were developed, and with the great strides that were made in the field of electronics, the foundations were laid for the development of the present generation of computers. The first electronic digital computer called ENIAC, standing for Electronic Numerical Integrator and Calculator, was completed in 1946, and also about this time the first general purpose electronic analog computer was built. Since then, of course, developments have come thick and fast, major steps forward, particularly in the digital computing field, being a result of the development of transistors and more recently of integrated circuits.

Two types of computer have been mentioned, digital and analog, and we can perhaps get a clearer idea about why they are necessary if we consider the kind of problem which can be solved reasonably well on both types.

1.1. Types of Problem to be Solved on Computers

Probably the major requirements for automatic calculating machines have been to carry out calculations which, although not difficult, require a considerable and sometimes prohibitive number of man-hours if they are to be done manually. For this type of work time is not a variable in the problem, and the main requirement is that the calculations be carried out in a time scale to suit the person requiring the results. The requirement for solving this type of problem was the main stimulus for the development of automatic digital computers.

Another class of problem is where one of the variables is time, or can be represented by time. These problems arise in the investigation of mechanical, electrical, and chemical responses such as in aircraft, autopilot, nuclear reactor and process control systems. These are in general characterized by having differential equations describing their behaviour, and this is the type of problem with which we will be mainly concerned.

As an example, let us consider a simple mass spring damper system as illustrated in Fig. 1.1, where a mass M is suspended by a spring with stiffness K and damping coefficient D. A force F is applied to the mass, and we want to compute its displacement

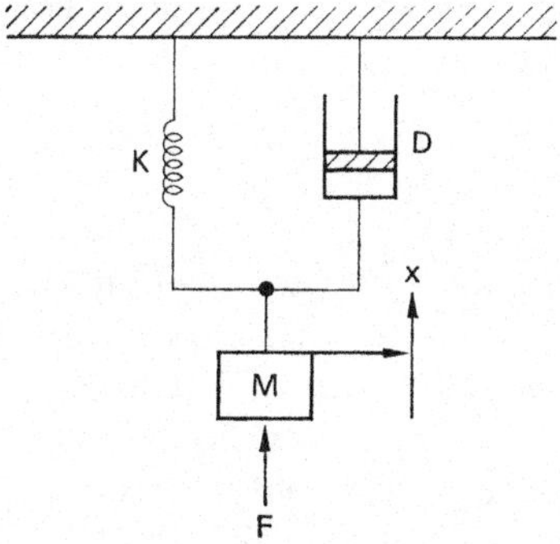

FIG. 1.1. Mass spring damper system.

x, from the initial position, as a function of time. To set up the equation of motion it is necessary to look at the forces acting on the mass. The application of the force F causes the mass to move, and as the spring is compressed or extended we get a force opposing the motion, proportional to the amount of compression or extension. There is also a damping force opposing the motion, proportional to the velocity of the mass. We therefore have the three forces acting on the mass:

$$\text{the applied force} = +F,$$

$$\text{the spring force} = -Kx,$$

$$\text{and the damping force} = -D\frac{dx}{dt}.$$

If we apply Newton's second law, which states that the mass of a body multiplied by its acceleration equals the applied force, we get

$$M\frac{d^2x}{dt^2} = F - Kx - D\frac{dx}{dt} \tag{1.1}$$

It is sometimes convenient to consider $M(d^2x/dt^2)$ as an inertia force, so that we could write equation (1.1) as a force balance equation, where the forces generated in the system oppose the applied force. Thinking about the system in this way, we would have written the equation

$$M\frac{d^2x}{dt^2} + D\frac{dx}{dt} + Kx = F \tag{1.2}$$

which is of course the same as equation (1.1). Having written down equation (1.2), it is then convenient to convert it for computing purposes to the form of equation (1.1).

The next step is to draw up a flow diagram of computations which we would have to carry out in order to solve this equation. Such a flow diagram is shown in Fig. 1.2. Starting at the left-hand

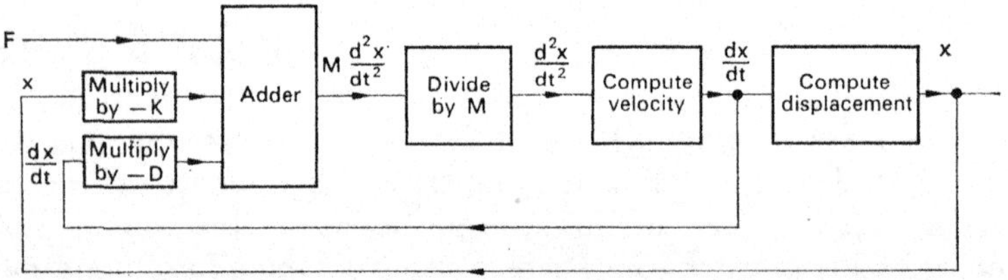

FIG. 1.2. Flow diagram of computation.

side, we have first an adding unit into which are summed the three forces appearing on the right-hand side of equation (1.1), multiplied by the appropriate constants. These are the applied force F, the spring force, dependent on the present value of x, and the damping force, dependent on the present value of dx/dt.

The output of the adder is therefore $M(d^2x/dt^2)$. Dividing this by M gives the acceleration, and the next block computes the present value of velocity which is a function of present and past values of d^2x/dt^2. The next block is similar, computing the present value of displacement x from present and past values of dx/dt. As is typical in this type of problem, the present values of dx/dt and x are fed back to provide the inputs to the adding unit. To start the problem, it is necessary to know, and set in, the initial values of x and dx/dt and apply the force F. Once the starting conditions have been established, the system will continuously compute the value of x with respect to time. If the changes in the computed x occur at the same rate as in the system being simulated, the computer is said to be operating in real time. For some systems the computed results may occur at faster or slower rates than in the physical system, in which case the computer is said to be time-scaled.

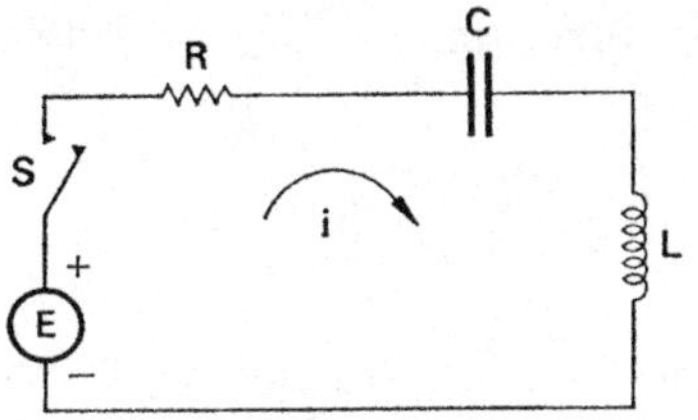

FIG. 1.3. Electrical system.

Before considering how the necessary computations could be carried out, we will derive the equations describing the behaviour of the current in the electrical system shown in Fig. 1.3. This consists of a resistor, capacitor, inductor and d.c. voltage source E, connected in series with a switch. It is required to compute the value of the current in the circuit, as a function of time, from the instant at which the switch is closed. The differential equation describing the behaviour of i can be obtained by equating the sum of the voltages across the circuit elements to the voltage source. Considering the various circuit elements we have

the voltage across $R = iR$,

the voltage across $L = L\dfrac{di}{dt}$,

and the voltage across $C = \dfrac{1}{C}\displaystyle\int_0^t i\,dt + e_0$.

e_0 is the initial voltage across C, which we will take equal to zero, and the switch is closed at time $t = 0$. Equating the sum of these voltages to the voltage source, we obtain the equation

$$L\frac{di}{dt} + iR + \frac{1}{C}\int_0^t i\,dt = E \tag{1.3}$$

If we change the dependent variable in the equation from current to the charge on the capacitor, by replacing $\int_0^t i\,dt$ by q, we obtain the equation

$$L\frac{d^2q}{dt^2} + R\frac{dq}{dt} + \frac{1}{C}q = E \tag{1.4}$$

which is the same form as equation (1.2). We could therefore use the computing circuit of Fig. 1.2, with the appropriate changes in the constants, to calculate q as a function of time. The behaviour of the current in the circuit, which is what we really want to compute, is obtained at the output in Fig. 1.2 marked velocity.

We have, therefore, a direct analogy between the behaviour of the variables in the mechanical system and those in the electrical system, and by studying the behaviour of one we could predict the behaviour of the other. As complex mechanical systems are difficult and expensive to make, it is extremely useful to be able to predict their behaviour by studying the analogous electrical network.

1.2. Computing Systems

Let us now consider the methods which could be used to carry out the necessary computations to solve equations (1.2) and (1.4). Looking at Fig. 1.2 we see that there are a number of mathematical operations to be carried out, addition, multiplication, division by constants and integration. One type of computer would consist of a collection of units capable of performing the necessary operations. To solve the problem an appropriate number of them would be connected together, in the same way as the blocks are connected in Fig. 1.2. As all the units would operate at the same time, such a computer is referred to as a simultaneous or parallel computer. Another type of computer would have only one calculating unit and this would be shared by all sections of the problem. To solve the problem, the calculating unit would carry out the calculations for each of the blocks in turn, and some form of memory would be necessary to store the results of the calculations. This type of computer is generally referred to as a sequential or serial computer.

It is now necessary to consider the type of signals which could be used to represent variables in the computers. These again can be broken into two classes, analog signals and digital signals. With analog signals the problem variable is represented by a continuously varying quantity, whereas with digital signals the variable is represented by a quantized quantity, that is a quantity which changes only in discrete steps. The two types of signal are illustrated in Fig. 1.4. In analog computers the signals will be voltages, currents, mechanical displacements, etc., and one limit on accuracy is the precision with which these can be measured. Because of the mode of operation of the computing units, accuracy is also dependent on how accurately resistors or capacitors can be made, or mechanical parts machined or constructed. In the electronic analog computer, computing unit accuracies of better than 0·01% are possible, but due to the accumulation of errors when units are interconnected, problem solution accuracies will vary from 0·1% to several %. In digital computers the quantized levels of the signal will be represented by numbers held in binary coded form, that is numbers having a radix of 2 instead of the familiar radix of 10. The advantage of the binary code is the fact that only 0 and 1 are necessary, and these can be represented in the computer by two levels of voltage, the absolute values of which are not critical. For those readers unfamiliar with the binary code, Table 1.1 shows some decimal numbers with their binary equivalents. The accuracy with which a signal is represented in the computer depends on the size of the steps from one quantization level to another, and this is a function of the number of

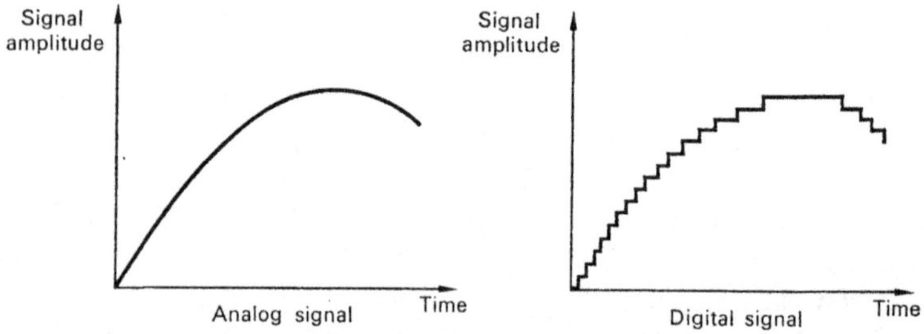

FIG. 1.4. Typical analog and digital signals.

digits in the numbers representing the levels. For a number with 7 binary digits, the least significant digit, which is equivalent to the change in quantization levels, is just less than 1% of the maximum value of the number. Increasing the number of digits to 14, the least significant one is less than 0·01% of the maximum value. If the maximum value of the number is kept the same, this is equivalent to increasing the number of decimal places. It is therefore possible, in theory, to represent a number to any required accuracy by increasing the number of digits. From what we have said in this section, it becomes clear that there are four possible types of computer, parallel or serial analog and parallel or serial digital. Of the four, the parallel analog and serial digital are the most widely used, the parallel digital to a limited extent, mainly for special purpose computers, and the serial analog hardly at all. Because of the continual decrease in the price of electronic components, particularly with the advent of integrated circuits and the future possibilities of large-scale integration, it may be that the parallel digital computer, present forms of which are known as digital differential analysers, will in the future

TABLE 1.1

Decimal number	Binary equivalent
0	0
1	1
2	10
3	11
4	100
5	101
6	110
7	111
8	1000
9	1001
10	1010
20	10100
30	11110
40	101000
50	110010
100	1100100

assume greater importance. In this book our main interest is in the parallel analog computer, but in the chapter on hybrid computing we will be looking at the combination of serial digital and parallel analog. We will therefore at this stage take a brief look at the main features of the serial digital computer.

1.3. Digital Computers

In a digital computer, the only mathematical operation that can be carried out directly is addition, but this is capable of being done at a rate of up to a million times a second. All other mathematical operations have to be broken down into formulae which only require a series of additions to be carried out. Multiplication of two numbers, say 5 and 4, essentially reduces to adding 5+5+5+5, although modern computers use a faster technique. In order to carry out a sequence of calculations, it is necessary to have a set of instructions in the computer as well as the numerical information to be manipulated. These instructions tell the computer what operations to carry out and in what sequence. To be able to operate successfully the digital computer needs five major units, an input unit, a store, an arithmetic unit, an output unit and a control unit, typically connected as shown in Fig. 1.5. The full lines are signal paths and the broken lines control

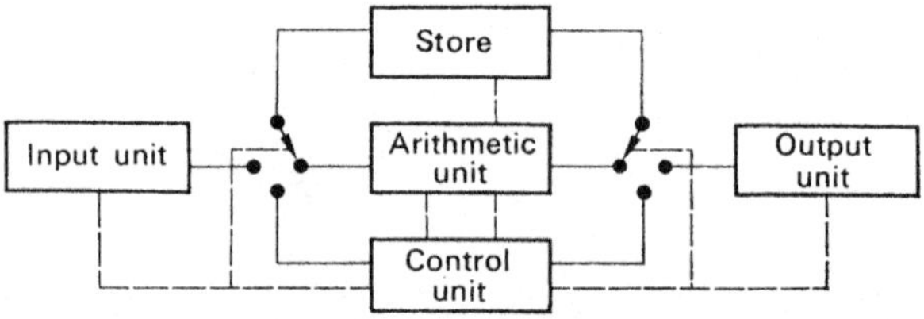

FIG. 1.5. Block diagram of general purpose digital computer.

operations. Information can be fed into the computer on punched paper tape or cards, and out of the computer on a typewriter, line printer, or graph plotter, as well as paper tape and cards. Before running a problem on the computer, it is necessary to prepare a program of instructions and information. To read this into the machine, switches on the control unit are set to connect the input equipment to the store and the instructions and information are then read from the tape or cards and put into specified locations in the store. To run the problem, the control unit is then given the address of the first instruction to be obeyed and the start button is pressed. The instructions are then fed in sequence from the store into the control unit. This calls information from the store to the arithmetic unit for processing, and then sends the results to the store for further processing at a later time, or to the output equipment. Although the computer operates at a very high speed, some complex calculations, where a large number of operations have to be carried out, may take quite a long time.

A program to solve the second order differential equation for the mass spring damper system or the electrical system would evaluate the output of each of the blocks of Fig. 1.2 in turn. The program would start with the two blocks at the left-hand side, and the results of each calculation would be stored for future use. For the first evaluation of the output of the blocks, the given initial values of x and dx/dt are used as input quantities, and on succeeding evaluations the most recently calculated values are taken. Each of the quantities can be updated only once per series of calculations, and the amount of time required for each series fixes the length of step along the time axis. If this step is so large that the number of points calculated on the output graph per cycle of the solution is very small, it will be necessary to reduce the step size. As the speed of the computer is limited this can only be done by time scaling the solution so that it is obtained in a time much greater than real time.

1.4. Examples of System Mathematical Models

In this section we will consider some typical mechanical and electrical systems, and derive differential equations describing the behaviour of variables in the systems.

Systems described by first order linear ordinary differential equations. Examples of these are shown in Fig. 1.6. For the

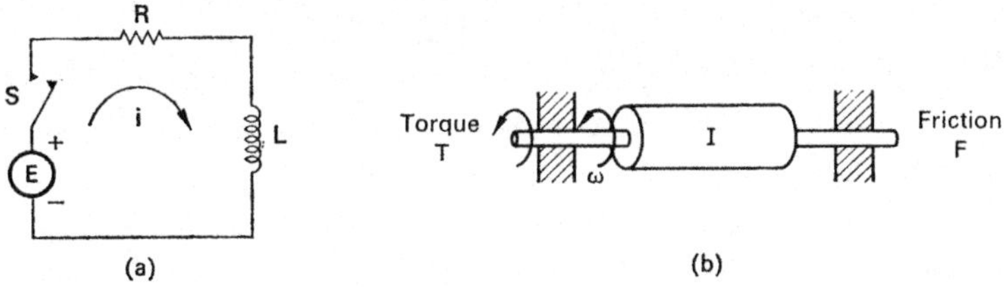

FIG. 1.6. Systems described by first order linear differential equations.

electrical system of Fig. 1.6(a), if we equate the voltages in the circuit after the switch is closed, we obtain the equation

$$L\frac{di}{dt}+iR = E \tag{1.5}$$

In the mechanical system of Fig. 1.6(b) a torque T is applied to the rotating mass, with inertia I and bearing friction F, causing it to rotate at ω radians per second. If we use the concept of inertia force and equate forces in the system we obtain the equation

$$I\frac{d\omega}{dt}+F\omega = T \tag{1.6}$$

Systems with two degrees of freedom. For the system of Fig. 1.7, we can obtain the equations of motion by considering the forces

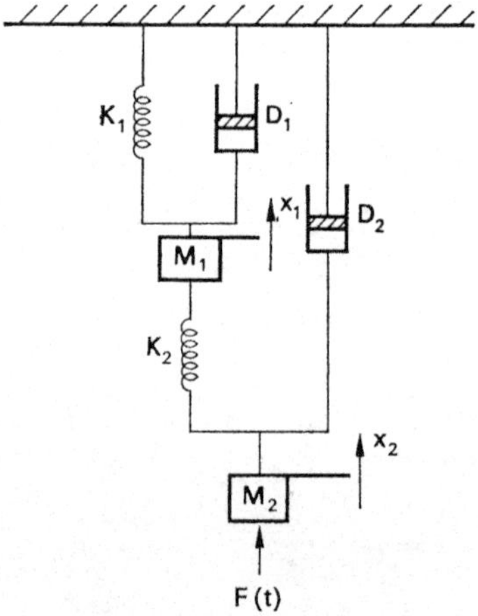

FIG. 1.7. Mechanical system with two degrees of freedom

acting on each mass. The mass M_1 has forces due to the springs K_1, K_2 and the damper D_1, and mass M_2 has forces due to the spring K_2, the damper D_2 and the applied force $F(t)$. Equating the forces acting on each mass, we get the following equations:

$$M_1 \frac{d^2x_1}{dt^2} + D_1 \frac{dx_1}{dt} + K_1x_1 + K_2(x_1 - x_2) = 0 \tag{1.7}$$

and

$$M_2 \frac{d^2x_2}{dt^2} + D_2 \frac{dx_2}{dt} + K_2(x_2 - x_1) = F(t) \tag{1.8}$$

If we wanted to compute the behaviour of x_1 resulting from the application of $F(t)$ to the system, we could eliminate the variable x_2 and obtain a fourth order differential equation for x_1. There is, however, no advantage in doing this, and if we are going to solve the equations on a simultaneous type of computer it is in fact an advantage to retain the system equations in their simplest form.

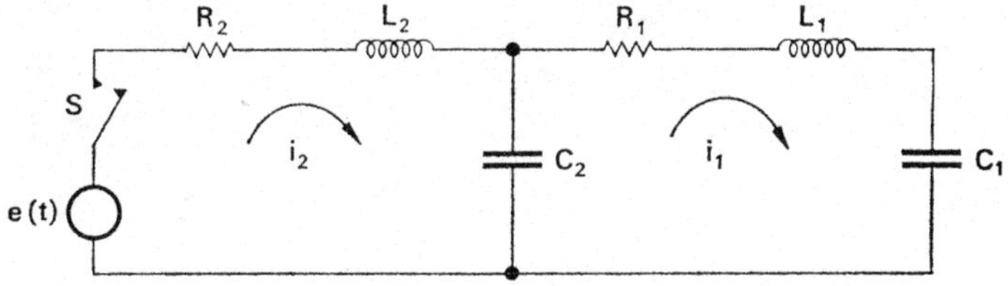

FIG. 1.8. Electrical system with two degrees of freedom.

Again, we can consider an analogous electrical network as shown in Fig. 1.8. Equating voltages in the two loops, after switch S is closed we obtain the equations

$$L_1 \frac{di_1}{dt} + R_1 i_1 + \frac{1}{C_1} \int_0^t i_1 dt + \frac{1}{C_2} \int_0^t (i_1 - i_2)\, dt = 0 \tag{1.9}$$

and

$$L_2 \frac{di_2}{dt} + R_2 i_2 + \frac{1}{C_2} \int_0^t (i_2 - i_1)\, dt = e(t) \tag{1.10}$$

for the case where the initial voltages on the capacitors are zero. If these equations were written in terms of the charges on the capacitors C_1 and C_2 they would be converted into the same form as those for the mechanical system.

For any mechanical system consisting of a number of masses interconnected by springs and dampers, or electrical system consisting of capacitors interconnected by resistors and inductors, we can obtain a set of second order linear differential equations, one for each mass or capacitance in the system.

CHAPTER 2

Theory and Operation of the Basic Units of an Electronic Analog Computer

THIS chapter will show how the generalized computing units introduced in Chapter 1 are realized in the electronic analog computer. The various units can be classified into two groups, those which are linear in operation such as summers, inverters, integrators and constant multipliers and those which are nonlinear such as multipliers and function generators.

2.1. The Operational Amplifier

This is the fundamental unit in the electronic analog computer, and as it is necessary to be able to amplify signals over a band of frequencies from d.c. upwards, a direct coupled amplifier is used. An idealized operational amplifier would have the following specification:

Infinite gain at all frequencies.

Zero phase shift at all frequencies.

Infinite input impedance.

Zero output impedance.

Output voltage zero for zero input voltage.

No noise signals generated in the amplifier.

As the amplifier will always be operating with negative feedback, there will be inversion of the signal between the input and output.

It is not possible to build an amplifier with this ideal specification, but it can be approximated over a range of frequencies. In this range, the errors in computation due to the amplifier are small in comparison to those introduced from other sources.

The change from valve to transistor amplifiers, in precision analog computers, did not take place generally until about 1964 for several reasons. Valve amplifiers were very good, reliable and inexpensive, and early transistor amplifiers were complex, expensive and with lower performance due to limitations of the early types of transistors. About 1964 the picture changed, with the availability of better and cheaper transistors. These gave improved performance, and largely eliminated the price differential between the two types of amplifier. A typical modern 100 V transistor amplifier specification is as follows:

Gain at d.c. between 10^7 and 10^8 falling to between 10^4 and 10^5 at around 1 Hz, staying constant to about 100 Hz, and thereafter decreasing linearily with frequency at 20 db per decade to give a gain bandwidth product between 1 MHz and 2 MHz.

Phase shift at 100 Hz about 0·001°.

Input impedance at d.c. about 1 MΩ.

Output impedance less than 100 Ω.

Output voltage adjustable to zero with zero input, but with drift referred to input of 1 μV per week at constant temperature.

Noise generated in the amplifier, referred to the input, of less than 20 μV R.M.S.

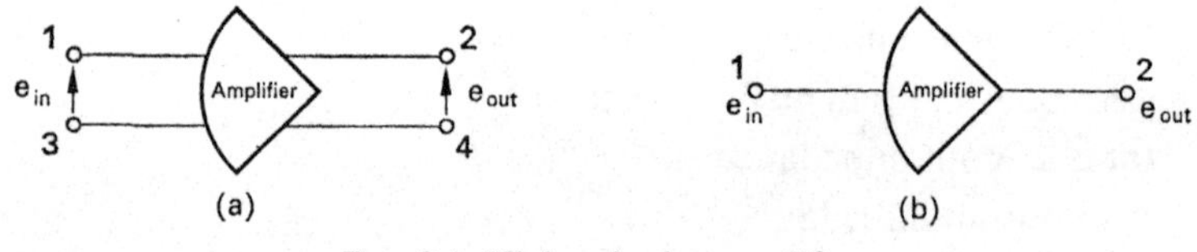

FIG. 2.1. High gain d.c. amplifier.

An amplifier is a four-terminal device as shown in Fig. 2.1(a), but as terminals 3 and 4 are common and generally connected to ground potential, they are omitted from diagrams, and the amplifier is drawn as in Fig. 2.1(b).

2.2. Linear Computing Units

Summation, multiplication by a constant, and integration with respect to time of voltages, can be carried out using an operational amplifier, if appropriate resistors and capacitors are connected to it as feedback and input elements.

Summation, multiplication by a constant and sign inversion. For these operations the operational amplifier is set up as shown in Fig. 2.2, with a resistor R_0 as the feedback element, and the input connected by resistors $R_1, R_2, \ldots, R_n$ to corresponding voltage sources $e_1, e_2, \ldots, e_n$. Consider the specification of the amplifier as being ideal except for the gain which we will take equal to $-k$.

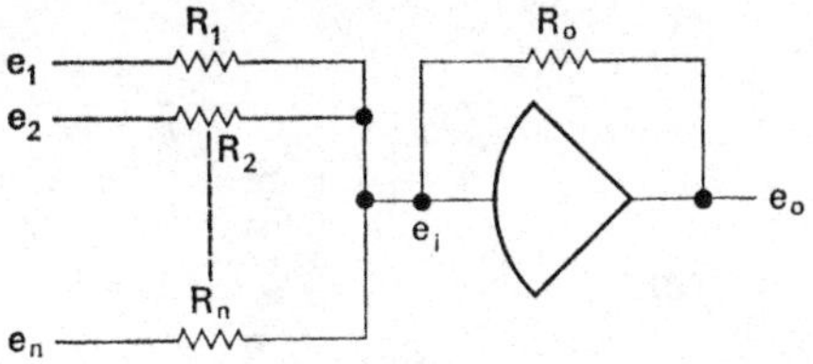

FIG. 2.2. Summing unit.

If the amplifier has infinite input impedance, no current flows into it, and therefore the sum of the currents in the resistors $R_1, R_2, \ldots, R_n$ must equal the current in the feedback resistor R_0. If the voltage at the input of the amplifier, which is generally referred to as the summing junction, is e_i, then equating the currents in the resistors $R_0, R_1, \ldots, R_n$ using Ohm's law, we get

$$\left[\frac{e_1-e_i}{R_1}\right]+\left[\frac{e_2-e_i}{R_2}\right]+\ldots+\left[\frac{e_n-e_i}{R_n}\right]=\left[\frac{e_i-e_0}{R_0}\right] \quad (2.1)$$

Now

$$e_0 = -ke_i \quad (2.2)$$

Giving

$$e_i = -\frac{e_0}{k} \quad (2.3)$$

Substituting this in equation (2.1) gives

$$\frac{1}{R_1}\left[e_1+\frac{e_0}{k}\right]+\frac{1}{R_2}\left[e_2+\frac{e_0}{k}\right]+\ldots+\frac{1}{R_n}\left[e_n+\frac{e_0}{k}\right] = -\frac{1}{R_0}\left[e_0+\frac{e_0}{k}\right] \tag{2.4}$$

By bringing all the terms in e_0 to the left-hand side, we get

$$e_0\left[\frac{1}{R_0}+\frac{1}{k}\left(\frac{1}{R_0}+\frac{1}{R_1}+\ldots+\frac{1}{R_n}\right)\right] = -\left[\frac{e_1}{R_1}+\frac{e_2}{R_2}+\ldots+\frac{e_n}{R_n}\right] \tag{2.5}$$

from which we obtain the expression

$$e_0 = -\left[\frac{R_0}{R_1}e_1+\frac{R_0}{R_2}e_2+\ldots+\frac{R_0}{R_n}e_n\right]\times$$

$$\times\left[\frac{1}{1+\frac{1}{k}\left(1+\frac{R_0}{R_1}+\frac{R_0}{R_2}+\ldots+\frac{R_0}{R_n}\right)}\right] \tag{2.6}$$

If k is large, the term

$$\frac{1}{k}\left(1+\frac{R_0}{R_1}+\ldots\frac{R_0}{R_n}\right)$$

in equation (2.6) tends to zero and can be neglected. This results in an expression

$$e_0 = -\left[\frac{R_0}{R_1}e_1+\frac{R_0}{R_2}e_2+\ldots+\frac{R_0}{R_n}e_n\right] \tag{2.7}$$

which is dependent only on the input voltages $e_1, e_2, \ldots, e_n$ and the values of the resistors $R_1, R_2, \ldots, R_n$. From this expression we see that with an amplifier set up as in Fig. 2.2, we can carry out the operations of summation, multiplication by a constant, and sign inversion.

Generally in commercial computers the amplifiers which are assigned for summation will have two values of resistors associated with them, 100 kΩ and 1 MΩ in 100 V computers, and 10 kΩ and 100 kΩ in 10 V computers. These are arranged as shown in

Fig. 2.3, and depending on which value of feedback resistor is selected, gains of 1 and 0·1, or 10 and 1 are obtainable. The number of input resistors available, between 4 and 8, will depend on the size of the computer.

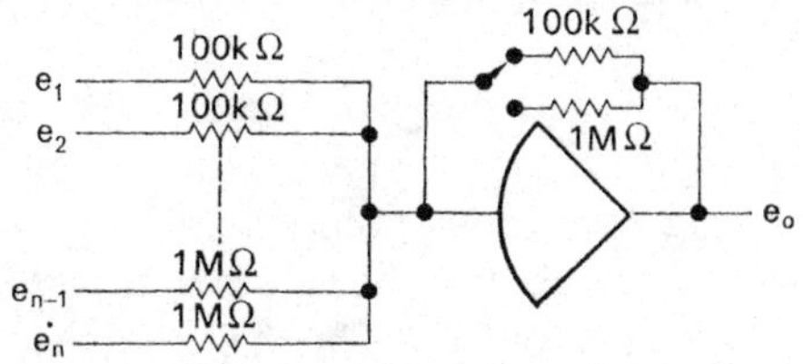

FIG. 2.3. Summing unit in 100 V computer showing typical resistor values.

Because it is often necessary to carry out the operation of sign inversion, a number of amplifiers are assigned as unity gain inverters with only one input resistor. This cuts down on resistors which are expensive and saves patch panel space.

Let us examine the validity of the statement that the term

$$\frac{1}{k}\left(1+\frac{R_0}{R_1}+\ldots+\frac{R_0}{R_n}\right)$$

in equation (2.6) can be neglected. The error in neglecting it is the difference between the right-hand sides of equations (2.6) and (2.7) which is

$$\left[\frac{R_0}{R_1}e_1+\frac{R_0}{R_2}e_2+\ldots+\frac{R_0}{R_n}e_n\right]\left[1-\frac{1}{1+\frac{1}{k}\left(1+\frac{R_0}{R_1}+\ldots+\frac{R_0}{R_n}\right)}\right] \tag{2.8}$$

Expressing this as a percentage of the required value of e_0 given by equation (2.7), we get

$$\text{the percentage error} = \frac{\frac{100}{k}\left(1+\frac{R_0}{R_1}+\ldots+\frac{R_0}{R_n}\right)}{1+\frac{1}{k}\left(1+\frac{R_0}{R_1}+\ldots+\frac{R_0}{R_n}\right)} \tag{2.9}$$

In a computation, the worst error would occur in a summer where all inputs are being used at their highest gain. For the case of an eight input summer, four gains of 10 and four gains of 1, the factor inside the brackets of equation (2.9) would be 45. For frequencies below 1 Hz where the amplifier gain is greater than 10^7, the error in e_0 is less than 0·00045%.

Summing amplifier accuracy is limited by the resistors, which are difficult and expensive to obtain with tolerances better than 0·01%. By putting low value potentiometers in series with the resistors, it is possible to adjust the values so that the ratios R_0/R_1, etc., are accurate to about 0·002%. To minimize the effects of temperature change, the resistors in the larger computers are kept in temperature stabilized enclosures.

The effects of finite amplifier gain become more important at frequencies above 1 Hz where the gain is decreasing. For the case of the eight input summer, there is an error of about 1% when the amplifier gain falls to 5000.

Integration. To operate as an integrator, an operational amplifier is set up as shown in Fig. 2.4, with a capacitor C as the feedback element,

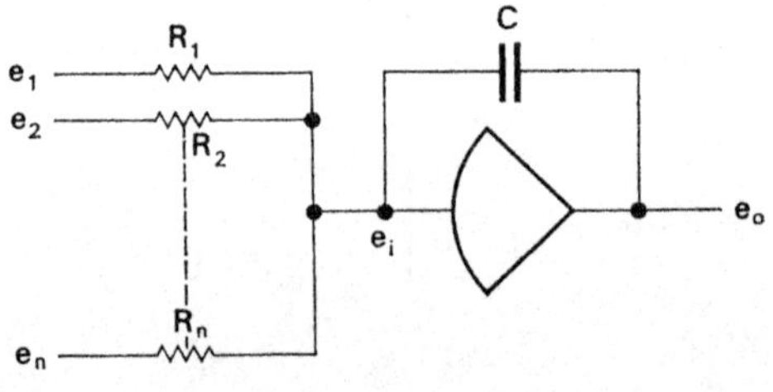

FIG. 2.4. Integrator unit.

back element, and a number of input resistors R_1 to R_n connected to voltage sources e_1 to e_n in the same way as for the summing unit. Again consider the specification of the amplifier as being ideal except for the gain, which will be taken as $-k$. As before, we can equate the sum of the currents in the input resistors with that in the feedback element. The current which flows in a capacitor depends on the rate of change of the voltage across the capacitor, and the value of the capacitor, and is given by $i = C(de/dt)$, where C is the value of the capacitor in farads and e is the voltage across it. For the integrator unit therefore

$$\left[\frac{e_1-e_i}{R_1}\right]+\left[\frac{e_2-e_i}{R_2}\right]+\ldots+\left[\frac{e_n-e_i}{R_n}\right] = C\frac{d}{dt}[e_i-e_0] \qquad (2.10)$$

Therefore, substituting $-(e_0/k)$ for e_i we get

$$\frac{1}{R_1}\left[e_1+\frac{e_0}{k}\right]+\frac{1}{R_2}\left[e_2+\frac{e_0}{k}\right]+\ldots+\frac{1}{R_n}\left[e_n+\frac{e_0}{k}\right] = -C\frac{d}{dt}\left[e_0\left(\frac{k+1}{k}\right)\right] \qquad (2.11)$$

Integrating both sides of equation (2.11) with respect to time and dividing through by $C[(k+1)/k]$ gives

$$e_0 = -\frac{k}{k+1}\left[\frac{1}{CR_1}\int_0^t\left(e_1+\frac{e_0}{k}\right)dt+\frac{1}{CR_2}\int_0^t\left(e_2+\frac{e_0}{k}\right)dt+\ldots+\frac{1}{CR_n}\int_0^t\left(e_n+\frac{e_0}{k}\right)dt-e_0|_{t=0}\right] \qquad (2.12)$$

where integration is assumed to start at time $t = 0$ and $e_0|_{t=0}$ is the value of e_0 at time $t = 0$. When k is very large $k/(k+1)$ tends to 1 and e_0/k tends to 0, therefore, to a close approximation, we can write equation (2.12):

$$e_0 = -\left[\frac{1}{CR_1}\int_0^t e_1\,dt+\frac{1}{CR_2}\int_0^t e_2\,dt+\ldots+\frac{1}{CR_n}\int_0^t e_n\,dt-e_0|_{t=0}\right] \qquad (2.13)$$

For the case where $CR_1 = CR_2 = \ldots = CR_n = 1$ and $e_0|_{t=0} = 0$, the amplifier output voltage is seen to equal minus the sum of the integrals, with respect to time, of the input voltages e_1 to e_n. The effect of different values of the time constants CR_1, CR_2, etc., is to introduce gain factors into the expression. The use of gain factors is dealt with in detail in Chapter 3.

To ensure that the integrator starts computing with the correct initial condition voltage, and to control its operations, special switching circuits are required. These are described in Chapter 4.

The amplifiers which are assigned for integration will have fixed components associated with them. The resistor values will be the same as in the summing unit 100 kΩ and 1 MΩ in 100 V computers, and 10 kΩ and 100 kΩ in 10 V computers. The selection of capacitors available will depend on the computer, but in general there will be four, 1 μF, 0·1 μF, 0·01 μF and 0·001 μF in a 100 V computer, and 10 μF, 1 μF, 0·1 μF and 0·01 μF in a 10 V computer. In conjunction with the input resistors, this gives a range of integrator gains 1, 10, 100, 1000, 10,000. Of course, for any particular value of feedback capacitor only two of these are available.

The error in e_0 due to the finite value of k is more difficult to calculate for the integrator unit than for the summing unit. However, if we look at equation (2.12), it is obvious that at low frequencies, where k is greater than 10^7, the maximum value of e_0/k in a 100 V computer is 10^{-5} V. This is a negligable percentage of the voltages e_1 to e_n which will always be arranged to have a maximum value approaching 100 V. The attenuation introduced by the factor $k/(k+1)$ will be too small to be measured.

The limitation on accuracy is imposed by the tolerances of the resistors and capacitors. Capacitors are difficult to manufacture to close tolerances, and it is necessary to use trimmers to adjust to the required accuracy. Because of temperature coefficient effects and leakage resistance, 0·01% is effectively the best that can be obtained, and to maintain this requires adjustment every few months.

Another factor which can affect the accuracy of integrators is the amount of leakage current into the amplifier input. This causes an insignificant error in summing amplifiers, but as the effect in integrators is one that increases with time, over a long period significant errors can build up. The leakage current causes an error current in the feedback capacitor, resulting in an error voltage. The value of this voltage is

$$e = \frac{1}{C}\int_0^t i\,dt,$$

if the initial voltage across the capacitor is zero, where C is the value of the capacitor in farads and i is the leakage current in amps.

If i is a constant, $e = it/C$.

For the case where the leakage current is 10^{-10} A and $C = 1\ \mu$F,

$$e = \frac{10^{-10}t}{10^{-6}} = 100t\ \mu\text{V},$$

i.e. the error voltage will increase at 100 μV/sec.

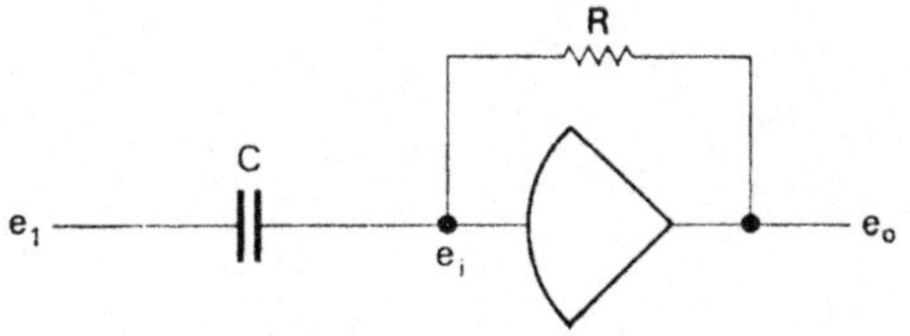

FIG. 2.5. Differentiator unit.

Differentiation. In theory this is possible using an operational amplifier set up as in Fig. 2.5, with a resistor R as feedback element and capacitor C as the input element. Equating currents in the input and feedback elements as before

$$C\frac{d}{dt}(e_1 - e_i) = \frac{e_i - e_0}{R} \tag{2.14}$$

$$e_i = -\frac{e_0}{k}$$

and with k large tends to zero.

Therefore

$$e_0 \text{ tends to } CR\frac{d}{dt}(e_1).$$

However, practical difficulties arise. The loading effect of the capacitor C when connected to the output of another amplifier decreases its stability. Also, any noise on e_1 is amplified more than the signal, because at higher frequencies the impedance of C is low. This causes e_0 to have a poor signal-to-noise ratio. Because of these difficulties, differentiators are very rarely used in analog computers. When differentiation is absolutely necessary, an approximate relationship is used, such as that given by the circuit of Fig. 2.6. This can be shown to approximate to differentiation over a band of frequencies, the upper frequency limit being determined by the $1/CR_1$ value.

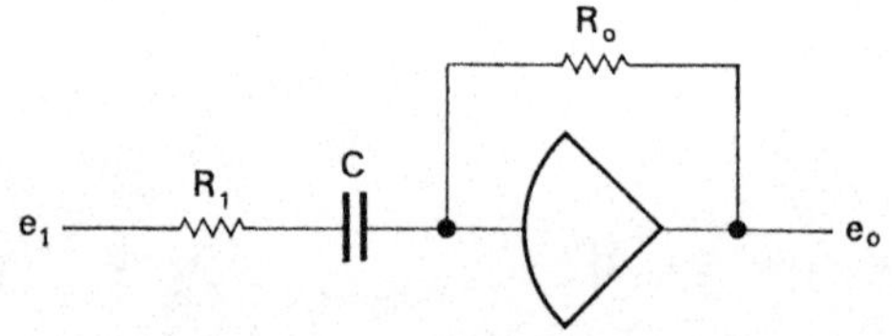

FIG. 2.6. Approximate differentiation circuit.

Multiplication by constants less than unity. As the summing and integrating units have a limited range of fixed gains, it is necessary to have another unit with continuous variation of gain from 0 to 1. This, when combined with the fixed gains in the summers and integrators, allows infinite variation of gain in the range from 0 to the maximum available. Generally potentiometers, as shown in Fig. 2.7, are used to achieve this. Some modern computers

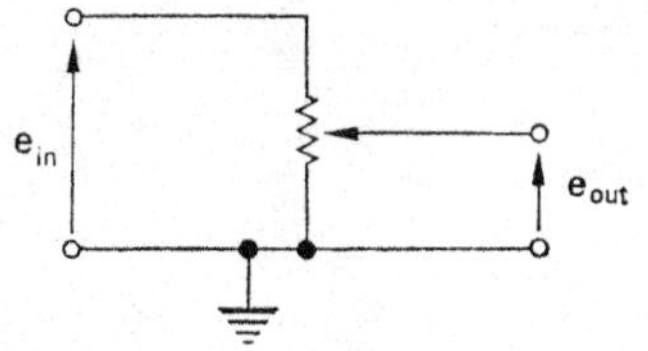

FIG. 2.7. Potentiometer.

designed for hybrid operation have optional attenuator networks available, which can be easily and quickly set up by a digital computer, and have much less phase shift than potentiometers. Potentiometers generally have one end connected to ground potential, so they can, like amplifiers, be shown as two terminal devices as in Fig. 2.8.

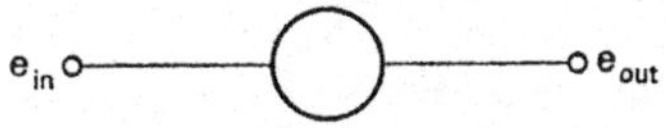

FIG. 2.8. Potentiometer symbol.

Consider the circuits shown in Fig. 2.9. If the total resistance of the potentiometer is R and the loading effect of R_1 on the potentiometer is ignored, then for the summing unit of Fig. 2.9(a)

$$e_0 = -\alpha \frac{R_0}{R_1} e_1 \tag{2.15}$$

and for the integrator of Fig. 2.9(b)

$$e_0 = -\frac{\alpha}{CR_1} \int_0^t e_1 dt + e_0|_{t=0} \tag{2.16}$$

where α can be set to any value between 0 and 1. The method of setting the value of α, which will be described in Chapter 4, allows for the loading effect of R_1 on R. The accuracy with which α can be set depends on the type of potentiometer used, and the method of setting. Ten-turn wirewound potentiometers are generally used, and these can be set to an accuracy of better than 0·01%.

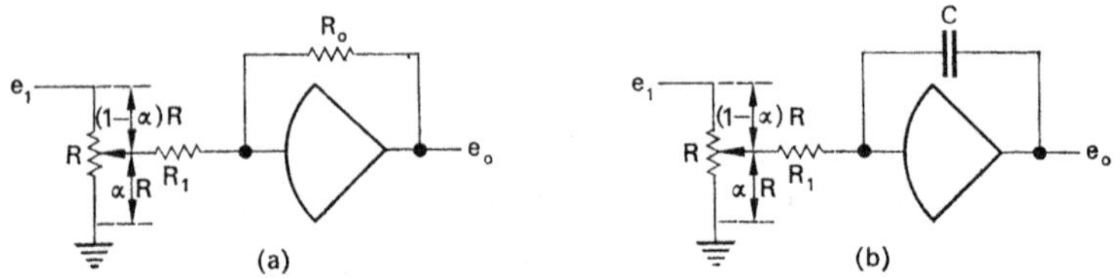

FIG. 2.9. Potentiometers associated with (a) summing unit, (b) integrator unit.

2.3. Nonlinear Computing Units

In the previous sections we showed how the operational amplifier, combined with linear passive electrical elements, could be used to perform basic mathematical operations. By the use of nonlinear passive elements or active elements such as diodes and transistors, combined with operational amplifiers, we can generate nonlinear functions and carry out multiplication of variables. This extends considerably the usefulness of the computer.

Servo-driven function generators. Consider the case where we want to generate a voltage y which is a function of the voltage x, as shown in Fig. 2.10. Using a servomechanism, Fig. 2.11, the voltage x is converted into a shaft rotation. This is used to position the wipers of a number of nonlinear or tapped potentiometers, so that the distance along the potentiometer winding is proportional to the value of x. For the case of a tapped potentiometer, the taps, which correspond to values of x: x_0, x_1, x_2, x_3, x_4, x_5, x_6, x_7, and x_8, are connected to corresponding voltage

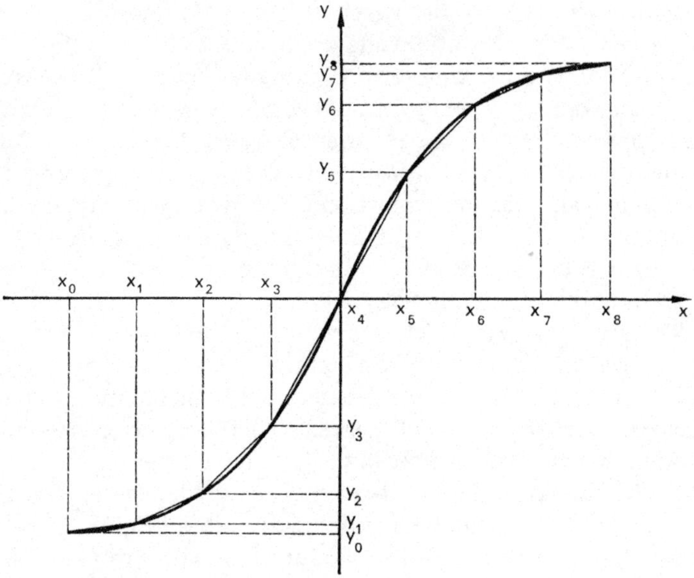

FIG. 2.10. Nonlinear function with straight line approximation.

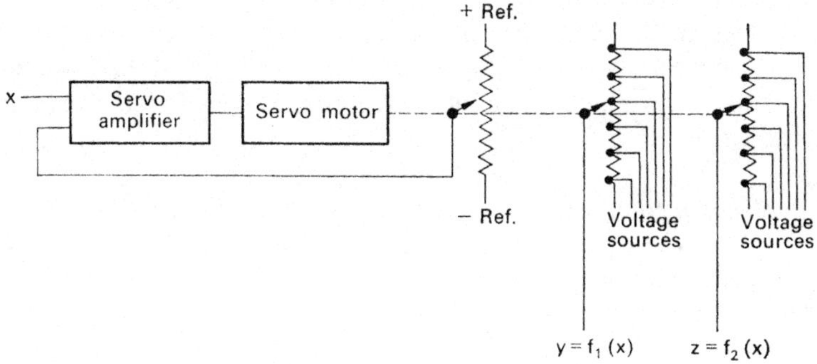

FIG. 2.11. Servo-driven function generator.

sources y_0 to y_8. As the wiper of the potentiometer traverses between taps, it picks off a voltage which is a linear interpolation between the two flanking taps. Plotting the output voltage from the potentiometer wiper against the voltage x, we obtain a straight line approximation to the required curve as shown in Fig. 2.10. Using this technique it is possible to generate an approximation to almost any required function, provided there are no discontinuities. Also, the maximum slope must not require voltage gradients between taps which will cause excessive current to flow in sections of the potentiometer.

The accuracy with which a function can be generated depends on the number of taps on the potentiometer and the slope of the function curve. A disadvantage with tapped potentiometers is that the taps are normally equally spaced so that large errors can occur where the radius of curvature of the function is small.

For functions which are frequently required, such as sine and cosine, specially wound potentiometers are available having a resistance law proportional to the function. These can be wound to close tolerance, allowing accurate generation of these functions. As the servomechanism is expensive, a number of potentiometers are normally connected to the shaft, some of which will be linear for multiplication of x by other variables. Multiplication will be described in a later section.

As the servomechanism will only work at low frequencies this imposes a limitation on the time scale of the computer solution. For this reason and because of the availability of cheaper and more accurate means of function generation, present day general purpose computers do not include servo-driven function generators.

Diode function generators. These are based on the approximation of diode action to that of a switch. Consider a diode as shown in Fig. 2.12(a), with a voltage e across it and current i flowing in it. The voltage/current relationship is shown in Fig. 2.12(b). If e is positive, and greater than about 0·5 V for a silicon diode, current flows, and when e is negative the reverse current is negligibly small. The diode approximates a switch with a small closed resistance, which is nonlinear at low voltage levels, and a finite off resistance. However, for the purpose of function generation, this is a good enough approximation and the nonlinear resistance at low voltage levels can be an advantage.

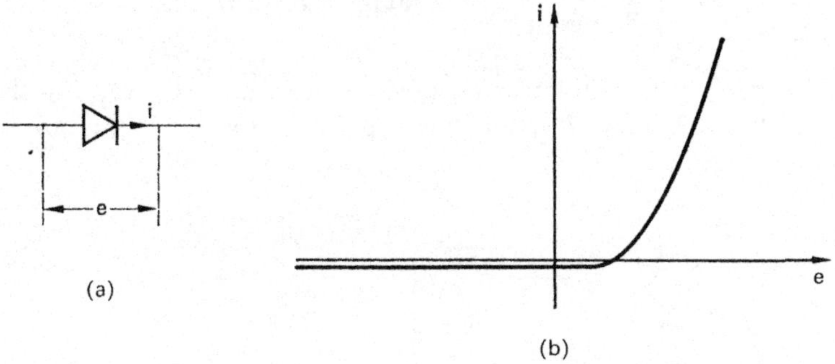

FIG. 2.12. (a) Solid state diode. (b) Diode characteristic.

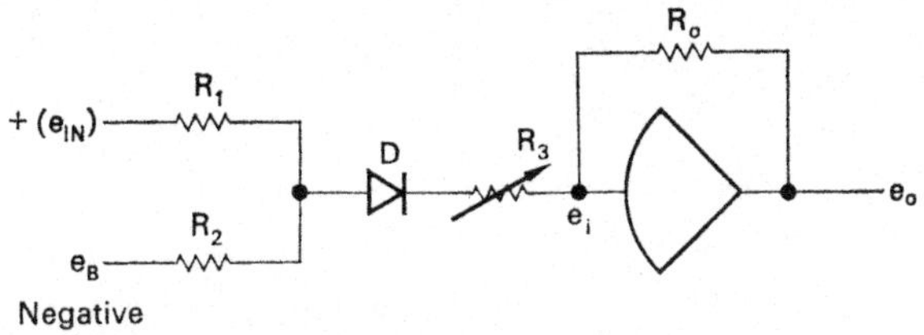

FIG. 2.13. Basic circuit for diode function generator.

The basic circuit used is shown in Fig. 2.13. Because of the high amplifier gain the voltage e_i is negligibly small, and for all practical purposes the amplifier input can be considered as being at earth potential. It is in fact often referred to as a virtual earth point. For the case where $R_1 = R_2$, when e_{IN} is less than e_B the diode D is biased off by the negative voltage at the junction of R_1 and R_2. No current can flow through it, apart from the negligibly small reverse current, and the voltage e_0 is zero. If e_{IN} is greater than e_B, the voltage at the junction of R_1 and R_2 becomes positive, and the diode D starts to conduct. We therefore get an output voltage as shown in Fig. 2.14, which is negative and has a value

$$e_0 = -\left[\frac{R_0}{R_D+R_3}\right] \text{[voltage at junction of } R_1 \text{ and } R_2\text{]} \quad (2.17)$$

where R_D is the forward resistance of the diode. By varying the values of R_1 and R_2, the break point in the e_0 curve can be

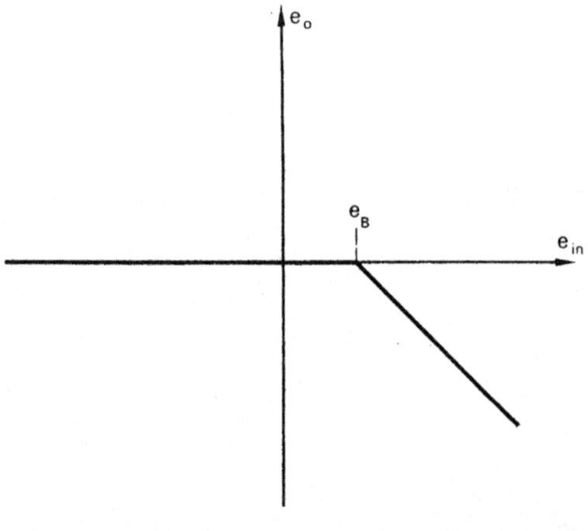

FIG. 2.14. Basic diode circuit characteristic.

moved along the e_{IN} axis. It is difficult to calculate accurate values for R_1, R_2, and R_3 because of the wide variations in the characteristics of any particular type of diode. In a variable function generator R_2 and R_3 are generally potentiometers, with switched series resistors. The segment is set up by adjusting R_2 so that the breakpoint occurs at the correct value of e_{IN} and R_3 to give the correct slope.

By selecting the sign of e_{IN} and e_B and the direction of the diode D, the part of the e_0 curve where D is conducting can be made to fall in any of the four quadrants of $\pm e_{IN}$, $\pm e_0$. In Fig. 2.15(a) we have the case already described, giving a segment in the fourth quadrant. In Fig. 2.15(b) where e_{IN} is inverted before being connected to the diode section, the diode will conduct when e_{IN} is negative and large enough so that $-(e_{IN})$ is positive and overcomes the negative bias. The output e_0 will be negative, giving a segment in the third quadrant. In Fig. 2.15(c)

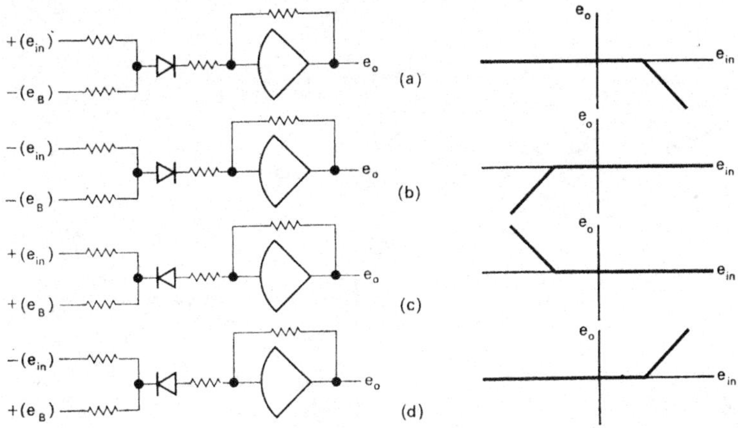

FIG. 2.15. Diode circuit configurations with their output characteristics.

and (d) the diode is reversed, and the sign of the bias voltage changed. The voltage e_{IN} is applied directly in Fig. 2.15(c) so that the diode conducts when e_{IN} is large enough negative to overcome the positive bias, and the output is positive giving a segment in the second quadrant. In Fig. 2.15(d) e_{IN} is inverted before being applied to the diode section. This results in the diode conducting when e_{IN} is positive, and as $-(e_{IN})$ is negative e_0 will be positive, giving a segment in the first quadrant.

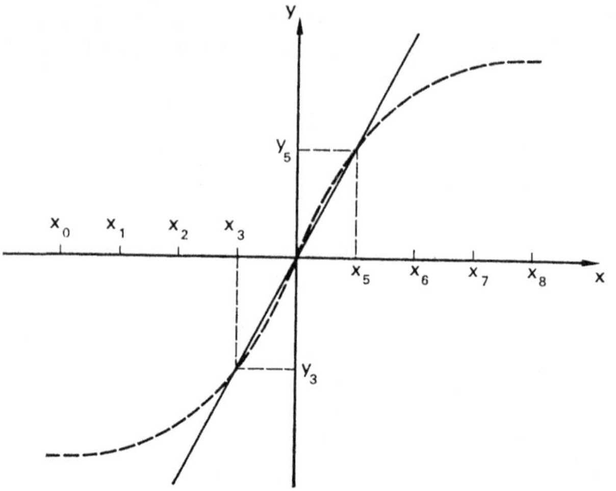

FIG. 2.16. Nonlinear function with linear section approximation to the region between x_3 and x_5.

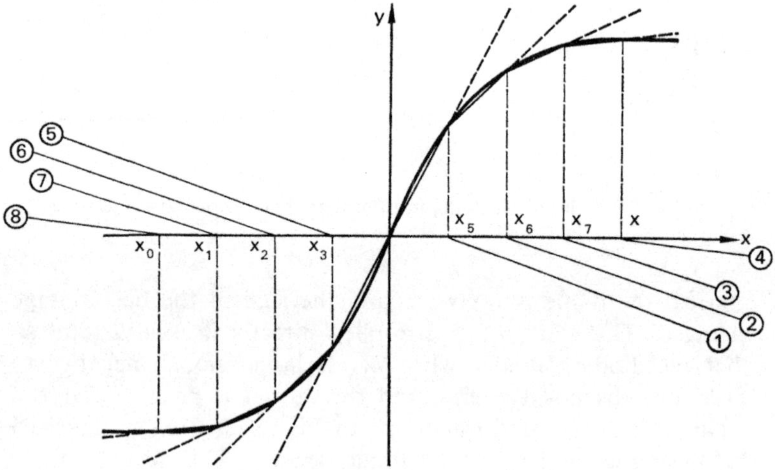

FIG. 2.17. Nonlinear function with straight line diode section approximation.

Let us now see how diode sections can be combined to generate an approximation to the curve of Fig. 2.10. The portion of the curve between x_3 and x_5 can be generated using a linear segment, that is one with no diode, where $y = +kx$. With just this segment we would of course get the linear relationship of Fig. 2.16 between y and x, where the broken line is the actual curve we wish to generate. If we add some diode sections at the input of the amplifier, as shown in the circuit of Fig. 2.18, we can build up an approximation to the curve as illustrated in Fig. 2.17. For this

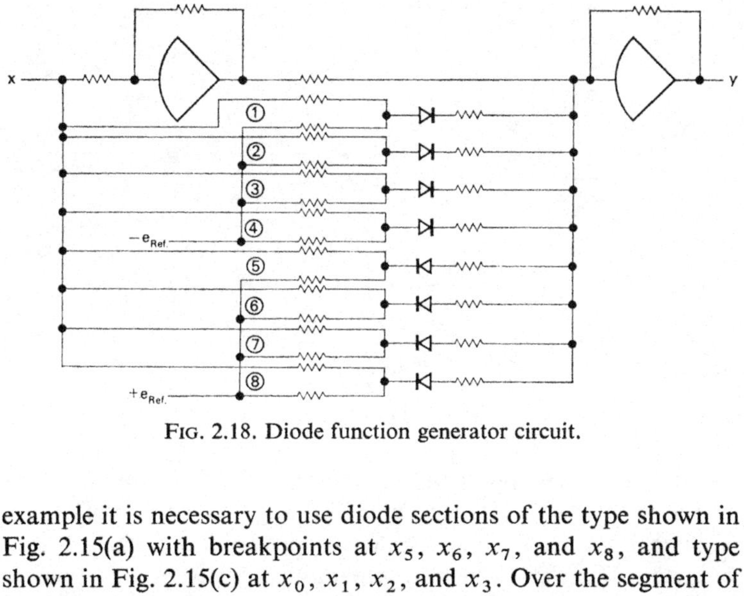

FIG. 2.18. Diode function generator circuit.

example it is necessary to use diode sections of the type shown in Fig. 2.15(a) with breakpoints at x_5, x_6, x_7, and x_8, and type shown in Fig. 2.15(c) at x_0, x_1, x_2, and x_3. Over the segment of the curve between x_3 and x_5 only the linear section is operating. Outside this range an appropriate number of diode sections conduct, so that the sum of their output voltages subtracted from that due to the linear section, gives a straight line approximation to the required function.

The accuracy with which the curve can be generated depends on the shape of the curve and the number of diode sections used.

One major advantage of the diode function generator, compared with the tapped potentiometer, is that the segments do not have to be equally spaced, which means that they can be tightly packed or well spaced out, depending on the curvature of the function.

In a variable function generator each segment is provided with switches and potentiometers so that it can be made to operate in any quadrant. A typical circuit is shown in Fig. 2.19. In addition

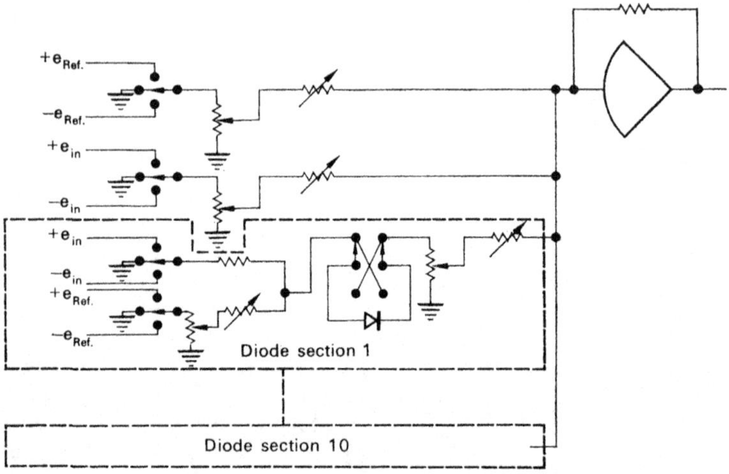

FIG. 2.19. Variable function generator circuit.

to the linear section, another section is added which can be connected to either the positive or negative reference supply voltage. This is used to bias the curve for zero input voltage. Most commercial variable function generators have ten diode segments, but it is possible to connect two or more of them in parallel when a greater number of segments are required.

Some of the larger modern machines have more complex function generators available. In these the potentiometers are replaced by attenuator networks, so that they can be set up by selection of points on a patch board, or from a digital computer. These are of course very much more expensive.

In any computer the manufacturer will also have a number of fixed function generators such as sine, cosine, square law and logarithmic law available. These need no setting up and as there are no switched resistors and potentiometers, they are more compact and have a better frequency response. This also means that they can be constructed more cheaply.

Multipliers

Multiplication of variables, accurately and cheaply, has until recently proved to be one of the most difficult operations to carry out on the electronic analog computer. Over the years many circuits have been designed, and used with limited success, but not many have been universally accepted. In the following sections only the most successful and widely used circuits will be described and discussed.

An ideal multiplier will accept input voltages x and y, and produce a product $z = (x.y)/u$, where u is a constant equal to the value of the computer reference voltage. It is necessary to divide the product $x.y$ by u to ensure that the voltage level of z does not exceed the maximum voltage level of the computer when x and y are at their maximum values of $\pm u$. The multiplier can be considered as a variable gain unit, in which the input voltage x is transferred to the output modified by a gain factor (y/u). The value of the gain factor varies over the range -1 to 1. To design an efficient multiplier, therefore, it is necessary to find a device whose gain can be linearily controlled over a wide range by a voltage. Devices whose gains are voltage dependent do not generally have a linear characteristic, but by the use of high gain operational amplifiers and feedback suitable devices can be found.

Let us consider the general case of a variable gain device having its gain controlled by the output of an operational amplifier, and with a constant input voltage u as shown in Fig. 2.20. Let the characteristic of the variable gain device be such that it has a gain $m_1(0)$ for zero input voltage and a variable term

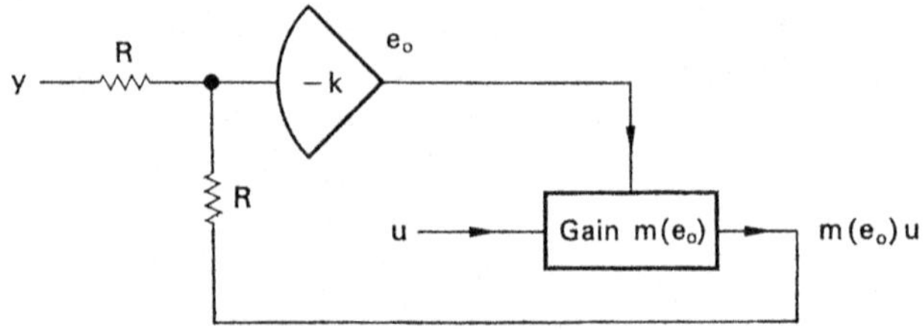

FIG. 2.20. Voltage controlled variable gain device.

$m_2(e_0).e_0$, where $m_2(e_0)$ can be positive or negative and is not necessarily linear. The device gain is

$$m(e_0) = m_1(0) - m_2(e_0).e_0 \tag{2.18}$$

If the amplifier gain is $-k$, then

$$e_0 = -k[y + m(e_0).u] \tag{2.19}$$

Substituting (2.19) in (2.18), we get

$$m(e_0) = m_1(0) - m_2(e_0).k[y + m(e_0).u] \tag{2.20}$$

giving

$$m(e_0)[1 + m_2(e_0).k.u] = m_1(0) - m_2(e_0).k.y \tag{2.21}$$

Therefore

$$m(e_0) = \frac{m_1(0) - m_2(e_0).k.y}{1 + m_2(e_0).k.u} \tag{2.22}$$

$$= -\frac{y}{u} + \frac{(y/u) + m_1(0)}{1 + m_2(e_0).k.u} \tag{2.23}$$

$$= -\frac{y}{u} + \frac{1}{k}\left[\frac{(y/u) + m_1(0)}{(1/k) + m_2(e_0).u}\right] \tag{2.24}$$

If k is large, the second term in equation (2.24) can be neglected giving

$$m(e_0) = -\frac{y}{u}$$

The effect of the feedback loop is to make the gain of the variable gain device proportional to the amplifier input voltage y.

If another device or a number of devices can be found having exactly the same gain versus gain setting characteristics, then it is possible to design a multiplier unit as shown in Fig. 2.21, where a number of the variable gain devices are set by the voltage e_0 to have gains y/u, resulting in output voltages $-(x.y)/u$, $-(w.y)/u$, etc. A number of types of multipliers based on this principal are available.

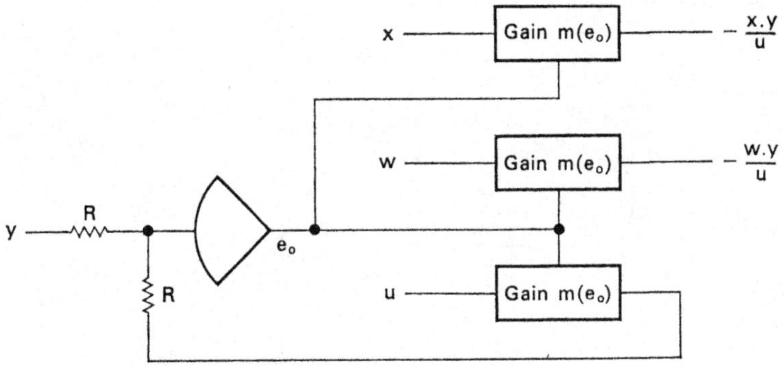

FIG. 2.21. Function multiplier using voltage controlled variable gain devices.

An alternative to using a variable gain device is to base multiplication on the mathematical relationship

$$(x+y)^2-(x-y)^2 = 4x.y$$

This is dependent only on being able to design units with an accurate square law characteristic. In modern machines this type of multiplier is most generally used.

Servo multipliers. Here the variable gain devices are potentiometers mounted in a group, with their wipers connected to a common shaft driven by a servo motor. This is shown diagrammatically in Fig. 2.22. In this case the gain setting voltage e_0 is converted into a shaft rotation, proportional to y/u, common to all potentiometers. Potentiometer 1 is the reference gain setting device and its output voltage provides the feedback to be compared with y. The ends of the other potentiometers are connected to the voltages to be multiplied by y, and the products appear at the appropriate wipers. The signs of the output voltages can be arranged to give a reversal of sign or not, depending on which

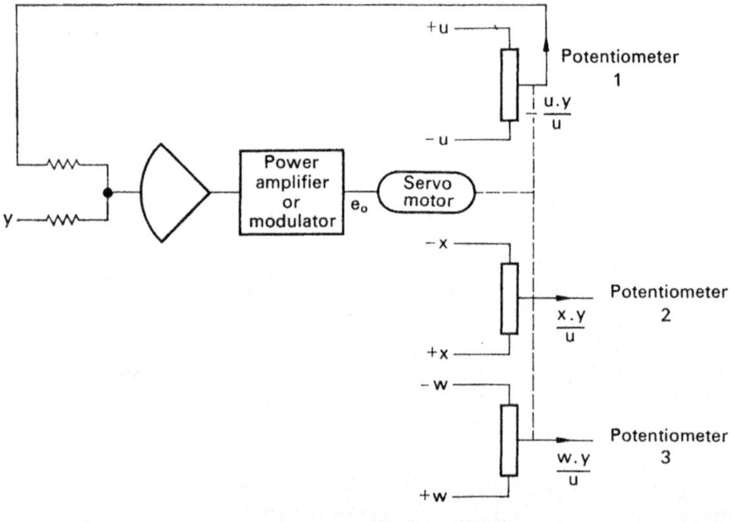

FIG. 2.22. Servo-driven multiplier.

sign of the input voltage the ends of the potentiometers are connected to. Accuracy of this type of multiplier is largely dependent on the similarity of the potentiometer windings, and how well they are aligned on the common shaft. Best accuracy is obtained by using multiturn potentiometers, as this gives better resolution. Because the servomechanism will only respond to low frequency input signals, servomultipliers have a very limited frequency band of operation, and their best accuracies are obtained at frequencies below 0·01 Hz. Typical accuracy figures are

0·025% at 0·01 Hz with 100% travel of the potentiometer wiper.
0·025% at 0·2 Hz with 20% travel of the potentiometer wiper.
0·1% at 0·1 Hz with 100% travel of the potentiometer wiper.
0·1% at 1·0 Hz with 20% travel of the potentiometer wiper.

Because servomultipliers have such a limited frequency band of operation, and also other types of multipliers with equal and better performance are now available, present-day general purpose computers do not include servomultipliers.

Time division multipliers. There are a number of different types of time division multiplier, but they all depend on modulating the mark to space ratio of a square wave by one input voltage, and the amplitude by the other input voltage. The resultant wave form when averaged, gives a voltage proportional to the product. In this type of multiplier the variable gain device is a switch, which is being cycled between closed and open at a high frequency. The ratio of the difference between the closed and open time and the period, is a measure of the gain.

A typical circuit is illustrated in Fig. 2.23(a), and the type of waveforms expected in Fig. 2.23(b). With switch 1 open and $y = 0$, the output of the integrator goes negative at u/CR_1 V/sec. When it reaches $-u$ volts, the comparator circuits operate and close all the switches. As the $-u$ input to the integrator has twice the gain of the $+u$ input, the output now reverses and goes in the positive direction at u/CR_1 V/sec. When it reaches $+u$ volts the comparator circuits again operate and open the switches. The output of the integrator again reverses sign and goes in the negative direction. If y remains zero, the output of the integrator will continue to oscillate between $\pm u$ volts at a frequency determined by the time constant CR_1 and the voltage u, with a mark to space ratio, of the time the switches are closed to the time they are open, of unity.

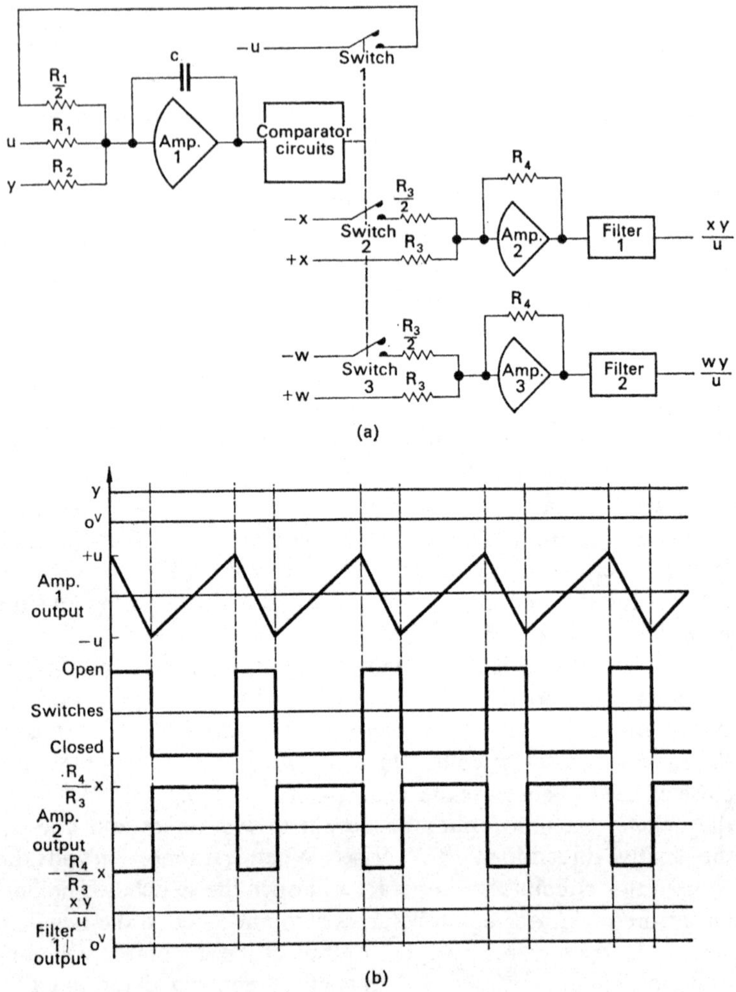

FIG. 2.23. Time division multiplier: (a) circuit, (b) typical waveforms.

If y is not zero, the mark to space ratio will be varied to be greater or less than unity depending on its sign. Typically in a 100 V computer, the pulse width or the closed time of the switch T_1 would equal $(0{\cdot}5+0{\cdot}003y)T$, where T is the period of one cycle of operation. This gives

$$T_1 = 0{\cdot}2T \quad \text{when} \quad y = -100\ \text{V}$$

$$T_1 = 0{\cdot}8T \quad \text{when} \quad y = +100\ \text{V}$$

Consider what happens at the output of amplifier 2. When switch 2 is closed, the output is

$$x\left(\frac{2R_4}{R_3}-\frac{R_4}{R_3}\right) = \frac{R_4}{R_3}.x$$

When switch 2 is open, the output is

$$-\frac{R_4}{R_3}.x$$

The average value of the output is therefore

$$\frac{\dfrac{R_4}{R_3}.x(T_1)-\dfrac{R_4}{R_3}x(T-T_1)}{T} = \frac{\dfrac{R_4}{R_3}x(2T_1-T)}{T}$$

$$= \frac{\dfrac{R_4}{R_3}x(T+0{\cdot}006y.T-T)}{T}$$

$$= 0{\cdot}006\frac{R_4}{R_3}x.y$$

If

$$\frac{R_4}{R_3} = \frac{1}{0{\cdot}006u},$$

then the average value of the output from amplifier 2 is $(x.y)/u$, and this is obtained by filtering. In a similar way, the average value of the output from amplifier 3 is $(w.y)/u$.

The repetition rate in the circuit must be high compared with the highest signal frequency. In practice, repetition rates between 1 kHz and 300 kHz are used. The accuracy of this type of multiplier can be high, with a static accuracy of 0·01% possible and dynamic errors within 2% up to a frequency of $\frac{1}{25}$ of the pulse repetition rate used.

Analog-to-digital multiplier. This type of multiplier is not commonly available with analog computers, but it is a good example of the variable gain device technique, and with the advent of hybrid computing it could become important because of its mode of operation. The variable gain device in this unit is a digital-to-analog converter, which is effectively a digitally set attenuator. The gain is dependent on the numbers of switches in the converter which are closed, and these are controlled by the output of a reversible counter. The contents of this are a digital representation of one of the multiplier input voltages.

A block diagram of an analog-to-digital multiplier is shown in Fig. 2.24. Consider the operation of the feedback loop with the digital-to-analog converter (1). Depending on the sign of the

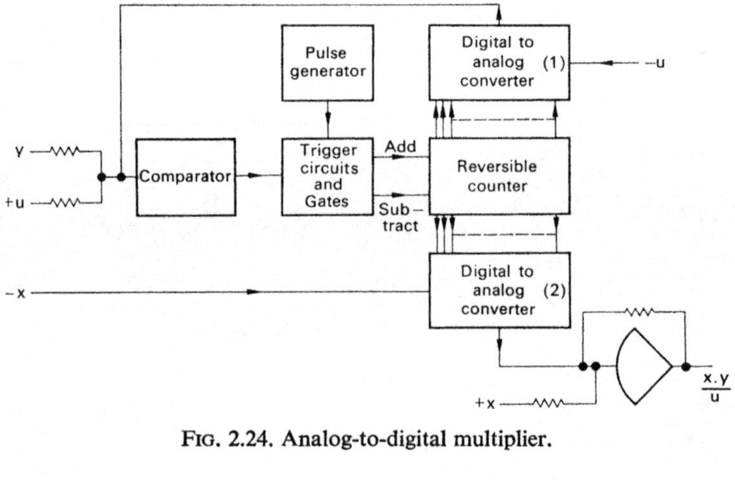

FIG. 2.24. Analog-to-digital multiplier.

sum of the voltages at the input of the comparator, its output will operate the trigger circuit to gate either add or subtract pulses to the reversible counter. The counter will count up or down until its output sets the gain of digital-to-analog converter (1), so that the voltage it feeds back to the comparator balances the sum of the voltages y and $+u$. The $+u$ voltage at the input of the comparator is to allow the circuit to handle both positive and negative values of y. For y zero the $+u$ voltage drives the counter to half full, and for y equal to $-u$ the counter is empty. Because of the biasing, the output of the digital-to-analog converter is $[(y/u)+1](-u)$. As y changes, the sign of the comparator output changes and pulses are gated to the reversible counter to maintain its contents at a digital value proportional to the value of y. If the reversible counter is used to drive another digital-to-analog converter fed by a voltage $-x$, its output would be $[(y/u)+1](-x)$. If the output of the digital-to-analog converter were summed with $+x$ into an amplifier, the output would be $(y.x)/u$. A number of digital-to-analog converters can be driven from the reversible counter to give products $(y.w)/u$, etc. This type of multiplier is capable of very high accuracy depending on the pulse generator and signal frequency. Typically for the case of a pulse generator of frequency 1 MHz, an accuracy of 0·01% is possible up to a y signal frequency of about 16 Hz, and 0·1% up to a y signal frequency of about 160 Hz.

Quarter square multiplier. This uses diode section function generators and summing amplifiers to set up the mathematical relationship

$$\tfrac{1}{4}[(x+y)^2-(x-y)^2] = x.y$$

A number of different circuit configurations are commonly used, and a typical one is shown in Fig. 2.25. Using amplifiers 1 and 2, the sums $-(x+y)$ and $-(x-y)$ are formed. The outputs of these amplifiers are connected to diode section squaring units arranged so that all possible sign combinations of x and y can be handled. The outputs of the squaring units are combined in amplifiers 3 and 4 to give the product $(x.y)/u$ at the output of amplifier 4. In some multipliers the forming of $(x+y)$ and $(x-y)$ is carried out in the squaring units. This can lead to a saving in amplifiers if both signs of x and y are available from the computation.

The quarter square multiplier is probably the most commonly used type in modern computers. It is very reliable, has good frequency response and requires little adjustment. At low frequencies accuracies of 0·01% are possible, providing enough diode sections are used in the squaring units. Bandwidths of greater than 10 kHz with 1% accuracy are obtainable.

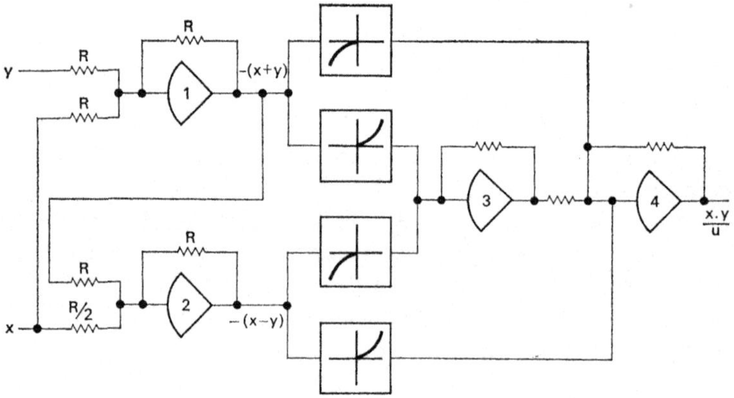

FIG. 2.25. Quarter square multiplier.

CHAPTER 3

Problem Preparation

BEFORE we can put a problem on the computer, it is necessary to carry out a considerable amount of preliminary work, formulating the correct equations, scaling the equations and drawing flow diagrams.

As we have seen in Chapter 1, the types of problem most suited for solution on an analog computer are linear and nonlinear ordinary differential equations, with constant or variable coefficients. Of these types of equations, linear differential equations can in general be easily solved analytically, but the methods often involve much tedious work. When it is necessary to investigate the effects of varying the coefficients, the amount of calculation can become prohibitive. The use of an analog computer allows the solution to be obtained quickly, and the effects of varying the coefficients are easily investigated merely by changing potentiometer settings. For this type of problem only summers, integrators, inverters and potentiometers are required. Linear differential equations with coefficients which are functions of the independent variable have been solved analytically only for particular cases. They can be solved with little difficulty on the analog computer, requiring multipliers in addition to the computing units mentioned above. Nonlinear differential equations are either very difficult or impossible to solve analytically, but their solution on an analog computer is only slightly more difficult than for linear equations. Function generators and discontinuous computing units are required in addition to those previously mentioned.

3.1. Flow Diagrams

Let us consider the procedure in preparing a simple problem, such as the mass spring damper system which we have already discussed in Chapter 1, so that it can be solved on an analog computer. The physical system is illustrated in Fig. 3.1, where a mass of M kg is suspended from a support by a spring with stiffness K N/m and a damper with damping coefficient D N/m/sec.

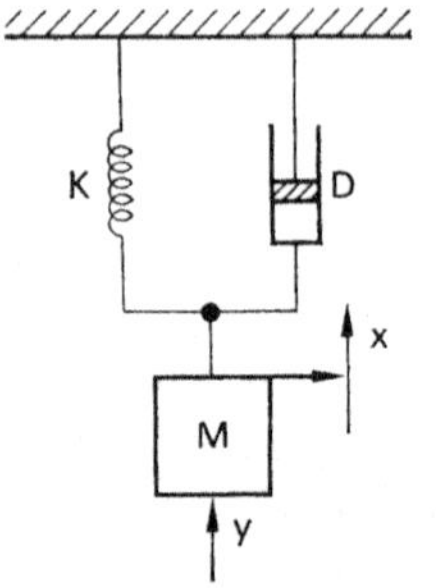

FIG. 3.1. Mass spring, damper system

A force of y N is applied to the system and the displacement of the mass from its initial position is x m. Using Newton's laws of motion, the differential equation describing the behaviour of this system has been shown to be

$$M\frac{d^2x}{dt^2}+D\frac{dx}{dt}+Kx = y \tag{3.1}$$

Rearranging the equation by dividing through by M and taking the highest derivative of x to the left-hand side, we get

$$\frac{d^2x}{dt^2} = \frac{y}{M}-\frac{D}{M}\frac{dx}{dt}-\frac{K}{M}x \tag{3.2}$$

To set this up on an analog computer, we first assume that voltages representing the three terms on the right-hand side of the equation are available. These are then summed with the appropriate signs to produce a voltage representing d^2x/dt^2. Integrating d^2x/dt^2 gives a voltage $-(dx/dt)$ and integrating again we get a voltage x. As all computing units in an analog computer operate in parallel, the voltages dx/dt and x can be fed back to provide the appropriate input terms. The other input voltage, representing the applied force, can be generated in the computer or fed from an external source. The complete flow diagram is shown in Fig. 3.2.

Considering the operation of the circuit, we can see the analogy between it and the physical system. In the physical system when y

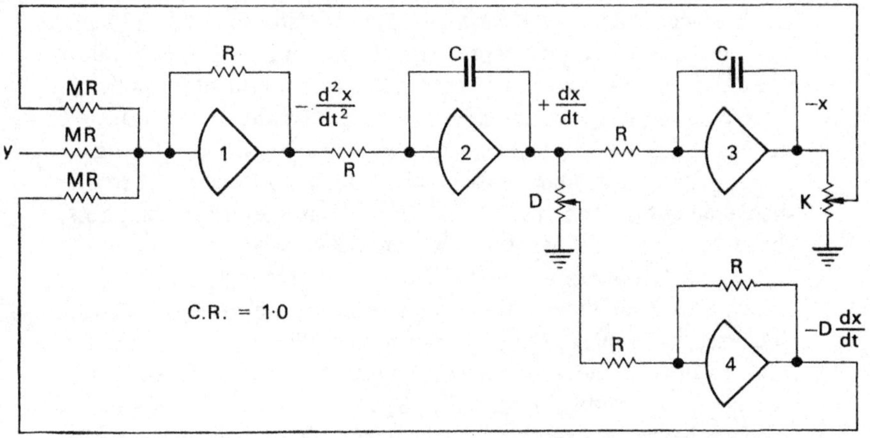

FIG. 3.2. Four-amplifier circuit for solution of second order linear differential equation

is zero the mass is at rest, its position from the point of suspension being dependent on the value of the mass, and the spring stiffness. When a step function of force y is applied, it gives the mass an acceleration of y/M m/sec^2. This causes it to have velocity and hence displacement from its initial position. If the mass was not connected to the spring and damper, and there was no air friction resistance, it would continue to accelerate at y/M m/sec^2. However, as the mass moves the spring is compressed or extended, with a resulting force opposing the applied force proportional to the compression or extension of the spring. There is also a damper force opposing the applied force, proportional to the velocity of the mass. The mass will eventually take up a new steady state position, and its transient behaviour before settling down will depend on the values of the various constants in the system.

Now consider the behaviour of the voltages at the outputs of the amplifiers in the computer circuit of Fig. 3.2. When the voltage representing y is zero, the outputs of all the amplifiers will also have a steady state zero value. As the system is linear, it is convenient to take the initial position of the mass as a reference point. This is represented by zero volts at the output of amplifier 3, and all displacements are then measured with respect to this. When a step function of voltage representing y is applied to the circuit a voltage proportional to y/M appears at the output of amplifier 1. This is integrated by amplifier 2, to give a voltage at its output proportional to the velocity of the mass dx/dt. This is again integrated by amplifier 3 to give a voltage proportional to the displacement of the mass x. If there were no feedback paths, the output of amplifier 1 would remain constant corresponding to constant acceleration in the physical system. When the feedback paths are connected, voltages proportional to displacement and velocity, representing the spring and damper forces, are fed back to oppose the voltage representing the applied force y. The voltage at the output of amplifier 3, when plotted with respect to time, behaves in exactly the same way as the displacement of the mass in the physical system, eventually settling down to a steady state value.

In the circuit diagram of Fig. 3.2 all the derivatives of x have been generated, and a total of four amplifiers is required. In many cases the highest derivative in the system may be of no interest and need not be formed. This will in general result in a saving in the number of amplifiers required, as use is made of the fact that summation can be carried out at the input of an integrator. The spring mass damper system could then be simulated with three amplifiers. Integrating both sides of equation (3.2) with respect to t, we get

$$\frac{dx}{dt} = \int_0^t \left(\frac{y}{M} - \frac{D}{M}\frac{dx}{dt} - \frac{K}{M}x\right) dt + \left.\frac{dx}{dt}\right|_{t=0} \tag{3.3}$$

$$\frac{dx}{dt} = \frac{1}{M}\int_0^t \left(y - D\frac{dx}{dt} - Kx\right) dt, \quad \text{if} \quad \left.\frac{dx}{dt}\right|_{t=0} = 0 \tag{3.4}$$

Equation (3.4) can be set up on a computer using the circuit of Fig. 3.3.

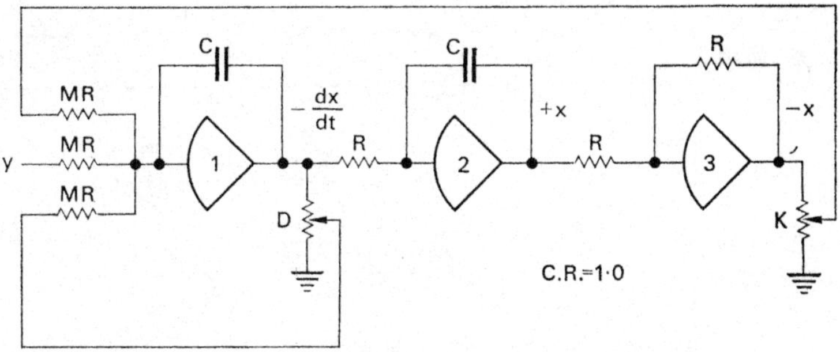

FIG. 3.3. Three-amplifier circuit for solution of second order linear differential equation

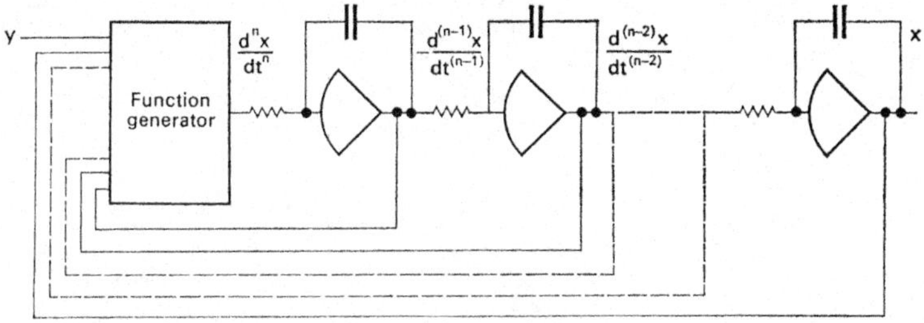

FIG. 3.4. Circuit for solution of *n*th order differential equation.

In the general case of an *n*th order differential equation expressed in the form

$$\frac{d^n x}{dt^n} = f\left(t, y, \frac{dx}{dt} \cdots \frac{d^{(n-1)}x}{dt^{(n-1)}}\right), \tag{3.5}$$

the computer circuit would be as shown in Fig. 3.4.

Where the computer circuit contains a large number of amplifiers, it is inconvenient to draw all the amplifier input resistors and feedback components. A set of standard symbols have therefore been developed, allowing the computer flow diagrams to be drawn in simplified form, which is clearer and more easily understood. Some of these standard symbols are shown in Fig. 3.5 and a complete set is given in Appendix 2.

ELEMENT	SYMBOL	FUNCTION	NOTES
Summer	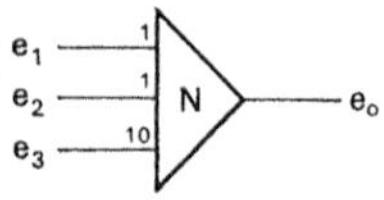	$e_o = -\left[e_1 + e_2 + 10e_3\right]$	N is amplifier number
Integrator	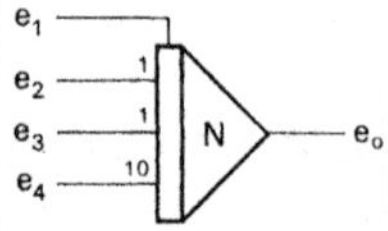	$e_o = -e_1 - \int_0^t (e_2 + e_3 + 10e_4)\,dt$	N is amplifier number
Potentiometer	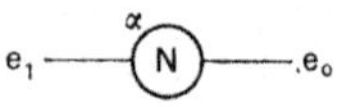	$e_o = \alpha e_1$	N is potentiometer number
Multiplier	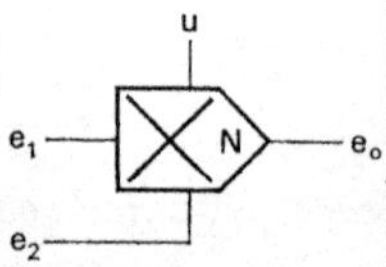	$e_o = \frac{e_1 e_2}{u}$ u is computer reference voltage	u input not generally shown N is multiplier number
Divider	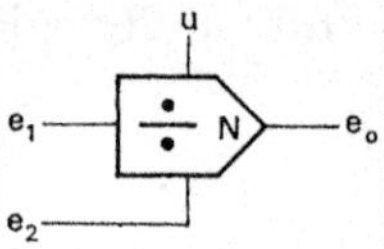	$e_o = u\frac{e_1}{e_2}$ u is computer reference voltage	u input not generally shown N is divider number

FIG. 3.5. Standard symbols for computing units.

Using standard symbols, Fig. 3.2 would be drawn as shown in Fig. 3.6, where for clarity the feedback paths have been left out. In complex systems, the feedback paths if drawn in tend to cause confusion.

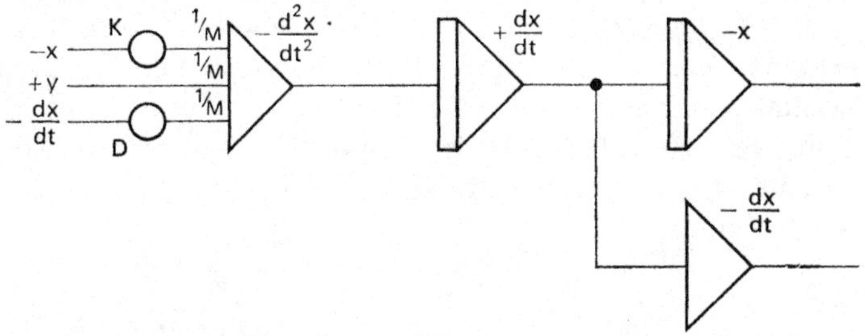

FIG. 3.6. Computer flow diagram for solution of a second order differential equation using standard symbols.

3.2. Time and Amplitude Scaling

When putting a problem on an analog computer, it is necessary to have scale factors which relate the computer variables, voltage and time, to the physical system variables. There are a number of methods of scaling problems for the computer, some of which are described in the following sections. Which ones are used depends on the individual, but it will be found in fact that they all have the same basic principles. Lack of knowledge of the principles of scaling can and has caused much confusion to analog computer users, and it is therefore very important that the student should understand, and be able to apply scaling techniques.

It is necessary to relate both the dependent and independent variables of the problem to be studied to the voltages and time in the computer. The dependent variables are related to voltages and this is referred to as amplitude scaling. The independent variable is related to time and this is referred to as time scaling.

Amplitude scale factors. In the computer, the variables of the system being studied are represented by voltages at the outputs of the amplifiers. The output range of all the amplifiers is the same, whereas the system variables may be distance, velocity, acceleration, angle, force, etc., with widely differing amplitude ranges. It is therefore necessary to select scale factors so that the ranges of all the problem variables, when converted to voltages, are the same. Selection of the scale factors is based on calculated or estimated maximum values of the problem variables, which are related to the maximum computer voltage. It is important that suitable scale factors are obtained, so that no amplifier output tries to exceed its maximum operating voltage, or has such a low value as to give a poor signal to noise ratio.

Time scale factors. In the majority of problems which are studied using an analog computer, the independent variable is time, but it is not necessary to have direct correspondence between computer time in seconds and problem time in seconds. Problem time scales may be years or microseconds, so it is convenient to introduce time scale factors which will make computer time scales in the range milliseconds or seconds. The important thing to remember in the choice of time scale factor is to select problem solution frequencies so that computer errors are minimized. When the independent variable of the problem is not time, the scale factor is chosen to give a convenient solution time on the computer, bearing in mind the frequencies that will be generated.

The choice of time scale factor is dictated by a number of considerations.

1. *The gain-bandwidth product of the computing elements.* It is important that frequencies generated in the problem solution are such that errors are not introduced by limitations in the specifications of the computing components. For example, at high frequencies amplifier gains are reduced, and phase shifts are introduced. If care is not taken, these effects can lead to large errors in the solution.

2. *Integrator drift.* If computing periods are too long, effects of drift voltages in integrators may become important.

3. *Dynamic capabilities of the recording equipment to be used.* This is an important factor to bear in mind. There is not much point in having a computer generating problem solutions accurately if the recording equipment is not capable of faithfully recording the computer voltages. This is particularly important when using electromechanical recording equipment which can only follow accurately very low frequency waveforms.

Taking the above three points into consideration will result in solution frequencies on the computer generally falling in the range 0·01 Hz to 10 Hz.

One important exception to these general rules is the case where the computer is being run in repetitive mode, with up to 1000 solutions per second. In this mode of operation, accuracy may be of secondary importance to the speed of operation.

3.3. Methods of Amplitude Scaling

Two methods for amplitude scaling of equations will be described and illustrated. However, examination of the methods will show that they are basically the same, and that the results are identical. Individual students may find one approach appeals to them more than the other.

The first method uses scale factors with dimensional units to relate the computer variables to the corresponding equation variables. Consider the case of a variable x, represented on the computer by a voltage which could have the symbol e_x. Then $e_x = a_x . x$, where a_x is a constant referred to as the scale factor, having the dimensions volts per unit of x.

In every computer there are two very stable reference voltage supplies, one positive and the other negative with respect to ground potential and equal in amplitude. It is convenient to consider the amplitude as 1 computer unit, and to measure amplifier output voltages in computer units. This has the advantage that programs can easily be exchanged between computers with different reference voltages. Also, multiplier outputs can simply be taken as the product of the inputs in computer units, whereas if the inputs were considered in volts, the output would be the product of the inputs divided by the computer reference voltage. The scale factor a_x will therefore have the dimensions computer units per unit of x. The term computer unit will be written C.U.

A value for the scale factor is obtained by relating the maximum operating value of the computer variable, which is 1 C.U., to the scale factor multiplied by the maximum value of the equation variable.

$$[e_x]_{max} = a_x[x]_{max}$$

Therefore

$$a_x = \frac{[e_x]_{max}}{[x]_{max}} \quad \text{C.U./unit of } x$$

$$= \frac{1}{[x]_{max}} \quad \text{C.U./unit of } x$$

Let us apply this method of amplitude scaling to the second order differential equation for the mass spring damper system of Fig. 3.1:

$$\frac{d^2x}{dt^2}+\frac{D}{M}\frac{dx}{dt}+\frac{K}{M}x = \frac{1}{M}y \tag{3.6}$$

This can be written using the dot notation for differentials

$$\ddot{x}+\frac{D}{M}\dot{x}+\frac{K}{M}x = \frac{1}{M}y \tag{3.7}$$

If the computer variables are $e_{x,2}$, $e_{x,1}$, $e_{x,0}$ and e_y, representing the equation variables $\ddot{x}$, $\dot{x}$, x, and y, then

$$e_{x,2} = a_{x,2}.\ddot{x}$$

$$e_{x,1} = a_{x,1}.\dot{x}$$

$$e_{x,0} = a_{x,0}.x$$

and

$$e_y = a_y.y$$

Maximum values for all the equation variables are calculated or estimated, and hence values for the scale factors are obtained as follows:

$$a_{x,2} = \frac{1}{[\ddot{x}]_{max}} \quad \text{C.U./m/sec}^2$$

$$a_{x,1} = \frac{1}{[\dot{x}]_{max}} \quad \text{C.U./m/sec}$$

$$a_{x,0} = \frac{1}{[x]_{max}} \quad \text{C.U./m}$$

$$a_y = \frac{1}{[y]_{max}} \quad \text{C.U./N}$$

If the equation variables are changed to computer variables, equation (3.6) can be rewritten as

$$\frac{e_{x,2}}{a_{x,2}} + \frac{D}{M}\frac{e_{x,1}}{a_{x,1}} + \frac{K}{M}\frac{e_{x,0}}{a_{x,0}} = \frac{1}{M}\frac{e_y}{a_y} \qquad (3.8)$$

Multiplying through by $a_{x,2}$ and keeping only $e_{x,2}$ on the left-hand side of the equation gives

$$e_{x,2} = \frac{1}{M}\frac{a_{x,2}}{a_y}[e_y] - \frac{D}{M}\frac{a_{x,2}}{a_{x,1}}[e_{x,1}] - \frac{K}{M}\frac{a_{x,2}}{a_{x,0}}[e_{x,0}] \qquad (3.9)$$

The coefficients of this equation are the gains for the inputs to amplifier 1 of Fig. 3.7. As the scale factors for all the variables are

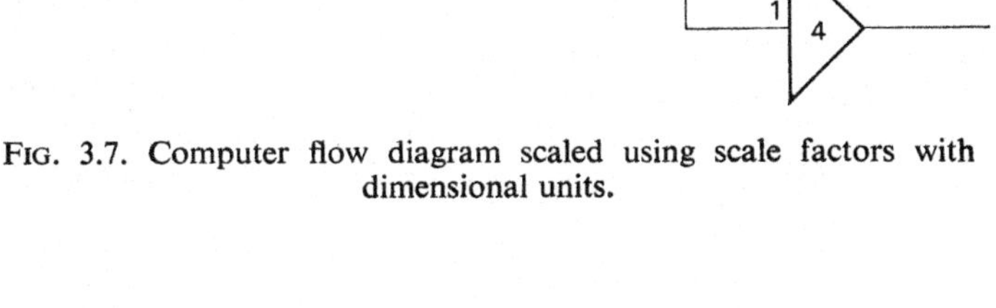

FIG. 3.7. Computer flow diagram scaled using scale factors with dimensional units.

different, it is necessary to obtain the integrator gains by writing down the equations relating $\dot{x}$ to $\ddot{x}$ and x to $\dot{x}$ and covering them to computer variables:

$$\dot{x} = \int_0^t \ddot{x}\, dt + \dot{x}\,|_{t=0} \tag{3.10}$$

This becomes in computer variables

$$\frac{e_{x,1}}{a_{x,1}} = \int_0^t \frac{e_{x,2}}{a_{x,2}}\, dt + \frac{e_{x,1}}{a_{x,1}}\bigg|_{t=0} \tag{3.11}$$

which multiplied through by $a_{x,1}$ gives

$$e_{x,1} = \frac{a_{x,1}}{a_{x,2}} \int_0^t e_{x,2}\, dt + e_{x,1}\,|_{t=0} \tag{3.12}$$

Similarly we have

$$x = \int_0^t \dot{x}\, dt + x\,|_{t=0} \tag{3.13}$$

which converting to computer variables in the same way as above gives

$$e_{x,0} = \frac{a_{x,0}}{a_{x,1}} \int_0^t e_{x,1}\, dt + e_{x,0}\,|_{t=0} \tag{3.14}$$

From equation (3.12) the gain of the first integrator, amplifier 2, in Fig. 3.7 is $a_{x,1}/a_{x,2}$ and from equation (3.14) the gain of the second integrator, amplifier 3, is $a_{x,0}/a_{x,1}$.

The effect of scaling is to distribute the gains in the loops so that all amplifiers will be operating over their full voltage range, but the total gain in the loop should of course be the appropriate coefficient in the original system equation. In Fig. 3.6 the gain round the loop of amplifiers 1, 2 and 3 is K/M which is the coefficient of x in equation (3.7). In the scaled computer diagram Fig. 3.7, the product of gains is

$$\frac{K}{M} \cdot \frac{a_{x,2}}{a_{x,0}} \cdot \frac{a_{x,1}}{a_{x,2}} \cdot \frac{a_{x,0}}{a_{x,1}}$$

equal to K/M which of course it should be. In the other loop, amplifiers 1, 2 and 4, the gain should be D/M which is the coefficient of $\dot{x}$ in equation (3.7). In Fig. 3.7 the gain is

$$\frac{D}{M} \cdot \frac{a_{x,2}}{a_{x,1}} \cdot \frac{a_{x,1}}{a_{x,2}}$$

equal to D/M.

The use of a symbol, such as e_x, for the computer voltage representing a variable x is not universal. Many computer users prefer to write the computer voltage as $(a_x x)$. Equation (3.9) would therefore be written,

$$(a_{x,2}\ddot{x}) = \frac{1}{M}\frac{a_{x,2}}{a_y}(a_y y) - \frac{D}{M}\frac{a_{x,2}}{a_{x,1}}(a_{x,1}\dot{x}) - \frac{K}{M}\frac{a_{x,2}}{a_{x,0}}(a_{x,0}x)$$

Using the second method of amplitude scaling the equation variables are normalized by dividing them by their maximum values. These are then equated to normalized computer variables. Consider a variable x with maximum value x_M. This is written in normalized form as $[x/x_M]$, which has a maximum value of 1 and is non-dimensional. This will be represented in the computer by a voltage e at the output of an amplifier, which in normalized form would be [e/ref. voltage], also having a maximum value of 1. The two normalized quantities can be equated giving

$$\left[\frac{x}{x_M}\right] = \left[\frac{e}{\text{ref. voltage}}\right]$$

For any particular value of the output voltage e the corresponding value of x is obtained as

$$x = \left[\frac{x_M}{\text{ref. voltage}}\right][e]$$

To convert the system equations into computer equations, all equation variables are written in normalized form with their coefficients multiplied by their maximum value.

To illustrate this method of scaling, we will again use the equation for the mass spring damper system of Fig. 3.1:

$$\ddot{x}+\frac{D}{M}\dot{x}+\frac{K}{M}x = \frac{1}{M}y$$

The normalized form of the variables will be

$$\left[\frac{\ddot{x}}{\ddot{x}_M}\right], \left[\frac{\dot{x}}{\dot{x}_M}\right], \left[\frac{x}{x_M}\right] \text{ and } \left[\frac{y}{y_M}\right]$$

and rewriting equation 3.7 using these we get

$$\ddot{x}_M\left[\frac{\ddot{x}}{\ddot{x}_M}\right]+\frac{D}{M}\dot{x}_M\left[\frac{\dot{x}}{\dot{x}_M}\right]+\frac{K}{M}x_M\left[\frac{x}{x_M}\right] = \frac{1}{M}y_M\left[\frac{y}{y_M}\right] \quad (3.15)$$

Dividing through by $\ddot{x}_M$ and taking everything to the right-hand side of the equation except $[\ddot{x}/\ddot{x}_M]$ gives

$$\left[\frac{\ddot{x}}{\ddot{x}_M}\right] = \frac{1}{M}\frac{y_M}{\ddot{x}_M}\left[\frac{y}{y_M}\right]-\frac{D}{M}\frac{\dot{x}_M}{\ddot{x}_M}\left[\frac{\dot{x}}{\dot{x}_M}\right]-\frac{K}{M}\frac{x_M}{\ddot{x}_M}\left[\frac{x}{x_M}\right] \quad (3.16)$$

The coefficients of the terms on the right-hand side are the gains for the inputs to amplifier 1 of Fig. 3.8.

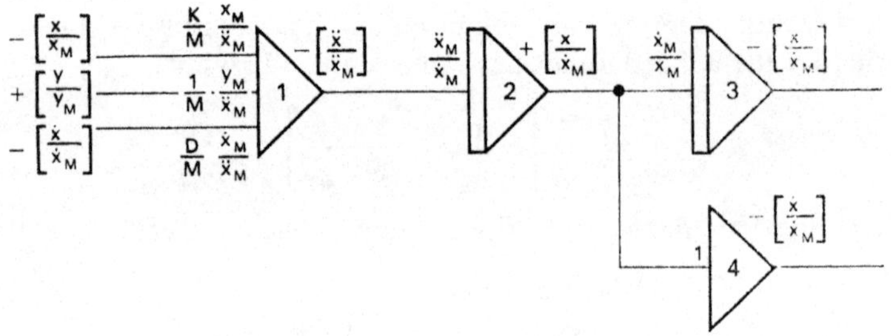

FIG. 3.8. Computer flow diagram scaled using normalized variables.

The integrator gains are obtained as in the previous method of scaling by writing down the equations relating $\dot{x}$ to $\ddot{x}$ and x to $\dot{x}$ and then converting them to normalized variables. We have therefore

$$\dot{x} = \int_0^t \ddot{x}\, dt + \dot{x}\,|_{t=0} \tag{3.17}$$

which becomes using normalized variables

$$\dot{x}_M \left[\frac{\dot{x}}{\dot{x}_M}\right] = \int_0^t \ddot{x}_M \left[\frac{\ddot{x}}{\ddot{x}_M}\right] dt + \dot{x}_M \left[\frac{\dot{x}}{\dot{x}_M}\right]\Bigg|_{t=0} \tag{3.18}$$

Dividing through by $\dot{x}_M$ gives

$$\left[\frac{\dot{x}}{\dot{x}_M}\right] = \frac{\ddot{x}_M}{\dot{x}_M} \int_0^t \left[\frac{\ddot{x}}{\ddot{x}_M}\right] dt + \left[\frac{\dot{x}}{\dot{x}_M}\right]\Bigg|_{t=0} \tag{3.19}$$

Similarly for

$$x = \int_0^t \dot{x}\, dt + x\,|_{t=0} \tag{3.20}$$

converting to normalized variables we get

$$\left[\frac{x}{x_M}\right] = \frac{\dot{x}_M}{x_M} \int_0^t \left[\frac{\dot{x}}{\dot{x}_M}\right] dt + \left[\frac{x}{x_M}\right]\Bigg|_{t=0} \tag{3.21}$$

The gain of the first integrator, amplifier 2 in Fig. 3.8, is from equation (3.19) $\ddot{x}_M/\dot{x}_M$, and that of the second integrator, amplifier 3, is from equation (3.21) $\dot{x}_M/x_M$.

It is again of interest to check the loop gains to ensure that they correspond to the coefficients of the system equation. For the loop of amplifiers 1, 2 and 3, the gain is

$$\frac{K}{M} \cdot \frac{x_M}{\ddot{x}_M} \cdot \frac{\ddot{x}_M}{\dot{x}_M} \cdot \frac{\dot{x}_M}{x_M} = \frac{K}{M},$$

which is the coefficient of x in equation (3.7) and therefore correct. For the loop of amplifiers 1, 2 and 4, the gain is

$$\frac{D}{M}\cdot\frac{\dot{x}_M}{\ddot{x}_M}\cdot\frac{\ddot{x}_M}{\dot{x}_M}=\frac{D}{M},$$

which is the coefficient of x in equation (3.7) and also correct.

The two methods of scaling should give computer flow diagrams with identical gains at the inputs of all the amplifiers. If this is so, it should be possible to show that the amplifier gains in Fig. 3.7 are the same as those in Fig. 3.8.

Consider the gains at the input of amplifier 1 in Fig. 3.7. These are

$$\frac{K}{M}\cdot\frac{a_{x,2}}{a_{x,0}},\quad \frac{1}{M}\cdot\frac{a_{x,2}}{a_y}\quad\text{and}\quad \frac{D}{M}\cdot\frac{a_{x,2}}{a_{x,1}}$$

If the scale factors are replaced by their values, in terms of the equation variables maximum value, the gains become

$$\frac{K}{M}\cdot\frac{1}{\ddot{x}_M}\cdot x_M,\quad \frac{1}{M}\cdot\frac{1}{\ddot{x}_M}\cdot y_M,\quad\text{and}\quad \frac{D}{M}\cdot\frac{1}{\ddot{x}_M}\cdot\dot{x}_M$$

which are the same as in Fig. 3.8.

The integrator gains of Fig. 3.7, $a_{x,1}/a_{x,2}$ and $a_{x,0}/a_{x,1}$ become in terms of maximum values $1/\dot{x}_M\,.\,\ddot{x}_M$ and $1/x_M\,.\,\dot{x}_M$ which are the gains in Fig. 3.8.

The two methods of amplitude scaling therefore give the same computer flow diagram.

3.4. Methods of Time Scaling

There are two methods of carrying out time scaling, by changing the time scale of the equations or by changing the time scale on the computer. The method used will depend on the equations of the system being studied. When the frequencies in the physical system are very high or very low, it will be found that the equations have coefficients with values ranging over several decades. In this case it is often convenient to time scale the equations, thus bringing the values of all coefficients into the same decade. When the frequences in the physical system are within a decade of suitable frequencies for the computer, it is generally better to only carry out amplitude scaling of the equations, and then do any time scaling necessary on the computer. Modern computers, particularly the larger ones, have facilities for changing the time scales of all integrators by factors of 10, 100 and 1000.

Changing the time scale of the equations. The independent variable of the equations is replaced by a new variable τ, and the equations in τ are instrumented on the computer. In most problems the equation independent variable will be time in seconds t, in which case $\tau = a_\tau t$ and a_τ will be a constant. In problems where the independent variable is not time a_τ will have dimensions seconds per unit of the independent variable. An example would be the equation for the displacement of a beam, where the independent variable is distance along the beam. In this case distance along the beam would be represented by time on the computer and a_τ would have dimensions seconds per foot.

Considering the more general case where the independent variable of the equations is time, we have the situation where a_τ sec on the computer is equivalent to 1 sec of time for the original system. Therefore if a_τ is greater than unity, the solution is slowed down, and if a_τ is less than unity it is speeded up.

Let us see what effect time scaling has on the derivatives of the equations.

If

$$\tau = a_\tau t \tag{3.22}$$

then

$$\frac{d}{dt} = \frac{d}{d\left(\dfrac{\tau}{a_\tau}\right)} = a_\tau \frac{d}{d\tau} \tag{3.23}$$

$$\frac{d^2}{dt^2} = \frac{d}{d\left(\dfrac{\tau}{a_\tau}\right)}\left[a_\tau \frac{d}{d\tau}\right] = a_\tau^2 \frac{d^2}{d\tau^2} \tag{3.24}$$

and

$$\frac{d^n}{dt^n} = a_\tau^n \frac{d^n}{d\tau^n} \tag{3.25}$$

These equations show that the derivatives in the computer time scale are the derivatives in the physical system time scale divided by a_τ raised to the power of the appropriate derivative. If a_τ is greater than unity, the values of all the derivatives, in the computer time scale, are reduced. Consider the mass spring damper system of Fig. 3.1. When the solution is slowed down the frequency is lower and therefore the velocity and acceleration must be lower. Conversely, when a_τ is less than unity the solution frequency is higher and therefore the velocity and acceleration must be greater.

Substituting from equations (3.22) to (3.24) into equation (3.6) for the mass spring damper system we get

$$a_\tau^2 \frac{d^2x}{d\tau^2} + \frac{D}{M} a_\tau \frac{dx}{d\tau} + \frac{K}{M} x = \frac{1}{M} y \tag{3.26}$$

Dividing through by a_τ^2 gives

$$\frac{d^2x}{d\tau^2} + \frac{D}{M} \frac{1}{a_\tau} \frac{dx}{d\tau} + \frac{K}{M} \frac{1}{a_\tau^2} x = \frac{1}{M} \frac{1}{a_\tau^2} y \tag{3.27}$$

which is the time scaled equation to be solved on the computer.

For a second order differential equation with no damping, that is the coefficient of dx/dt is zero, and with the coefficient of d^2x/dt^2 unity, the solution frequency, in radians, is given by the square root of the coefficient of the x term. For the mass, spring, damper system of equation (3.6), the solution frequency is therefore $\sqrt{(K/M)}$ radians per second. This means that if the system is disturbed, the mass will oscillate with a frequency of $1/2\pi\sqrt{(K/M)}$ Hz. The system of equation (3.27) has a solution frequency of $(1/2\pi a_\tau)\sqrt{(K/M)}$. It can be seen from this that the period for one cycle on the computer is a_τ times the period for one cycle of the physical system.

Changing the time scale on the computer. In this case the system equations are only amplitude scaled and then put directly on the computer. Time scaling is carried out by changing the time constants of all the integrators, which are the only time dependent units, by the required time scale factor a_τ. As the integrator gains are the reciprocal of the integrator time constants, the change is effected by dividing all integrator gains by a_τ. The result of this is that for a_τ greater than unity the integrator gains are decreased and for a_τ less than unity they are increased. The equation for an integrator as shown in Fig. 3.9 is

$$e_0(t) = -\frac{1}{CR}\int_0^t e_1(t)\,dt + e_0(t)\,|_{t=0} \tag{3.28}$$

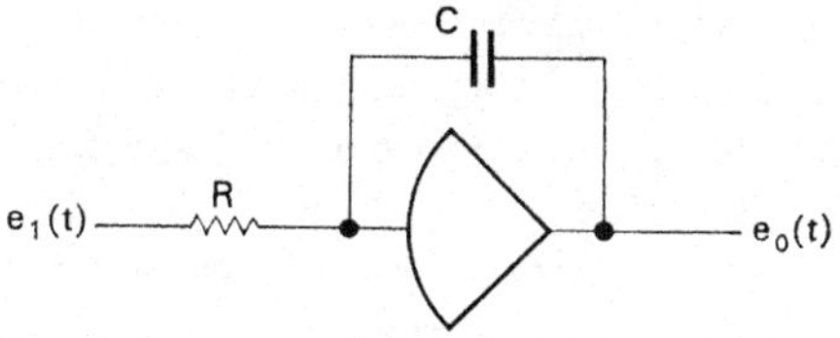

FIG. 3.9. Integrator unit.

where CR is the time constant of the integrator in seconds. If we want the integrator to operate in a new time scale τ, where $\tau = a_\tau t$, it is necessary to change its time constant by the factor a_τ so that

$$e_0(\tau) = -\frac{1}{a_\tau CR}\int_0^t e_1(\tau)\,dt + e_0(\tau)\,|_{\tau=0} \tag{3.29}$$

The unit will always integrate with respect to t; this is something which is fundamental and cannot be changed. What we are doing is altering the gain so that voltages in the system which occur at time t, before it is time scaled, occur at time $a_\tau t$ after it is time scaled.

Consider an integrator with $CR = 1$ for the case where $e_1(t)$ is a step of 10 V applied at time $t = 0$ sec, and $e_0(t)\,|_{t=0}$ is zero:

$$e_0(t) = -\int_0^t [10]\, dt = -10t \text{ V} \tag{3.30}$$

Therefore after 1 sec $e_0 = -10$ V. If we time scale the integrator to slow it down by a factor of 5, i.e. $a_\tau = 5$ and $\tau = 5t$, then

$$e_0(\tau) = -\frac{1}{5}\int_0^\tau [10]\, dt = -2\tau \tag{3.31}$$

For e_0 to reach -10 V requires 5 sec, which means that by changing the time constant the integrator is operating so that at the end of 5 sec its output is the same as it was after 1 sec before it was changed. The integrator can therefore be considered as operating in an expanded time scale. The effect of changing all integrator time constants by a_τ is to decrease or increase, depending on whether a_τ is greater or less than unity, the solution frequency of the equations.

When this method of time scaling is used, if the time scales of the recorded results are marked so that $a_\tau t$ sec appears as t sec, then the effect of time scaling can be ignored. This means that measurements can be taken directly from the records and no time scale conversion factor is required. When the equations are time scaled it is not possible to do this. Measurements are made with respect to the actual time scale of the recording and conversion factors, as given by equations (3.22) to (3.25), applied to get the required results.

3.5. Estimation of Maximum Values and Frequencies

In order to scale the equations of the physical system so that they are in a suitable form to put on the computer, it is necessary to know, or be able to estimate, maximum values of the variables and frequencies in the solution of the equations. It is therefore important when formulating the equations, to put down an estimate of the maximum values variables are likely to obtain, and the expected frequencies in the solution. These are often known from the characteristics of the physical system, or from previous knowledge of similar systems. It is sometimes possible to obtain maximum values and frequencies from the equations. This can be done for second order linear differential equations, which occur very frequently in the study of physical systems.

Consider the mass, spring, damper system of Fig. 3.1 with the equation of motion for the mass

$$M\ddot{x}+D\dot{x}+Kx = y \tag{3.1}$$

As shown in Appendix 1, this can be written in the generalized form

$$\ddot{x}+2\zeta\omega_n\dot{x}+\omega_n^2 x = \frac{y}{M} \tag{3.32}$$

where ω_n is the natural frequency of the system when the damping coefficient is zero, and ζ is the damping ratio. The value of ζ is 0 for zero damping and 1 for critical damping.

3.6. Examples of the Application of Scaling Techniques

EXAMPLE 1. Consider the mass, spring, damper system of Fig. 3.1 with the following values of constants,

$$M = 1 \text{ kg}$$
$$K = 100 \text{ N/m}$$
$$D = 6 \text{ N/m/sec}$$

Let the maximum value of the applied force y be 50 N and $x\,|_{t=0} = \dot{x}\,|_{t=0} = 0$.

Equation (3.7) becomes

$$\ddot{x}+6\dot{x}+100x = y \tag{3.33}$$

Comparing the coefficients of equation (3.33) with the generalized coefficients of equation (3.32) shows that the natural frequency of the system ω_n is 10 rad/sec and the damping ratio ζ is 0·3. For this system, time scaling of the equation is not necessary. If the solution is to be recorded using a plotting table, time scaling by a factor of 10 can be done on the computer.

If y is a step of force applied at time $t = 0$, the mass will oscillate and then settle down to a steady state displacement. When this happens the $\ddot{x}$ and $\dot{x}$ terms in equation (3.33) are zero, and the steady state displacement of the mass is obtained from the solution of $100x_{ss} = y$, where x_{ss} is the steady state value of x. For the case when y is the maximum value of 50 N, $x_{ss} = 0{\cdot}5$ m. If there was no damping term in the equation its solution would be, from Appendix 1,

$$x = x_{ss}(1 - \cos \omega_n t) \tag{3.34}$$

The maximum value of x is when $\cos \omega_n t = -1$,

$$x_M = 2x_{ss} \tag{3.35}$$

Differentiating equation (3.34) we have

$$\dot{x} = x_{ss}\omega_n \sin \omega_n t \tag{3.36}$$

with a maximum value, when $\sin \omega_n t = 1$

$$\dot{x}_M = \omega_n x_{ss} \tag{3.37}$$

Differentiating equation (3.36) we have

$$\ddot{x} = x_{ss}\omega_n^2 \cos \omega_n t \tag{3.38}$$

with a maximum value, when $\cos \omega_n t = 1$

$$\ddot{x}_M = \omega_n^2 x_{ss} \tag{3.39}$$

For the system which we wish to simulate on the computer the damping is small, so for scaling purposes take the maximum values of the variables as those obtained from equations (3.35), (3.37) and (3.39). We have therefore

$$x_M = 1 \text{ m}$$
$$\dot{x}_M = 5 \text{ m/sec}$$
$$\ddot{x}_M = 50 \text{ m/sec}^2$$

Amplitude scaling the equation using the method of scale factors with dimensional units, the computer variables will be $e_{x,2}$, $e_{x,1}$, $e_{x,0}$ and e_y, with corresponding scale factors $a_{x,2}$, $a_{x,1}$, $a_{x,0}$ and a_y. The values of the scale factors are

$$a_{x,2} = \frac{1}{50} \text{ C.U./m/sec}^2$$

$$a_{x,1} = \frac{1}{5} \text{ C.U./m/sec}$$

$$a_{x,0} = \frac{1}{1} \text{ C.U./m}$$

$$a_y = \frac{1}{50} \text{ C.U./N}$$

Writing equation (3.33) in computer variables, we get

$$\frac{e_{x,2}}{a_{x,2}} + 6\frac{e_{x,1}}{a_{x,1}} + 100\frac{e_{x,0}}{a_{x,0}} = \frac{e_y}{a_y} \tag{3.40}$$

and putting in the values of the scale factors and rearranging the equation gives

$$e_{x,2} = e_y - 0{\cdot}6\, e_{x,1} - 2e_{x,0} \tag{3.41}$$

The equations relating $e_{x,1}$ to $e_{x,2}$ and $e_{x,0}$ to $e_{x,1}$ are obtained as shown in section 3.3 and are given by equations (3.12) and (3.14).

$$e_{x,1} = \frac{a_{x,1}}{a_{x,2}} \int_0^t e_{x,2}\, dt + e_{x,1}\,|_{t=0} \tag{3.12}$$

$$e_{x,0} = \frac{a_{x,0}}{a_{x,1}} \int_0^t e_{x,1}\, dt + e_{x,0}\,|_{t=0} \tag{3.14}$$

Putting in the values of the scale factors gives

$$e_{x,1} = 10 \int_0^t e_{x,2}\, dt + 0 \tag{3.42}$$

$$e_{x,0} = 5\int_0^t e_{x,1}\,dt+0 \tag{3.43}$$

We now have all the information necessary to draw the computer flow diagram as shown in Fig. 3.10.

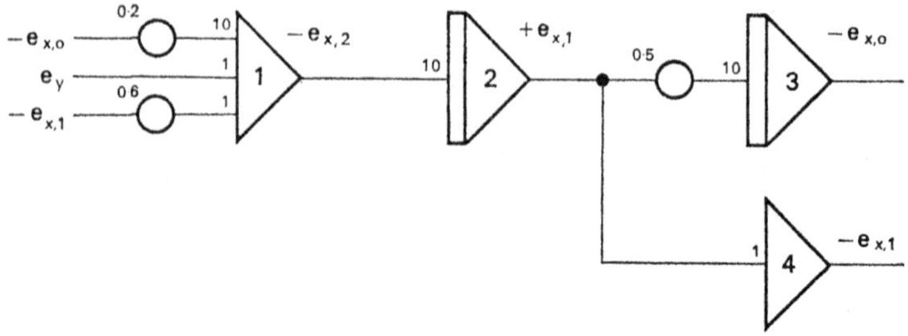

FIG. 3.10. Computer flow diagram for mass spring damper system.

Checking the gains round the two loops, we have 100 in the loop of amplifiers 1, 2 and 3, and 6 in the loop of amplifiers 1, 2 and 4. These are the coefficients of x and $\dot{x}$ in equation (3.33) and are therefore correct.

If the amplitude scaling is carried out using the method of normalized variables, the normalized form of the variables would be $[\ddot{x}/50]$, $[\dot{x}/5]$, $[x/1]$ and $[y/50]$, where the maximum values of the variables are those obtained previously.

The computer equations would then be, using equations (3.16), (3.19) and (3.21)

$$\left[\frac{\ddot{x}}{50}\right] = \left[\frac{y}{50}\right] - 0{\cdot}6\left[\frac{\dot{x}}{5}\right] - 2\left[\frac{x}{1}\right] \tag{3.44}$$

$$\left[\frac{\dot{x}}{5}\right] = 10\int_0^t \left[\frac{\ddot{x}}{50}\right] dt+0 \tag{3.45}$$

$$\left[\frac{x}{1}\right] = 5\int_0^t \left[\frac{\dot{x}}{5}\right] dt+0 \tag{3.46}$$

The coefficients of these three equations are the same as those in equations (3.41), (3.42) and (3.43), and the computer flow diagram for solving them would be the same as Fig. 3.10, with $e_{x,2}$, $e_{x,1}$, $e_{x,0}$ and e_y replaced by $[\ddot{x}/50]$, $[\dot{x}/5]$, $[x/1]$ and $[y/50]$.

For a computer set up as in Fig. 3.10, the amplifier output voltages plotted with respect to time are shown in Fig. 3.11.

EXAMPLE 2. Consider a simplified suspension system for one wheel of a car, as shown in Fig. 3.12.

M_1 is a quarter of the mass of the car = 300 kg
M_2 is the mass of a wheel and axle = 30 kg
K_1 is the spring constant = 14,700 N/m
K_2 is the tyre spring constant = 60,300 N/m

D is the shock absorber damping constant in N/m/sec., which is to be varied in order to optimize the performance of the suspension system.

x_1 is the displacement of the car body.
x_2 is the displacement of the wheel and axle.
y is the change in the road level

The equations of motion for the two masses are

$$M_1\ddot{x}_1+D(\dot{x}_1-\dot{x}_2)+K_1(x_1-x_2) = 0 \qquad (3.47)$$

$$M_2\ddot{x}+D(\dot{x}_2-\dot{x}_1)+K_1(x_2-x_1)+K_2(x_2-y) = 0 \qquad (3.48)$$

Putting in the values of the coefficients we have

$$300\ddot{x}_1+D(\dot{x}_1-\dot{x}_2)+14{,}700(x_1-x_2) = 0 \qquad (3.49)$$

$$30\ddot{x}_2+D(\dot{x}_2-\dot{x}_1)+14{,}700(x_2-x_1)+60{,}300(x_2-y) = 0 \qquad (3.50)$$

If we divide through the equations by the coefficients of the highest derivatives we get

$$\ddot{x}_1+\frac{D}{300}(\dot{x}_1-\dot{x}_2)+49x_1-49x_2 = 0 \qquad (3.51)$$

$$\ddot{x}_2+\frac{D}{30}(\dot{x}_2-\dot{x}_1)+2500x_2-490x_1-2010y = 0 \qquad (3.52)$$

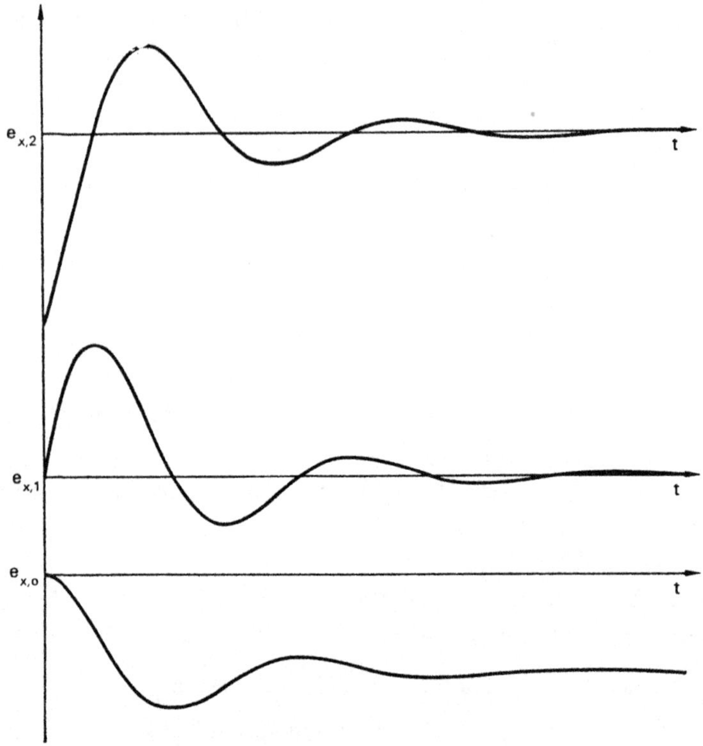

FIG. 3.11. Amplifier output voltages for the circuit of Fig. 3.10 with step input.

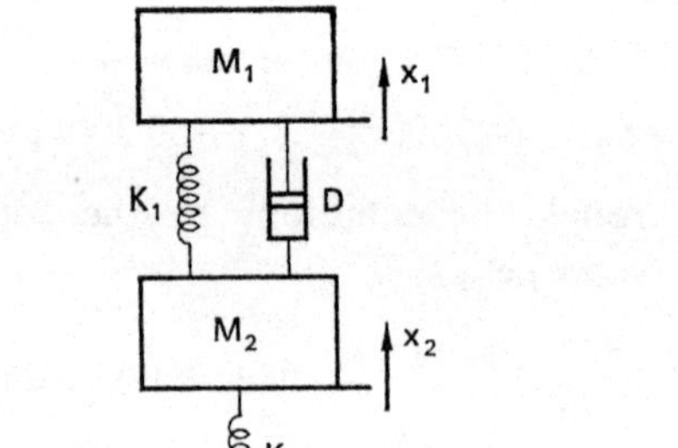

FIG. 3.12. Suspension system for one wheel of car.

To obtain an estimate of the frequencies in the solution of the problem, consider equations (3.51) and (3.52) with no cross-coupling terms:

$$\ddot{x}_1+\frac{D}{300}\dot{x}_1+49x_1 = 0 \tag{3.53}$$

$$\ddot{x}_2+\frac{D}{30}\dot{x}_2+2500x_2 = 2010y \tag{3.54}$$

The natural frequency of equation (3.53), ω_{M_1} is 7 rad/sec and of equation (3.54), ω_{M_2} is 50 rad/sec. The equations can be put on the computer without time scaling. If records are to be made using a plotting table, a time scale factor of 10 could be introduced by reducing all integrator gains by 10.

To estimate the maximum values of the variables, first find the steady state displacement of x_1 and x_2 for the maximum amplitude of step input of y. In the steady state all derivatives of x_1 and x_2 are zero, therefore from equations (3.51) and (3.52)

$$49x_1-49x_2 = 0 \tag{3.55}$$

$$2500x_2-490x_1-2010y = 0 \tag{3.56}$$

If the maximum step of y is 0·1 m

$$(x_1)_{ss} = (x_2)_{ss} = y = 0{\cdot}1 \text{ m}$$

where subscript ss refers to steady state value.

To allow for the case where D is small, i.e. the system is lightly damped, take the maximum values of x_1 and x_2 as twice their steady state values

$$(x_1)_M = 0{\cdot}2 \text{ m}$$

$$(x_2)_M = 0{\cdot}2 \text{ m}$$

The maximum values of the derivatives of x_1 and x_2 are estimated in the same way as for the simple mass spring damper system, equations (3.36) to (3.39). Use the steady state values of x_1 and x_2

and the natural frequencies ω_{M_1} and ω_{M_2} obtained from equations (3.53) and (3.54). Therefore estimate

$$(\dot{x}_1)_M = (x_1)_{ss}.\omega_{M_1} = 0{\cdot}7 \text{ m/sec}$$

$$(\ddot{x}_1)_M = (x_1)_{ss}.\omega_{M_1}^2 = 4{\cdot}9 \text{ m/sec}^2$$

$$(\dot{x}_2)_M = (x_2)_{ss}.\omega_{M_2} = 5 \text{ m/sec}$$

$$(\ddot{x}_2)_M = (x_2)_{ss}.\omega_{M_2}^2 = 250 \text{ m/sec}^2$$

Using the method of dimensional scale factors for amplitude scaling, let the computer variables be

$$e_{x_1},\ e_{\dot{x}_1},\ e_{\ddot{x}_1},\ e_{x_2},\ e_{\dot{x}_2},\ e_{\ddot{x}_2},\text{ and } e_y,$$

having corresponding scale factors

$$a_{x_1},\ a_{\dot{x}_1},\ a_{\ddot{x}_1},\ a_{x_2},\ a_{\dot{x}_2},\ a_{\ddot{x}_2},\text{ and } a_y$$

The values of the scale factors are obtained using the estimated maximum values

$$a_{x_1} = \frac{1}{0{\cdot}2} = 5 \text{ C.U./m}$$

$$a_{\dot{x}_1} = \frac{1}{0{\cdot}7} = 1{\cdot}43 \text{ C.U./m/sec}$$

$$a_{\ddot{x}_1} = \frac{1}{4{\cdot}9} = 0{\cdot}204 \text{ C.U./m/sec}^2$$

$$a_{x_2} = \frac{1}{0{\cdot}2} = 5 \text{ C.U./m}$$

$$a_{\dot{x}_2} = \frac{1}{5} = 0{\cdot}2 \text{ C.U./m/sec}$$

$$a_{\ddot{x}_2} = \frac{1}{250} = 0{\cdot}004 \text{ C.U./m/sec}^2$$

$$a_y = \frac{1}{0{\cdot}1} = 10 \text{ C.U./m}$$

It is not necessary to use the exact value of the scale factor obtained by the above calculations. Generally the number can be rounded off to a convenient lower value. This should only result in a small reduction in the excursion of the voltage representing the variable. Of the above scale factors it is convenient to round off $a_{\dot{x}_1}$ and $a_{\ddot{x}_1}$.

Take

$$a_{\dot{x}_1} = 1{\cdot}25 \text{ C.U./m/sec}$$

and

$$a_{\ddot{x}_1} = 0{\cdot}2 \text{ C.U./m/sec}^2$$

We can now rewrite equations (3.51) and (3.52) using computer variables as

$$\frac{e_{\ddot{x}_1}}{a_{\ddot{x}_1}} + \frac{D}{300}\left(\frac{e_{\dot{x}_1}}{a_{\dot{x}_1}} - \frac{e_{\dot{x}_2}}{a_{\dot{x}_2}}\right) + 49\frac{e_{x_1}}{a_{x_1}} - 49\frac{e_{x_2}}{a_{x_2}} = 0 \tag{3.57}$$

$$\frac{e_{\ddot{x}_2}}{a_{\ddot{x}_2}} + \frac{D}{30}\left(\frac{e_{\dot{x}_2}}{a_{\dot{x}_2}} - \frac{e_{\dot{x}_1}}{a_{\dot{x}_1}}\right) + 2500\frac{e_{x_2}}{a_{x_2}} - 490\frac{e_{x_1}}{a_{x_1}} = 2010\frac{e_y}{a_y} \tag{3.58}$$

Putting in the values of the scale factors gives

$$\frac{e_{\ddot{x}_1}}{0{\cdot}2} + \frac{D}{300}\left(\frac{e_{\dot{x}_1}}{1{\cdot}25} - \frac{e_{\dot{x}_2}}{0{\cdot}2}\right) + 49\frac{e_{x_1}}{5} - 49\frac{e_{x_2}}{5} = 0 \tag{3.59}$$

$$\frac{e_{\ddot{x}_2}}{0{\cdot}004} - \frac{D}{30}\left(\frac{e_{\dot{x}_1}}{1{\cdot}25} - \frac{e_{\dot{x}_2}}{0{\cdot}2}\right) + 2500\frac{e_{x_2}}{5} - 490\frac{e_{x_1}}{5} = 2010\frac{e_y}{10} \tag{3.60}$$

from which we obtain $e_{\ddot{x}_1}$ and $e_{\ddot{x}_2}$ in terms of the other computer variables

$$e_{\ddot{x}_1} = -1{\cdot}96e_{x_1} + 1{\cdot}96e_{x_2} - \frac{D}{1875}(e_{\dot{x}_1} - 6{\cdot}25e_{\dot{x}_2}) \tag{3.61}$$

$$e_{\ddot{x}_2} = 0{\cdot}804e_y - 2e_{x_2} + 0{\cdot}392e_{x_1} + \frac{D}{9375}(e_{\dot{x}_1} - 6{\cdot}25e_{\dot{x}_2}) \tag{3.62}$$

Four more equations are required relating $e_{\dot{x}_1}$ to $e_{\ddot{x}_1}$, e_{x_1} to $e_{\dot{x}_1}$, $e_{\dot{x}_2}$ to $e_{\ddot{x}_2}$ and e_{x_2} to $e_{\dot{x}_2}$ and these are obtained as shown in Section 3.3.

$$e_{\dot{x}_1} = \frac{a_{\dot{x}_1}}{a_{\ddot{x}_1}} \int_0^t e_{\ddot{x}_1}\, dt + e_{\dot{x}_1}\big|_{t=0}$$

$$= 6{\cdot}25 \int_0^t e_{\ddot{x}_1}\, dt + 0 \tag{3.63}$$

Similarly

$$e_{x_1} = 4 \int_0^t e_{\dot{x}_1}\, dt + 0 \tag{3.64}$$

$$e_{\dot{x}_2} = 50 \int_0^t e_{\ddot{x}_2}\, dt + 0 \tag{3.65}$$

$$e_{x_2} = 25 \int_0^t e_{\dot{x}_2}\, dt + 0 \tag{3.66}$$

We now have all the information necessary to draw the computer flow diagram as shown in Fig. 3.13. The responses of e_{x_1} and e_{x_2} to a step change in y are shown in Fig. 3.14 for a number of values of D.

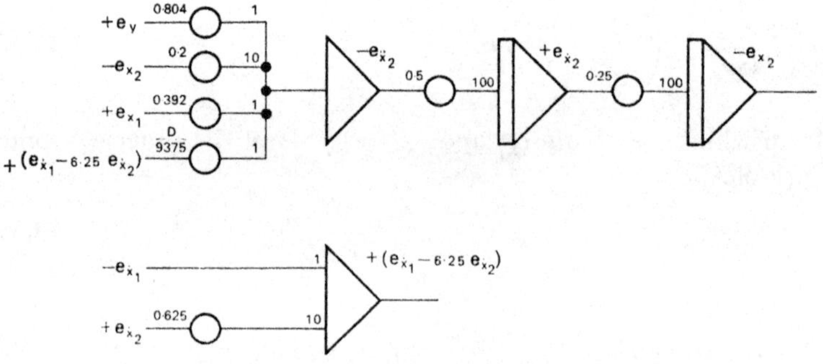

FIG. 3.13. Computer flow diagram for car suspension system.

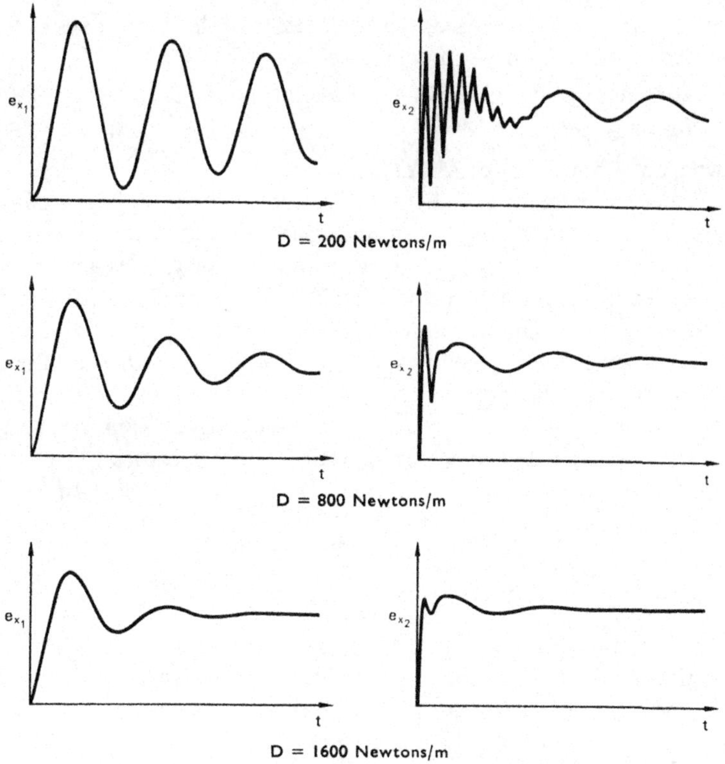

FIG. 3.14. Response of car suspension system to step inputs for a number of values of *D*.

3.7 Scaling of Higher Order Equations

We have seen that for second order equations or coupled second order equations we can make an estimate of the maximum value the variables are likely to attain. However, for equations of higher order it is much more difficult. An emperical rule, which works well, is suggested by A. S. Jackson in his book *Analog Computation*. Scaling is carried out using the method of normalized variables, and the maximum values are selected so as to make the values of all the coefficients of the derivatives in the scaled equation approximately unity.

Consider the nth order differential equation

$$a_n x^{(n)} + a_{n-1} x^{(n-1)} + \ldots + a_1 x^{(1)} + a_0 x^{(0)} = f(t) \qquad (3.67)$$

where $x^{(n)}$ is written for $d^n x/dt^n$.

Take the case where all the initial conditions of the variables are zero, and $f(t)$ is a step of amplitude A units. For the instant just after the step is applied, $x^{(0)}$ and all derivatives up to the $(n-1)$th are zero. The value of $x^{(n)}$ is A/a_n and if the system is stable it is its maximum value. As t tends to infinity, the derivatives of x go to zero and a steady state value of $x^{(0)} = A/a_0$ is attained. To allow for the possibility of lightly damped roots, take the maximum value of $x^{(0)}$ as twice its steady state value $= 2A/a_0$.

Using normalized variables, equation (3.67) becomes

$$A\left[\frac{x^{(n)}}{A/a_n}\right] + x_M^{(n-1)} . a_{n-1}\left[\frac{x^{(n-1)}}{x_M^{n-1}}\right] + \ldots + x_M^{(1)} . a_1\left[\frac{x^{(1)}}{x_M^{(1)}}\right]$$

$$+ 2A\left[\frac{x^{(0)}}{2A/a_0}\right] = f(t) \qquad (3.68)$$

A restriction in the selection of the maximum values is that the sequence of maxima must continually increase or decrease.

The rule is best illustrated by an example. Consider the equation

$$x^{(4)} + 16x^{(3)} + 153x^{(2)} + 550x^{(1)} + 2500x^{(0)} = f(t) \qquad (3.69)$$

where $x^{(3)}|_{t=0} = x^{(2)}|_{t=0} = x^{(1)}|_{t=0} = x^{(0)}|_{t=0} = 0$, and $f(t)$ is a step of maximum amplitude 2500 units. The maximum value of $x^{(4)}$ which occurs just after the step of $f(t)$ is applied is 2500 and the steady state value of $x^{(0)}$ is 1. For scaling purposes take the maximum value of $x^{(0)}$ as twice the steady state value, i.e.

$$x_M^{(0)} = 2$$

Writing equation (3.69) using normalized variables gives

$$2500\left[\frac{x^{(4)}}{2500}\right] + 16.x_M^{(3)}\left[\frac{x^{(3)}}{x_M^{(3)}}\right] + 153.x_M^{(2)}\left[\frac{x^{(2)}}{x_M^{(2)}}\right] + 550.x_M^{(1)}\left[\frac{x^{(1)}}{x^{(1)}}\right]$$

$$+ 5000\left[\frac{x^{(0)}}{2}\right] = 2500\left[\frac{f(t)}{2500}\right] \qquad (3.70)$$

Dividing through the equation by 2500 we have

$$\left[\frac{x^{(4)}}{2500}\right]+\frac{16.x_M^{(3)}}{2500}\left[\frac{x^{(3)}}{x_M^{(3)}}\right]+\frac{153.x_M^{(2)}}{2500}\left[\frac{x^{(2)}}{x_M^{(2)}}\right]+\frac{550.x_M^{(1)}}{2500}\left[\frac{x^{(1)}}{x_M^{(1)}}\right]$$

$$+2\left[\frac{x^{(0)}}{2}\right]=\left[\frac{f(t)}{2500}\right] \qquad (3.71)$$

Maximum values for the derivatives are selected so that all coefficients are approximately unity, except that for $x^{(0)}$ which is 2,

i.e.

$$x_M^{(3)} \simeq \frac{2500}{16}, \text{ say } 150$$

$$x_M^{(2)} \simeq \frac{2500}{153}, \text{ say } 16$$

and

$$x_M^{(1)} \simeq \frac{2500}{550}, \text{ say } 4{\cdot}5$$

Substituting these maximum values in equation (3.71) and taking all terms to the right-hand side of the equation except $x^{(4)}$ we get

$$\left[\frac{x^{(4)}}{2500}\right]=\left[\frac{f(t)}{2500}\right]-0{\cdot}96\left[\frac{x^{(3)}}{150}\right]-0{\cdot}979\left[\frac{x^{(2)}}{16}\right]$$

$$-0{\cdot}99\left[\frac{x^{(1)}}{4{\cdot}5}\right]-2\left[\frac{x^{(0)}}{2}\right] \qquad (3.72)$$

The relations between the normalized variable form of the derivatives are obtained as in Section 3.3.

$$\left[\frac{x^{(3)}}{150}\right] = \frac{2500}{150}\int_0^t \left[\frac{x^{(4)}}{2500}\right] dt + 0$$

$$= 16{\cdot}66 \int_0^t \left[\frac{x^{(4)}}{2500}\right] dt \tag{3.73}$$

$$\left[\frac{x^{(2)}}{16}\right] = \frac{150}{16}\int_0^t \left[\frac{x^{(3)}}{150}\right] dt + 0$$

$$= 9{\cdot}375 \int_0^t \left[\frac{x^{(3)}}{150}\right] dt \tag{3.74}$$

$$\left[\frac{x^{(1)}}{4{\cdot}5}\right] = \frac{16}{4{\cdot}5}\int_0^t \left[\frac{x^{(2)}}{16}\right] dt + 0$$

$$= 3{\cdot}55 \int_0^t \left[\frac{x^{(2)}}{16}\right] dt \tag{3.75}$$

$$\left[\frac{x^{(0)}}{2}\right] = \frac{4{\cdot}5}{2}\int_0^t \left[\frac{x^{(1)}}{4{\cdot}5}\right] dt + 0$$

$$= 2{\cdot}25 \int_0^t \left[\frac{x^{(1)}}{4{\cdot}5}\right] dt \tag{3.76}$$

Using equations (3.72) to (3.76), the computer flow diagram to solve the equation can be drawn, as shown in Fig. 3.15. The voltages representing x and all the derivatives plotted with respect

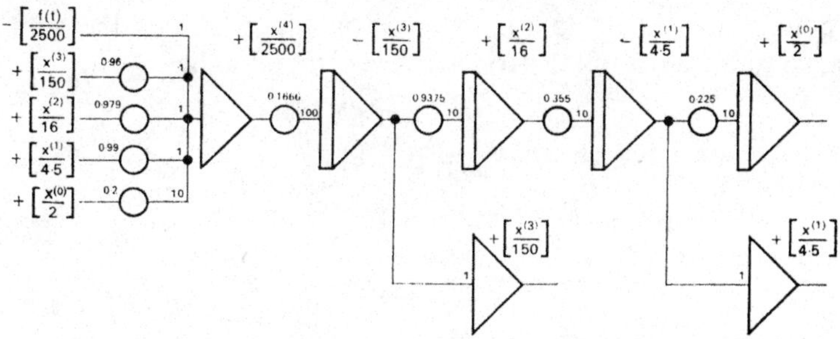

FIG. 3.15. Computer flow diagram for fourth order differential equation.

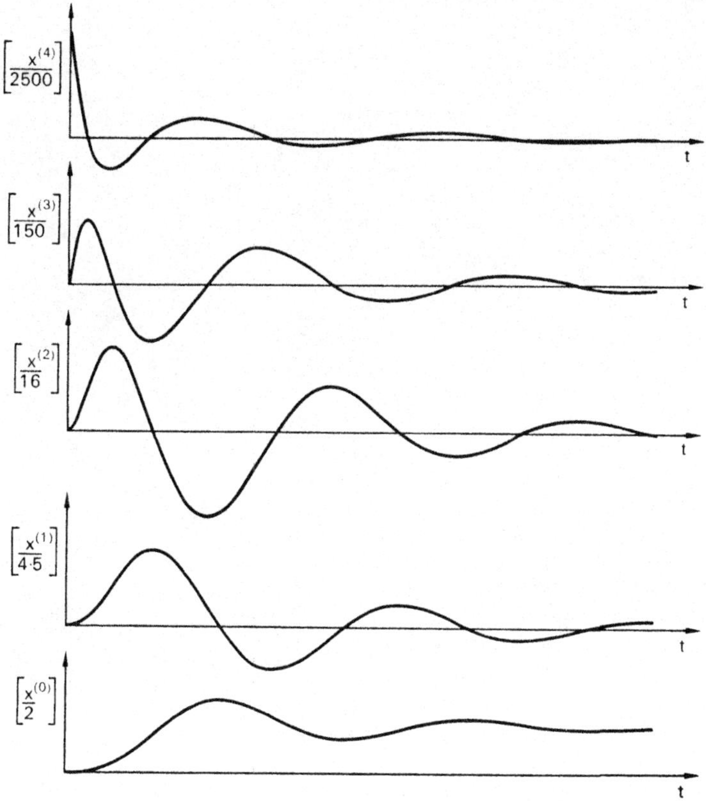

FIG. 3.16. Responses of voltages at outputs of amplifiers of Fig. 3.15 for step input $f(t)$.

to time are shown in Fig. 3.16. From these graphs the actual maximum values of the derivatives were found to be

$$x_M^{(0)} = 1{\cdot}52$$

$$x_M^{(1)} = 3{\cdot}51$$

$$x_M^{(2)} = 14$$

and

$$x_M^{(3)} = 100$$

which correspond approximately with the estimated values.

CHAPTER 4

Organization of the Computer and Checking Problem Set-ups

THE complexity of the organization and control of an analog computer depends on the size of the machine, and this is generally indicated by the number of operational amplifiers it contains. Computers vary in size from small machines with about ten to twenty amplifiers, to large systems with several hundred amplifiers. The amplifiers will be assigned as either summers, integrators or inverters, and as there are no definite rules about the proportions of any one type of unit, these vary from one manufacturer to another. There is also considerable variation in the number of nonlinear units available, a typical figure for a 250 amplifier machine being 100, a large proportion of which will be multipliers. The ratio of potentiometers to amplifiers will never be less than 1 and a more typical figure is 1·5.

On small computers it is not necessary to have a complex control and monitoring system. All the units are easily accessible, and any unnecessary sophistication only adds to the cost of the machine. On large computers a more complex control and monitoring system is justified, in order to simplify the setting up, checking and running of problems. It is important to make the machine as efficient as possible, bearing in mind the much higher capital expenditure and running costs.

In the following sections various organizational features common to all sizes of computer will be discussed.

4.1. Interconnection of Units

The number of computing units used, and the way they are interconnected, vary widely from one problem to another. It is therefore necessary to have a convenient and flexible method of interconnecting all the units, in any pattern. On modern machines this is done by bringing the inputs and outputs of the units to a central patchboard system, where they can be connected together using patch cords of various lengths. The patchboard system consists of a fixed patchbay with all the unit terminations on spring contacts, and removable patchboards which have holes in positions corresponding to the spring contacts on the patchbay. The interconnecting patch cords have pins on each end. When plugged into the patchboard they project through the back to mate with the spring contacts of the patchbay.

Patchboard systems are expensive, as they must be rigid and accurately constructed. This is necessary to ensure that all pins and spring contacts mate correctly with any configuration of patch cord connections. There are several advantages of having removable patchboards. Problems can be patched away from the computer while it is being used for another problem. Also the patched board can be stored, so that the problem can be run again at a later date without the necessity of repatching. This is important, as a considerable amount of time is generally required to patch and check out a problem set-up.

The size of the patchboard will depend on the number of holes required, their size and spacing. As it is necessary to have some means of identifying the holes, even when patch cords are inserted, there is a limit on how close together they can be. Usually holes are identified by a combination of colour and a simple legend. The layout of the patchboard differs from one computer to another, but for individual summers and integrators the arrangement shown in Fig. 4.1 is typical. The inputs will be labelled with the value of the resistor, or in some computers with the gain obtainable with the standard feedback element. The unit output is generally repeated several times so that connection to a number of other units can be made without using multiple type patch cords. Where a number of holes give access to the same point, this is usually indicated by lines joining them. Different colours will be used for the inputs, outputs, summing junction, and initial condition input areas. The feedback element will be a standard value of say 1 MΩ for summers and 1 μF for integrators, but there will be provision for selecting other values, either on the patchboard or by means of a switch on another panel.

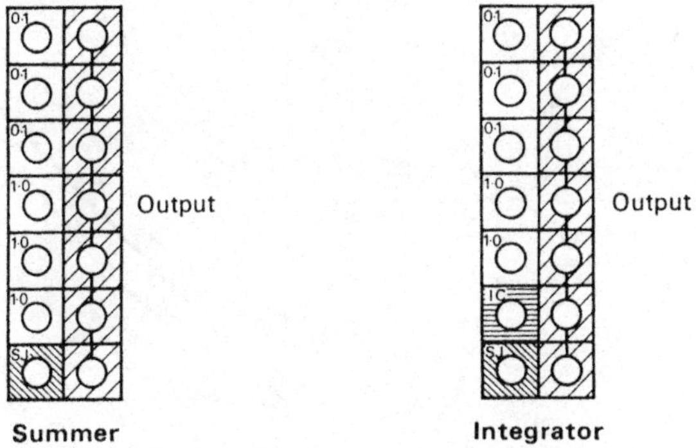

FIG. 4.1. Typical patchboard layout.

4.2. Setting Potentiometers

Before setting the potentiometers the problem must have been patched up and the patchboard inserted in the computer. This is necessary because the potentiometers have to be set up connected to the load they will be working into when computing.

Consider the potentiometer and amplifier configuration shown in Fig. 4.2a. If R_1 is infinite, there is a linear relationship between e_2 and the potentiometer wiper displacement as shown by curve 1 of Fig. 4.2b. In general R_1 will load the potentiometer, and the relation between e_2 and the wiper displacement is not linear but of the form shown by curve 2 of Fig. 4.2b, which is a function of the value of R_1. When setting up the potentiometer, the position of the wiper is adjusted so that e_2/e_1 is a value specified in the problem flow diagram. For this ratio to be correct, the adjustment must be made with the wiper loaded by a resistor of the same value as will be used in the computation. As R_1 could be one of a number of values, computers are organized so that potentiometers are set after the problem is patched, and therefore with the correct load resistors connected to them.

Most computers have a special POTENTIOMETER SET mode for carrying out the setting up operation. When this mode is selected,

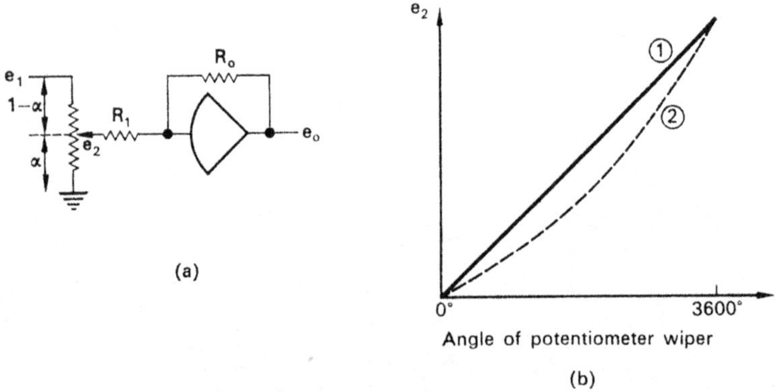

FIG. 4.2. Potentiometer loading.

overriding switches operate to connect the summing junction end of all input resistor groups either to ground or to the inputs of their respective amplifiers. In the latter case, additional relays connect low value feedback resistors across the amplifiers to ensure that their inputs are as close as possible to virtual earth, and also to ensure that they will not overload during the setting operation. Without this overriding mode the possibility exists of setting a potentiometer incorrectly, when the resistor it is feeding into is disconnected from its amplifier, and therefore not loading it.

A number of methods are used for setting potentiometers, and the important thing in all of them is that there must be no additional loading of the potentiometer wiper. In small and medium-size computers they are generally set manually, either by looking at their output with a high input impedance digital voltmeter or nulling against an accurate voltage source. The circuits for these two methods are shown in Fig. 4.3. The input and output of the potentiometer are connected to a double-pole switch. In the in-operated position the input of the potentiometer is connected to the patchbay and the output to only the patchbay. When the

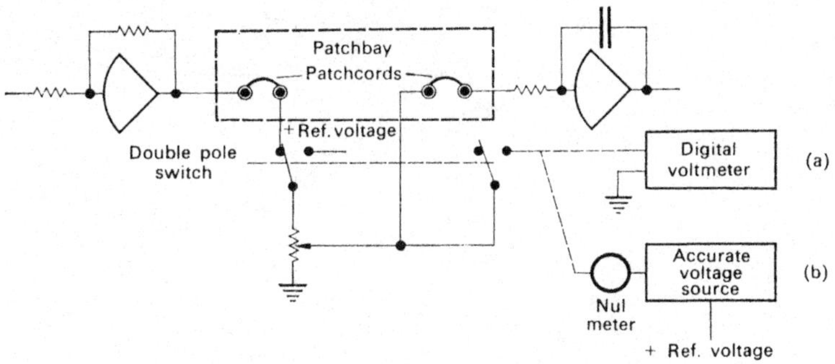

FIG. 4.3. Circuit for manually set potentiometers.

switch is operated, the input of the potentiometer is disconnected from the patchbay and connected instead to the positive reference voltage, and the output in addition to its connection to the patchbay is connected also to either (a) a digital voltmeter, or (b) a nulling circuit. If (a), the potentiometer is adjusted until the reading on the voltmeter is the reference voltage multiplied by the required potentiometer setting. For example, with a 100 V reference supply, if the potentiometer is to be set to 0·834 the digital voltmeter would read 83·4 V. If (b) the voltage source would be set to give an output of the reference voltage multiplied by the required setting, and the potentiometer then adjusted for zero reading on the null meter. For the example as in (a), the voltage source would be set to 83·4 V. The voltage source in some computers might be a very accurate potentiometer connected to the reference voltage. In these cases the reference potentiometer would be set to the required value, and the potentiometer being set adjusted for a zero on the null meter.

In large computers, where there are a great number of potentiometers to be set, manual setting is too slow and tedious, and all manufacturers have some means of automatic setting. This is generally done using a small servomotor attached to each potentiometer, and driven by a central servo amplifier. The connection

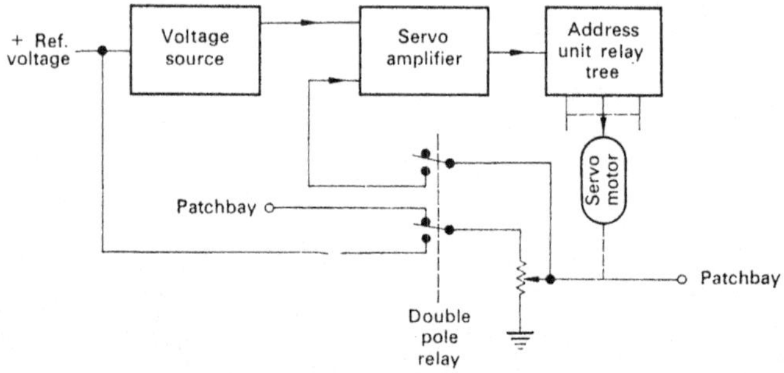

FIG. 4.4. Circuit for servo set potentiometers.

between the amplifier and the appropriate servomotor is made when the potentiometer is selected on an address unit. The system is illustrated in Fig. 4.4. The basic principle is the same as the nulling method for manual setting, except that in this case the null meter is replaced by a summing circuit at the input of the servo amplifier. To set a potentiometer, the computer is first put into the POTENTIOMETER SET mode, and then the potentiometer selected on the address unit. This connects the output of the servo amplifier to the servomotor for that potentiometer and operates a double-pole relay. The relay disconnects the top of the potentiometer from the patchbay, connecting it instead to the positive reference voltage, and connects the output to one input of the servo amplifier. The other input of the servo amplifier is connected to the output of a voltage source. This is set to the reference voltage multiplied by the required potentiometer setting. A button is then pressed to initiate the set operation. The servomotor drives the wiper of the potentiometer to a position so that its output voltage is equal to that from the voltage source. If the potentiometer has not set to the correct value within about 3 sec, a protection circuit disconnects the input to the servomotor, and a light comes on to warn the operator that there is a fault. With a servo set potentiometer system, it is possible, either with a special purpose digital unit or a digital computer, to set the potentiometers from punched paper tape or cards.

4.3. Control of the Problem

As the output voltages of the integrating units are dependent on time, in order to solve a problem on the computer it is essential to have some means of controlling their operation. This is necessary so that they can all be made to start integrating at the same time, with the correct initial condition voltages. Switching circuits are built into the units so that they can be put into one of three modes, RESET or INITIAL CONDITION, COMPUTE, and HOLD, controlled from a central source.

A typical control circuit for an integrating unit is illustrated in Fig. 4.5. In the RESET mode, switch S_1 is closed and S_2 is open.

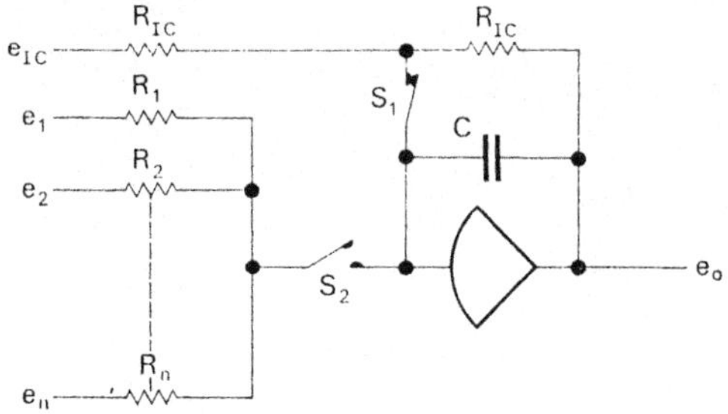

FIG. 4.5. Typical integrator control circuit.

If a constant voltage e_{IC} is applied, e_0 will charge up to $-e_{IC}$ as shown in Fig. 4.6, with a time constant determined by the value of the capacitor and the feedback resistor. Considering the case

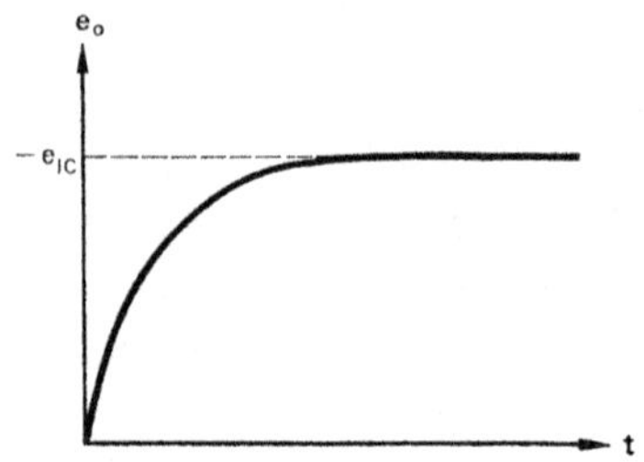

FIG. 4.6. Response of integrator unit to initial condition input.

of a perfect amplifier, where the input is a virtual earth point and no current flows into the amplifier, the current in the input resistor is equal to the sum of the currents in the feedback elements,

i.e.
$$\frac{e_{IC}}{R_{IC}} = -\left[\frac{e_0}{R_{IC}} + C\frac{d}{dt}(e_0)\right] \tag{4.1}$$

giving
$$\frac{d}{dt}(e_0) = -\frac{1}{CR_{IC}}[e_0 + e_{IC}] \tag{4.2}$$

which can be written
$$\frac{de_0}{e_0 + e_{IC}} = -\frac{dt}{CR_{IC}} \tag{4.3}$$

Integrating both sides, we get
$$\log_e(e_0 + e_{IC}) = -\frac{t}{CR_{IC}} + \log_e K \tag{4.4}$$

where K is a constant.

Therefore
$$e_0 + e_{IC} = Ke^{-t/(CR_{IC})} \tag{4.5}$$

At time $t = 0$, $e_0 = 0$.

Putting this in equation (4.5) we get

$$K = e_{IC}$$

Therefore

$$e_0 = -e_{IC}[1-e^{-t/(CR_{IC})}] \tag{4.6}$$

For e_0 to reach 0·01% of $-e_{IC}$, a time equal to at least $7CR_{IC}$ seconds is required.

In the COMPUTE mode, switch S_1 is opened and S_2 is closed. The unit then integrates the voltages e_1 to e_n with the appropriate gains, the integrated voltages adding to the initial condition voltage to which C has been charged in RESET. The value of e_0 at time t after the unit has been switched to COMPUTE is

$$e_0 = -\left[\frac{1}{CR_1}\int_0^t e_1 dt + \frac{1}{CR_2}\int_0^t e_2 dt + \ldots + \frac{1}{CR_n}\int_0^t e_n dt + e_{IC}\right] \tag{4.7}$$

In the HOLD mode, both switches S_1 and S_2 are open. With a perfect amplifier and capacitor no current would flow in C, and e_0 would remain at the value it had when the unit was switched to HOLD. However, in practice there will be a small current into the amplifier, and leakage across the capacitor. These will cause the capacitor voltage and hence e_0 to change slowly with time. For a drift corrected transistor amplifier with a 1 μF polystyrene capacitor, drift rates of less than 10 μV/sec are possible. For larger or smaller capacitors, the drift rates are correspondingly decreased or increased.

The three integrator modes can be controlled in a number of ways. For slow-speed real time computation, where a COMPUTE period of seconds or even minutes is required, the control will be manual, either from a multiway switch or a set of push buttons. The computer would first be put in RESET mode to set the integrator initial conditions. It would then be switched to COMPUTE and the solution displayed on an oscilloscope with a low-speed time base, or plotted using some form of pen recorder. At any time during or at the end of the COMPUTE period, the operator could put the computer into the HOLD mode, thus stopping the computation and freezing all voltage levels. This would allow him to measure voltages or change system parameters. Afterwards he could go back to the COMPUTE mode, in which case the computation would carry on from the point it had reached when put into HOLD mode, or he could go back to the RESET mode. A typical sequence of events is illustrated in Fig. 4.7.

In modern computers with wide bandwidth computing units, it is possible to compress the problem time scale considerably without decreasing the accuracy of solution too much. This means that COMPUTE periods of as low as 1 msec are possible. When

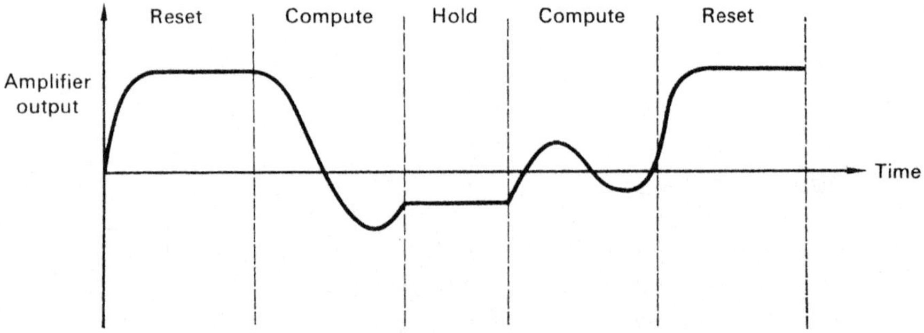

FIG. 4.7. Typical sequence of events at output of integrator unit.

operating with fast time scales, the computer is run in a repetitive mode, the integrators being automatically recycled from RESET to COMPUTE by means of a clock waveform. The problem solution is displayed on an oscilloscope, the time base of which is synchronized with the COMPUTE control signal so that a steady picture is available on the screen. With this type of operation, it is possible to assess quickly the effects on the solution of changing parameter values and initial condition levels.

For low-speed operation of the computer and repetition rates with COMPUTE periods of not less than 100 msec, reed relays can be used for the switches in the integrators. These are available with operate times of 0·5 msec matched within 50 μsec. For faster repetition rates, solid state electronic switches having operate times of less than 1 μsec are essential. It also becomes necessary to have initial condition circuits with very fast RESET.

A typical high-speed circuit using field effect transistor switches for switching between RESET and COMPUTE is shown in Fig. 4.8. Switches S_1 and S_2 are the field effect transistor switches and S_3 is a reed relay switch. In RESET, switch S_1 which is a single-pole on-off switch is closed, and S_2, which is a single-pole change-over

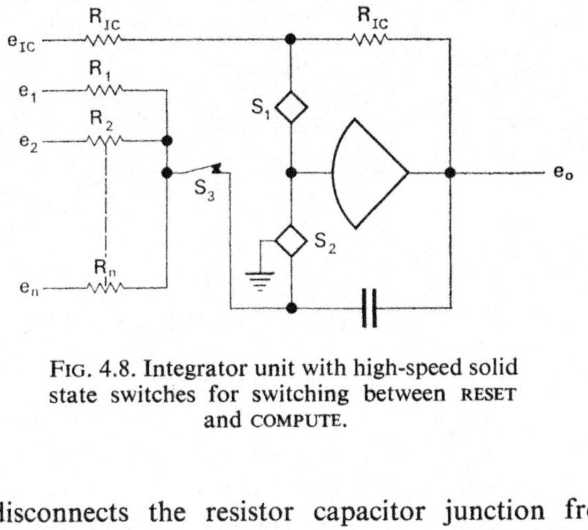

FIG. 4.8. Integrator unit with high-speed solid state switches for switching between RESET and COMPUTE.

switch, disconnects the resistor capacitor junction from the amplifier and connects it to ground. The amplifier is now connected as an inverter with a capacitor from its output to ground. When e_{IC} is applied, e_0 changes immediately to $-e_{IC}$ and C charges up to this voltage, with a time constant depending on its value and whatever resistance is in series with it. It is generally necessary to have a small series resistor to limit the amplifier output current required. For a 1 μF capacitor, and a 10 V amplifier with a maximum current output of 20 mA, a 500 Ω resistor in series with C would be required. The time constant of 0·5 msec would therefore require a RESET period of at least 3·5 msec for the initial condition to set within 0·01%. This compares with 70 msec for the circuit of Fig. 4.5, where a 10 kΩ resistor would probably be used. When switched to COMPUTE, S_1 opens and S_2 connects the resistor capacitor junction to the input of the amplifier instead of to ground. The amplifier is now connected as an integrating unit with an initial condition voltage of $|-e_{IC}$. If it is desired to put the unit into HOLD, switch S_3 is opened disconnecting the input voltages from the amplifier. A field effect transistor switch cannot be used in this position, because of its finite ON impedance which would be in series with all the input resistors. For S_1 and S_2, which are inside the amplifier feedback loops, the ON impedance does not matter. Because of the slow speed of operation of S_3, integrators using this method of switching could not be put into HOLD when running in high speed repetitive operation. This, however, imposes little restriction as the HOLD mode should not be necessary when running repetitively.

4.4. Checking the Problem Set-up

After the problem has been patched and the potentiometers set, it is advisable to carry out a static check of the problem to see that the patching and coefficient settings are correct. In RESET, all units apart from the integrators are operating normally, and will have output voltages depending on the values of the integrator initial conditions. Part of a typical circuit with the voltages appearing at the outputs of the various units in RESET is shown in Fig. 4.9.

To get a complete check of scaling, patching, coefficient and initial condition setting, the static check voltages should be calculated from the original system equations using the appropriate scale factors. For example, if the equations for Fig. 4.9 are

$$\ddot{x} = -1{\cdot}5\dot{x} - 50x$$

and

$$z = x \, . \, y$$

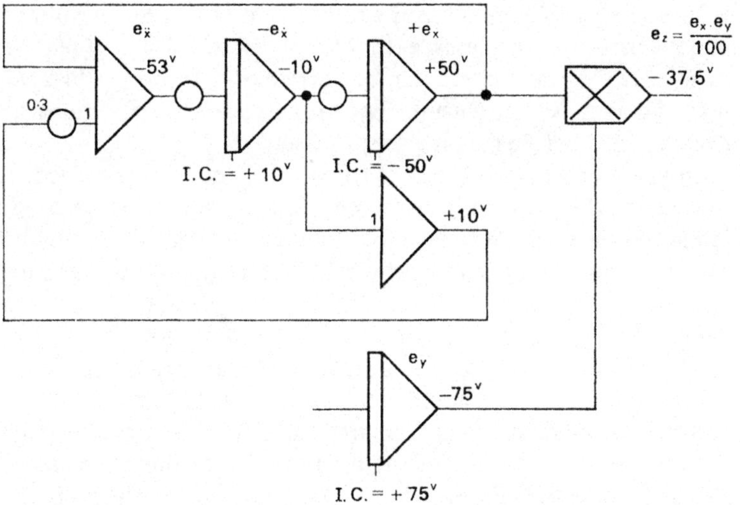

FIG. 4.9. Circuit with static check voltages.

with $\dot{x}\,|_{t=0} = 1$ unit, $x\,|_{t=0} = +0{\cdot}5$ units, and $y\,|_{t=0} = -1{\cdot}5$ units and the scale factors are

$$a_{\ddot{x}} = 0{\cdot}02 \text{ C.U./unit}, a_{\dot{x}} = 0{\cdot}1 \text{ C.U./unit}, a_x = 1 \text{ C.U./unit}$$

$$a_y = 0{\cdot}5 \text{ C.U./unit, and } a_z = 0{\cdot}5 \text{ C.U./unit.}$$

Putting the initial values of $\dot{x}$, x and y in the equations gives

$$\ddot{x}\,|_{t=0} = -26{\cdot}5 \text{ units and } z\,|_{t=0} = -0{\cdot}75 \text{ units}$$

Converting to computer voltages we get for a 100 V computer

$$e_{\ddot{x}}\,|_{t=0} = -53 \text{ V} \qquad e_{\dot{x}}\,|_{t=0} = +10 \text{ V}$$

$$e_x\,|_{t=0} = +50 \text{ V} \qquad e_y\,|_{t=0} = -75 \text{ V}$$

$$e_z\,|_{t=0} = -37{\cdot}5 \text{ V}$$

all of which correspond with the voltages in the figure.

In some problems, all or nearly all initial condition voltages may be zero. In such cases, extra initial conditions can be patched in so that the static check can be carried out. In doing this, care must be exercised to ensure that all extra initial conditions are disconnected before running the problem.

In some computers a DERIVATIVE CHECK mode is provided. In this mode the summing junctions of the input resistors of the integrators are disconnected from their amplifiers so that the sum of the voltages being fed to individual integrators can be measured on a digital voltmeter. With this facility it is possible to check the complete problem set-up before starting to compute.

The computer can now be switched to COMPUTE to obtain the problem solution. It will often be found that the correct solution will not be obtained at the first attempt. Even if the patching and coefficient settings are correct, it may be that the scale factors selected are not suitable. As a result, some of the amplifier output voltages will exceed their normal operating range. This will be indicated by overload lamps on the appropriate amplifiers. If the overloads have been caused by wrong scaling it will be necessary to rescale the appropriate parts of the equations. As an additional check on the operation of a complex problem it may be advisable to obtain a digital computer solution of the problem for one set of parameters, and compare the results from the two machines.

During the investigation of the problem, which may be carried out over a period of days or weeks, a log should be kept of all changes in patching and coefficient settings. The operation of the computer should also be checked each morning. This can be done by running the last solution of the previous day and comparing the results.

4.5. Output Equipment

As the problem solutions are generally graphs of the behaviour of amplifier output voltages plotted with respect to time, it is necessary to have some form of equipment which will indicate and record this behaviour. Most well-equipped laboratories will have a number of different types of recording equipment available. Depending on how the results of a particular problem are to be presented, the appropriate one is chosen. Some or all of the following types of recording equipment will be available either in the computer or easily accessible.

Digital voltmeter. This is an essential piece of equipment in medium size and large computers and is generally mounted in the console. As it can only read steady-state voltages, its main use is in the setting up of the problem and running static checks. The accuracy of measurement is good, generally 0·01%.

Oscilloscope. This is extremely useful when doing initial runs of the problem to check the behaviour of the computer set-up. If the problem is run in reduced time scale under the control of the repetitive operation unit, a continuous picture of the solution can be obtained. This kind of presentation is an invaluable aid to the operator when checking for errors and tracking them down. Permanent records can, of course, be obtained by photography, for which purpose a polaroid camera with its fast processing of film is probably most useful. This method of observing and recording the computer solutions will only give accuracies within a few per cent.

Plotting table. This is probably the most widely used type of recording equipment with analog computer installations. Voltages can be recorded with respect to time or to each other with a best accuracy of 0·1%. The majority have only one pen, but some are available with two. When it is necessary to record more than one amplifier output, this can be done on a number of successive computer runs, and providing the time base of the plotting table is generated in the computer the results will be synchronized. This allows direct comparisons to be made between the traces.

Because plotting tables are electromechanical devices, the position of the arm and pen being controlled by servo-mechanisms, their frequency response is limited. The band-width is about 5 Hz, so for maximum accuracy the solution frequencies recorded should not be greater than about 0·1 Hz.

Pen recorder. This is another widely used form of output recorder. The accuracy is not as good as the plotting table, about 1·0%, but it has a better frequency response, up to 100 Hz. It can be obtained with up to eight channels. The results are always plotted with respect to time.

Ultra-violet recorder. This is similar to the pen recorder, with the same accuracy, but as the pen is replaced by a light beam the frequency response can be much better. Galvanometers can be obtained for these recorders with a natural frequency of 15 kHz allowing recording of frequencies to 10 kHz. Recorders are available with up to thirty-six channels. These recorders use a special photographic paper which can be developed by exposure to a light source. When developed by this method the records are not permanent, although methods of stabilizing the traces are available, as continuous exposure to light causes the background to darken until the trace is lost. For permanent records which can be handled in well-lighted conditions proper photographic development is required.

Printer. This is useful when used in conjunction with the digital voltmeter, for printing out the values of potentiometer settings and amplifier steady-state voltages.

CHAPTER 5

Solution of Variable Coefficient and Nonlinear Differential Equations

As mentioned at the beginning of Chapter 2, these two types of equations are difficult or impossible to solve analytically, whereas for linear ordinary differential equations an analytical solution can always be found.

The variable coefficient linear ordinary differential equation is of the same form as the constant coefficient linear ordinary differential equation, except that some of the coefficients are functions of the independent variable. In many cases the independent variable is time, and these equations are generally referred to as time-varying ordinary differential equations. A typical example of a time-varying equation is the Mathieu equation, which arises for example, in the study of frequency modulation:

$$\frac{d^2y}{dt^2}+(a-2b\cos\omega t)y = 0 \tag{5.1}$$

Nonlinear ordinary differential equations have no fixed form. They may have terms which involve powers and products of derivatives and nonlinear functions of the dependent variables. A typical example is the equation for the motion of a pendulum:

$$\frac{d^2\theta}{dt^2}+\frac{g}{r}\sin\theta = 0 \tag{5.2}$$

where g is the acceleration due to gravity, and r is the length of the pendulum from the point of suspension to the centre of gravity of the weight. In the equation we have a term which is a nonlinear function of the dependent variable.

The solution of variable coefficient differential equations is linear, that is the Principle of Superposition holds, and the only reason for classing them in a chapter with nonlinear differential equations is that for the solution of both types on an analog computer nonlinear computing units are required.

5.1. Generation of Functions of Time $y = f(t)$

For the solution of variable coefficient differential equations on an analog computer, where the independent variable is represented by time, the generation of functions of time is necessary. If the function and its first n derivatives are continuous, it can be generated as the solution of an nth order differential equation, where the value of n depends on the type of function. In general only linear computing units are required, but for some functions it will be necessary to have multipliers as well. The following examples will serve to illustrate this technique.

EXAMPLE 1.

$$y = t^2 \tag{5.3}$$

Differentiating, we get

$$\dot{y} = 2t \tag{5.4}$$

$$\ddot{y} = 2 \tag{5.5}$$

y can therefore be generated using two integrators in cascade with zero initial conditions, and a constant input voltage applied to the first one.

Scaling is carried out using the methods of Chapter 3. Consider the case where t_{max} is 10 sec. Then y_{max} is 100 and $\dot{y}_{max}$ is 20. We therefore obtain the following scale factors

$$a_y = \frac{1}{100}\ \text{C.U./sec}^2$$

$$a_{\dot{y}} = \frac{1}{20}\ \text{C.U./sec}$$

$$a_y = \frac{1}{2}\ \text{C.U./unit}$$

Substituting these in equations (5.3) to (5.5) gives computer voltages

$$e_y = \frac{t^2}{100}\ \text{C.U.} \tag{5.6}$$

$$e_{\dot{y}} = \frac{t}{10}\ \text{C.U.} \tag{5.7}$$

$$e_{\ddot{y}} = 1\ \text{C.U.} \tag{5.8}$$

The equations for the integrators are:

$$e_{\dot{y}} = \frac{a_{\dot{y}}}{a_{\ddot{y}}} \int_0^t e_{\ddot{y}}\, dt + e_{\dot{y}} \big|_{t=0}$$

$$= 0{\cdot}1 \int_0^t e_{\ddot{y}}\, dt + 0 \tag{5.9}$$

and

$$e_y = \frac{a_y}{a_{\dot{y}}} \int_0^t e_{\dot{y}}\, dt + e_y \big|_{t=0}$$

$$= 0{\cdot}2 \int_0^t e_{\dot{y}}\, dt + 0 \tag{5.10}$$

The scaled computer flow diagram and output waveforms are shown in Fig. 5.1.

EXAMPLE 2.

$$y = e^{-at} \tag{5.11}$$

Differentiating, we get

$$\dot{y} = -ae^{-at}$$

$$= -ay$$

The maximum value of y is when $t = 0$ and for equation (5.11) $y_{max} = 1$. Scaling is very simple, the scale factor for y being 1 C.U./unit and therefore $e_y = y$. The flow diagram and output waveform are shown in Fig. 5.2. The value of y at $t = 0$ is set as

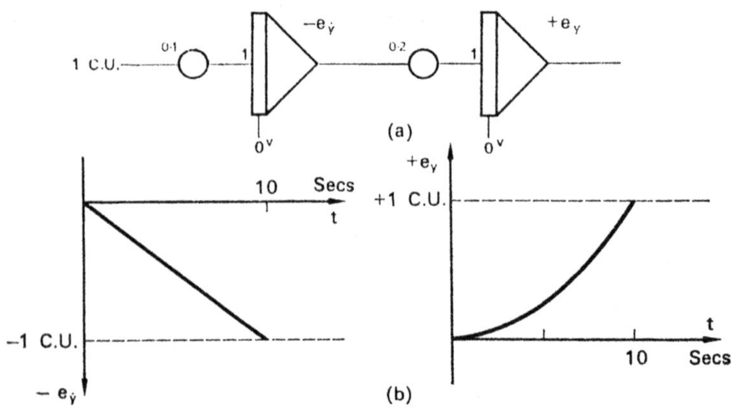

FIG. 5.1. Computer flow diagram for generating a voltage proportional to t^2, and output waveforms.

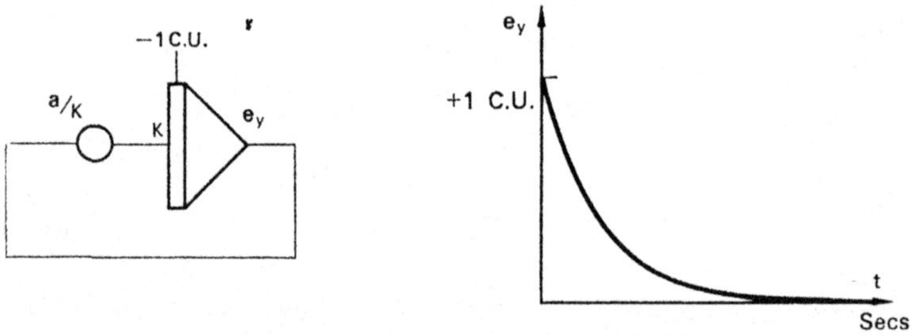

FIG. 5.2. Generation of voltage proportional to e^{-at}.

initial condition on the integrator, and the integrator gain is selected so that a/K is less than 1.

EXAMPLE 3.

$$y = \sin \omega t \tag{5.12}$$

Differentiating, we get

$$\dot{y} = \omega \cos \omega t$$
$$\ddot{y} = -\omega^2 \sin \omega t$$
$$= -\omega^2 y$$

which is the equation for simple harmonic motion. The maximum values are $y_{max} = 1$, $\dot{y}_{max} = \omega$, and $\ddot{y}_{max} = \omega^2$. The scale factors will therefore be

$$a_y = 1 \text{ C.U./unit}$$

$$a_{\dot{y}} = \frac{1}{\omega} \text{ C.U./unit}$$

$$a_{\ddot{y}} = \frac{1}{\omega^2} \text{ C.U./unit}$$

giving computer voltages

$$e_y = \sin \omega t \tag{5.13}$$

$$e_{\dot{y}} = \cos \omega t \tag{5.14}$$

$$e_{\ddot{y}} = -\sin \omega t \tag{5.15}$$

The equations for the integrators are

$$e_{\dot{y}} = \omega \int_0^t e_{\ddot{y}}\, dt + e_{\dot{y}} \,|_{t=0} \tag{5.16}$$

$$e_y = \omega \int_0^t e_{\dot{y}}\, dt + e_y \,|_{t=0} \tag{5.17}$$

At $t = 0$, $\sin \omega t = 0$ and $\cos \omega t = 1$. Therefore $e_{\dot{y}} \,|_{t=0} = 1$ and $e_y \,|_{t=0} = 0$.

The computer flow diagram and output waveforms are shown in Fig. 5.3.

EXAMPLE 4.

$$y = \frac{1}{1+t} \quad \text{for} \quad -1 < t < \infty \tag{5.18}$$

Differentiating, we get

$$\dot{y} = -\frac{1}{(1+t)^2} = -y^2$$

If t is in the range 0 to ∞

$$y_{max} = 1 \quad \text{and} \quad \dot{y}_{max} = 1$$

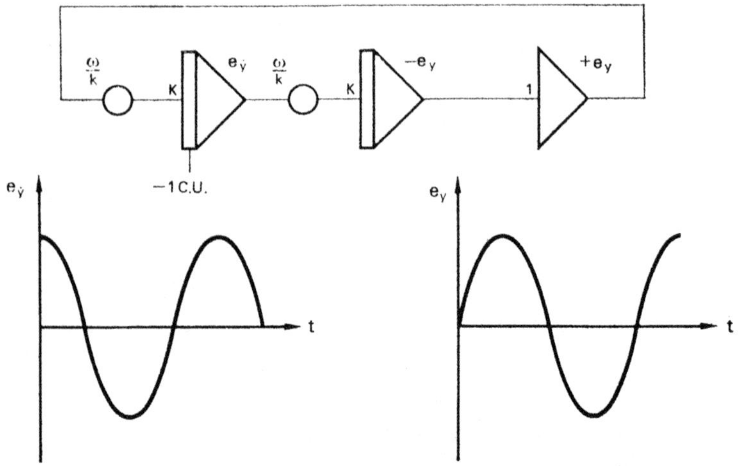

FIG. 5.3. Generation of voltage proportional to sin ωt and cos ωt.

Therefore $a_y = a_{\dot{y}} = 1$ C.U./unit, giving

$$e_y = y \quad \text{and} \quad e_{\dot{y}} = \dot{y}$$

At $t = 0$, $y = 1$, and this can be set as initial condition on the integrator. The computer flow diagram and output waveform are shown in Fig. 5.4.

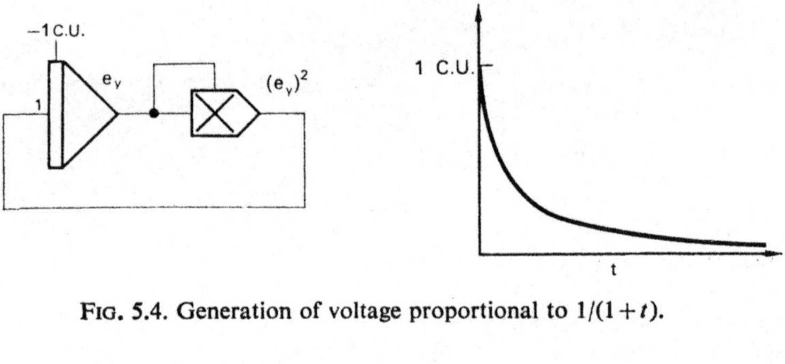

FIG. 5.4. Generation of voltage proportional to $1/(1+t)$.

5.2. Solution of Variable Coefficient Differential Equations

A typical example of this type of equation, as stated at the beginning of the chapter, is the Mathieu equation, which arises in the description of a number of physical systems. We will consider the case of frequency modulation. Figure 5.5 shows the

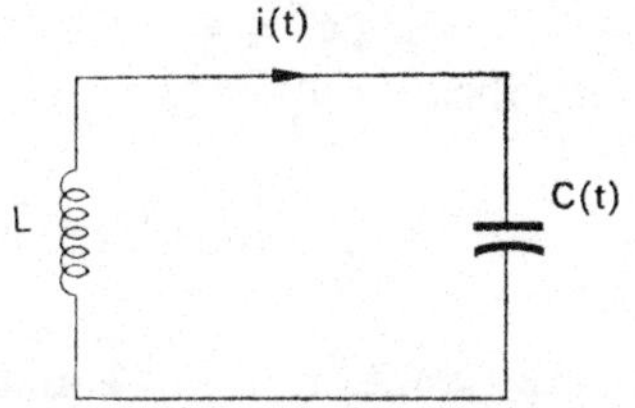

FIG. 5.5. Tank circuit for controlling the frequency of an oscillator.

tank circuit for controlling the frequency of an oscillator, where the inductance and capacitance are ideal elements. To modulate the frequency, the capacitance C can be varied so that its value at time t is given by

$$C(t) = C_0(1+a\cos\omega_1 t)$$

The equation for the current in the coil is

$$L\frac{d^2i}{dt^2}+\frac{i}{C(t)} = 0 \tag{5.19}$$

Substituting for $C(t)$ we get

$$\frac{d^2i}{dt^2}+\frac{i}{LC_0(1+a\cos\omega_1 t)} = 0 \tag{5.20}$$

As only a small variation in the resonant frequency is required a will be $\ll 1$. We can therefore expand $1/(1+a\cos\omega_1 t)$ as a series and use only the first two terms:

$$\frac{1}{1+a\cos\omega_1 t} = 1-a\cos\omega_1 t+a^2\cos^2\omega_1 t+\dots$$

$$\simeq 1-a\cos\omega_1 t$$

Equation (5.20) therefore becomes

$$\frac{d^2i}{dt^2}+\omega_0^2(1-a\cos\omega_1 t)i = 0 \tag{5.21}$$

where ω_0^2 has been substituted for $1/LC_0$, which is in the form of the Mathieu equation. Let us take the case where $\omega_0 = 10^7$ rad/sec, ω_1 is 10^6 rad/sec, $a = 0{\cdot}1$, $i\,|_{t=0} = 10$ mA and $di/dt\,|_{t=0} = 0$. Putting these in equation (5.21) we get

$$\frac{d^2i}{dt^2}+(10^{14}-10^{13}\cos 10^6 t)i = 0 \tag{5.22}$$

As the frequencies in the solution of this equation are high, it will be necessary to introduce time scaling. The range of coefficients is large so it is convenient to time scale the equation.

Let the time scale factor $a_\tau = 10^7$. Therefore

$$\tau = 10^7 t$$

$$\frac{d}{d\tau} = \frac{1}{10^7}\frac{d}{dt}$$

$$\frac{d^2}{d\tau^2} = \frac{1}{10^{14}}\frac{d^2}{dt^2}$$

Substituting these in equation (5.22) we get

$$10^{14}\frac{d^2i}{d\tau^2}+10^{14}(1-0{\cdot}1\cos 0{\cdot}1\tau)i = 0$$

which divided by 10^{14} becomes

$$\frac{d^2i}{d\tau^2}+(1-0{\cdot}1\cos 0{\cdot}1\tau)i = 0 \tag{5.23}$$

The initial value of i is 10 mA, and if the coefficient of i were constant this would also be the maximum value. The effect of varying C or i is not known, but as a is small, it should be safe to assume a maximum value for i of 20 mA. The maximum values of $di/d\tau$ and $d^2i/d\tau^2$ are given by

$$\left(\frac{di}{d\tau}\right)_M = \omega_0 i_M$$

and

$$\left(\frac{d^2i}{d\tau^2}\right)_M = \omega_0^2 i_M$$

For the time-scaled equation ω_0 is 1 rad/sec. Therefore

$$\left(\frac{di}{d\tau}\right)_M = 20 \text{ mA/sec}$$

and

$$\left(\frac{d^2i}{d\tau^2}\right)_M = 20 \text{ mA/sec}^2$$

i and its derivatives can all have the same value of scale factor, i.e.

$$a_{i(0)} = a_{i(1)} = a_{i(2)} = 0{\cdot}05 \text{ C.U./unit}$$

where $i^{(n)} = d^n i/d\tau^n$.

Writing equation (5.23) in computer variables, we get

$$\frac{e_{i(2)}}{0{\cdot}05} + \frac{e_{i(0)}}{0{\cdot}05}(1 - 0{\cdot}1 \cos 0{\cdot}1\tau) = 0$$

which becomes

$$e_{i(2)} = -e_{i(0)} + 0{\cdot}1 e_{i(0)} \cos 0{\cdot}1\tau \tag{5.24}$$

Writing the equations for the integrators in the usual way we get

$$e_{i(2)} = \int_0^t e_{i(2)}\, dt + e_{i(1)}\,|_{t=0} \tag{5.25}$$

$$e_{i(0)} = \int_0^t e_{i(1)}\, dt + e_{i(0)}\,|_{t=0} \tag{5.26}$$

The initial conditions are

$$e_{i(1)}\,|_{t=0} = 0$$

$$e_{i(0)} = a_{i(0)}i^{(0)}\,|_{t=0} = 0{\cdot}5 \text{ C.U.}$$

The cos $0{\cdot}1\tau$ is generated as illustrated by Example 3 of Section 5.1. The computer diagram for solving equations (5.24) to (5.26) is shown in Fig. 5.6.

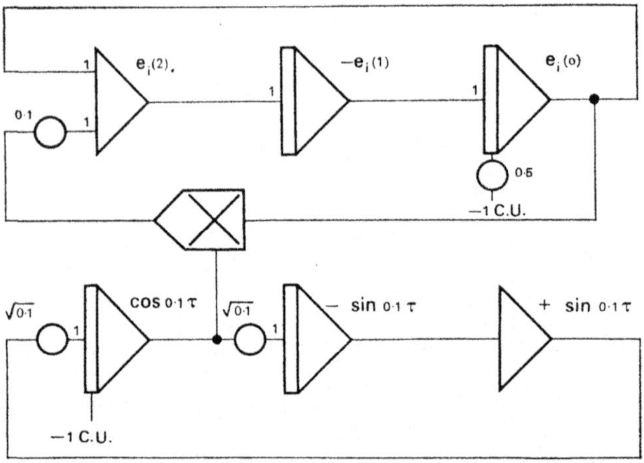

FIG. 5.6. Computer flow diagram for solution of the Mathieu equation.

Another example of a variable coefficient differential equation is the Legendre equation, which is important in some branches of physics and engineering:

$$(1-x^2)\frac{d^2y}{dx^2} - 2x\frac{dy}{dx} + n(n+1)y = 0 \qquad (5.27)$$

For integer values of n the solutions of the equation are polynomials called Legendre polynomials, and the general polynomial $P_n(x)$ is given by the series

$$P_n(x) = \sum_{r=0}^{N}(-1)^r \frac{(2n-2r)!}{2^n r!(n-r)!(n-2r)!}\,x^{(n-2r)}$$

where for n even, $N = n/2$, and for n odd, $N = (n-1)/2$.

For the case $n = 6$

$$P_6(x) = \tfrac{1}{16}(231x^6 - 315x^4 + 105x^2 - 5) \tag{5.28}$$

To generate this on an analog computer we want to set up the equation with x replaced by t

$$(1-t^2)\ddot{y} - 2t\dot{y} + 42y = 0 \tag{5.29}$$

with the initial conditions obtained from equation (5.28)

$$y\,|_{t=0} = -\tfrac{5}{16}, \qquad \dot{y}\,|_{t=0} = 0$$

We will only consider the time interval $0 \leqq t < 1$ sec, since at $t = 1$ $\ddot{y}$ is infinite.

For the purpose of scaling, equation (5.29) can be considered as a second order differential equation with maximum frequency and maximum y as t tends to 1. If we divide through by $(1-t^2)$ we get

$$\ddot{y} - \frac{2t}{1-t^2}\dot{y} + \frac{42}{1-t^2}y = 0 \tag{5.30}$$

At $t = 0{\cdot}95$, $\sqrt{[42/(1-t^2)]} \simeq 20$, which could be considered as the radian frequency for scaling purposes. The initial value of y is $-\tfrac{5}{16}$ units, but as the damping term causes y to diverge take $y_{max} = 1$ unit. On the usual basis for estimating the maximum values for a second order equation, we can therefore take

$$\dot{y}_{max} = 20 \text{ units/sec} \quad \text{and} \quad \ddot{y}_{max} = 400 \text{ units/sec}^2.$$

Using these values the scale factors are as follows:

$$a_y = 1 \text{ C.U./unit}$$
$$a_{\dot{y}} = 0{\cdot}05 \text{ C.U./unit/sec}$$
$$a_{\ddot{y}} = 0{\cdot}0025 \text{ C.U./unit/sec}^2$$

and the computer variables are e_y, $e_{\dot{y}}$, and $e_{\ddot{y}}$. For programming on the computer, the best form for the equation is

$$\ddot{y} = t^2\ddot{y} + 2t\dot{y} - 42y \tag{5.31}$$

the t and t^2 terms being generated as in Example 1 of Section 5.1.

Consider the terms in t, and let $z = t^2$. If t_{max} is 1 sec, then instead of the scale factors being as in Example 1 of Section 5.1 we would have

$$a_z = 1 \text{ C.U./sec}^2$$
$$a_{\dot{z}} = 0{\cdot}05 \text{ C.U./sec}$$
$$a_{\ddot{z}} = 0{\cdot}5 \text{ C.U./unit}$$

We now have scale factors for all the variables and can convert equation (5.31) into computer variables as follows:

$$\frac{e_{\ddot{y}}}{a_{\ddot{y}}} = \frac{e_z}{a_z} \cdot \frac{e_{\ddot{y}}}{a_{\ddot{y}}} + \frac{e_{\dot{z}}}{a_{\dot{z}}} \cdot \frac{e_{\dot{y}}}{a_{\dot{y}}} - 42 \frac{e_y}{a_y} \tag{5.32}$$

and putting in the values of the scale factors gives

$$e_{\ddot{y}} = e_z . e_{\ddot{y}} + 0{\cdot}1 e_{\dot{z}} e_{\dot{y}} - 0{\cdot}105 e_y \tag{5.33}$$

We also have

$$e_{\ddot{z}} = 1 \text{ C.U.} \tag{5.34}$$

The necessary integrator gains are obtained in the usual way giving

$$e_{\dot{y}} = 20 \int_0^t e_{\ddot{y}}\, dt + e_{\dot{y}} \,|_{t=0} \tag{5.35}$$

$$e_y = 20 \int_0^t e_{\dot{y}}\, dt + e_y \,|_{t=0} \tag{5.36}$$

$$e_{\dot{z}} = \int_0^t e_{\ddot{z}}\, dt + e_{\dot{z}} \,|_{t=0} \tag{5.37}$$

$$e_z = 2 \int_0^t e_{\dot{z}}\, dt + e_z \,|_{t=0} \tag{5.38}$$

The initial conditions are

$$e_z \,|_{t=0} = e_{\dot{z}} \,|_{t=0} = e_{\dot{y}} \,|_{t=0} = 0$$

and

$$e_y \,|_{t=0} = a_y . y \,|_{t=0} = -\tfrac{5}{16} \text{ C.U.}$$
$$= -0{\cdot}3125 \text{ C.U.}$$

The computer flow diagram and a plot of the solution are shown in Fig. 5.7.

In order to be able to plot the solution using electro-mechanical recorders, it is necessary to change the time scale of the problem. This is easily done on the computer by decreasing all integrator gains by say a factor of 10, thus increasing the time of solution from 1 to 10 sec.

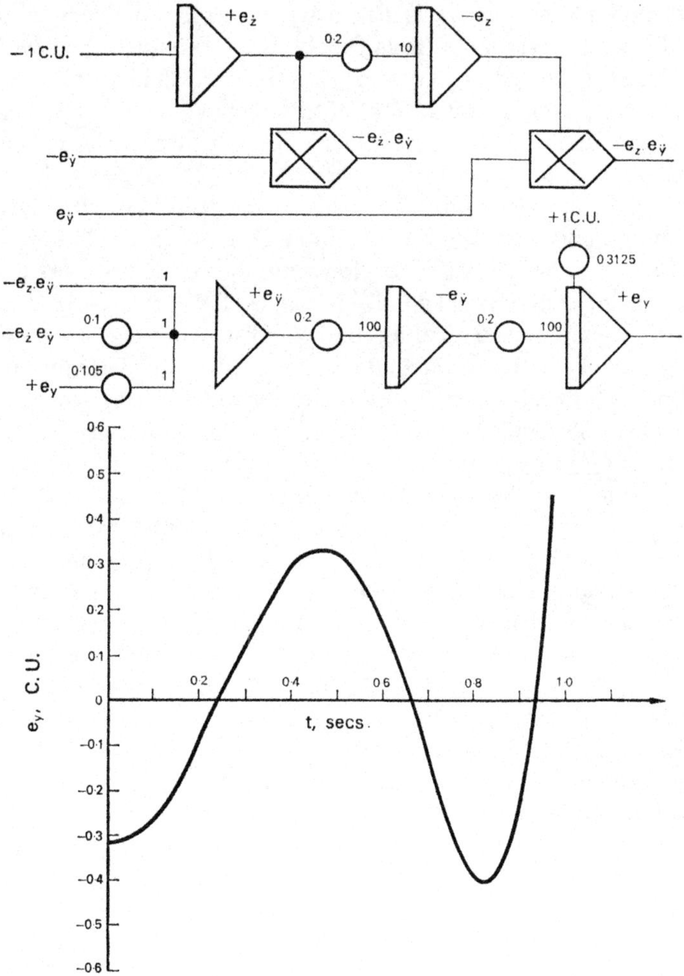

FIG. 5.7. Computer flow diagram for solution of Legendre equation and output waveform.

5.3. Solution of Nonlinear Differential Equations

The solution of nonlinear differential equations on an analog computer is no more difficult, though more complex, than the solution of linear equations. In addition to linear computing units and multipliers, it is necessary to have nonlinear units capable of generating various functions of variables. The basic methods for doing this have been described in Chapter 2.

In general the investigation of the behaviour of nonlinear equations on the computer will require much more time than would be necessary for linear ones. As the Principle of Superposition no longer holds, the form of the solution will change depending upon the values of the inputs and initial conditions. It will therefore be necessary to plot a number of solutions over a range of input and initial condition values, for each setting of the equation parameters. Scaling the equations for the computer will probably be more difficult, as the prediction of frequencies and maximum values are unlikely to be correct at the first attempt. In a linear system it is possible to reduce input levels and initial conditions until all units are working within their linear range. The maxima of the variables can then be measured so that a correct scaling can be obtained at the second attempt. With a nonlinear system this will probably not be possible, as nonlinear units will be working at a different part of their range and the resulting measured maxima may still not be sufficiently near the correct values to give satisfactory scaling. It is therefore sometimes necessary to have a number of attempts at scaling before satisfactory results are obtained.

One of the most common types of nonlinearity which occurs in physical systems is saturation. Examples are flux saturation of an inductor and limiting of the displacement of a spring.

Consider the mass, spring, damper system of Fig. 3.1 with a nonlinear spring having a characteristic which can be described by an equation of the form $F = Kx + Ax^3$, where F is the force applied to the spring, x is the displacement, K the constant for a linear spring, and A is the saturation constant. Using the force equation for the spring, the equation of motion of the mass becomes

$$\ddot{x}+D\dot{x}+Kx+Ax^3 = y \tag{5.39}$$

For the case where $y = K\cos\omega t$, equation (5.39) is known as Duffing's equation. Let us look at the effect of the cubic term on the motion of the mass. For small values of x the cubic term is negligible, and the spring acts like a linear one with natural frequency given by $\sqrt{K}$ rad/sec. For large values of x the spring becomes stiffer, if A is positive, and the frequency of oscillation is higher. If A were negative, the spring force would decrease with increasing x and the frequency of oscillation would decrease. Using Example 1 of Section 3.6 with the addition of a cubic term having $A = 1000$ gives

$$\ddot{x}+6\dot{x}+100x+1000x^3 = y \tag{5.40}$$

To scale the equation for the computer we have to consider the effect of the cubic term on the behaviour of the system over the range of values of y. If y has a maximum value of 300 N, then the

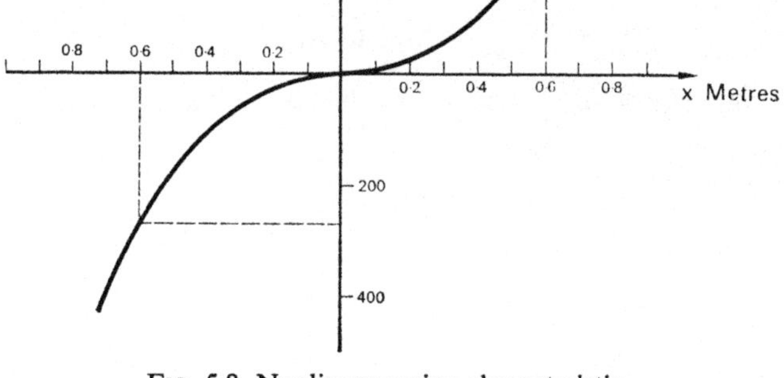

FIG. 5.8. Nonlinear spring characteristic.

force displacement curve for the spring would be as shown in Fig. 5.8. For the maximum value of y the displacement of the spring is just over 0·6 m. Considering a straight line from this point through the origin, we could make an estimate of the maximum frequency of oscillation based on the slope of this line. This would give a value between 21 and 22 rad/sec, and for scaling a value of 20 rad/sec could be used.

Take the maximum value of x as 0·75 m. Then $\dot{x}_{max}$ can be taken as $0{\cdot}75(20) = 15$ m/sec and $\ddot{x}_{max}$ can be taken as $0{\cdot}75(20)^2 = 300$ m/sec. The corresponding scale factors are therefore

$$a_x = \frac{1}{0{\cdot}75}\ \text{C.U./m}$$

$$a_{\dot{x}} = \frac{1}{15}\ \text{C.U./m/sec}$$

$$a_{\ddot{x}} = \frac{1}{300}\ \text{C.U./m/sec}^2$$

$$a_y = \frac{1}{300}\ \text{C.U./N}$$

Writing equation (5.40) in computer variables, we get

$$300e_{\ddot{x}} + 90e_{\dot{x}} + 75e_x + 1000(0{\cdot}75)^3 e_x = 300e_y$$

which becomes

$$e_{\ddot{x}} = e_y - 0{\cdot}3e_{\dot{x}} - 0{\cdot}25e_x - 1{\cdot}4e_x^3 \tag{5.41}$$

The integrator gains are calculated in the normal way giving

$$e_{\dot{x}} = 20\int_0^t e_{\ddot{x}}\,dt + e_{\dot{x}}\,|_{t=0} \tag{5.42}$$

$$e_x = 20\int_0^t e_{\dot{x}}\,dt + e_x\,|_{t=0} \tag{5.43}$$

The initial conditions $e_{\dot{x}}\,|_{t=0}$ and $e_x\,|_{t=0}$ are zero.

For equations (5.41) to (5.43) the computer flow diagram is shown in Fig. 5.9. In the example the cubic term has been generated using two multipliers, which is the quickest and best method of doing it. An alternative method would be to use a function generator set up to give a cube law output. If the nonlinear term had some arbitrary shape, a function generator would have to be used.

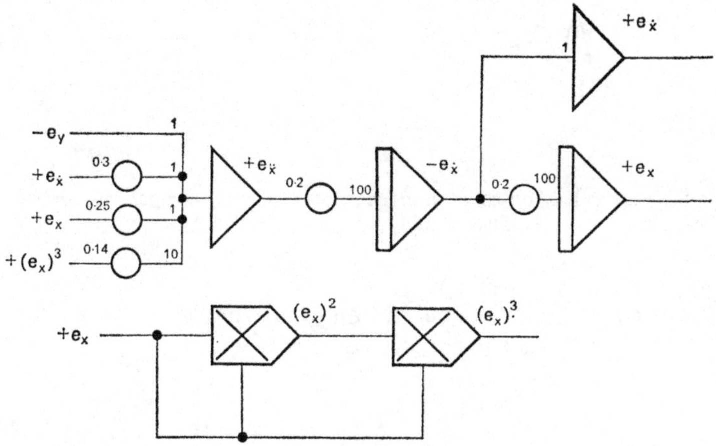

FIG. 5.9. Computer flow diagram for mass spring damper system with nonlinear spring.

For recording purposes, time scaling can be carried out on the computer by reducing all integrator gains by a factor of 10 or even 100. Recordings of the behaviour of the system for different amplitude steps of y are reproduced in Fig. 5.10, showing the increase in frequency and decrease in damping with increasing values of y.

A good example of a nonlinear equation is the Van der Pol equation, which describes the performance of a triode valve feedback oscillator of the form shown in Fig. 5.11. If the relation-

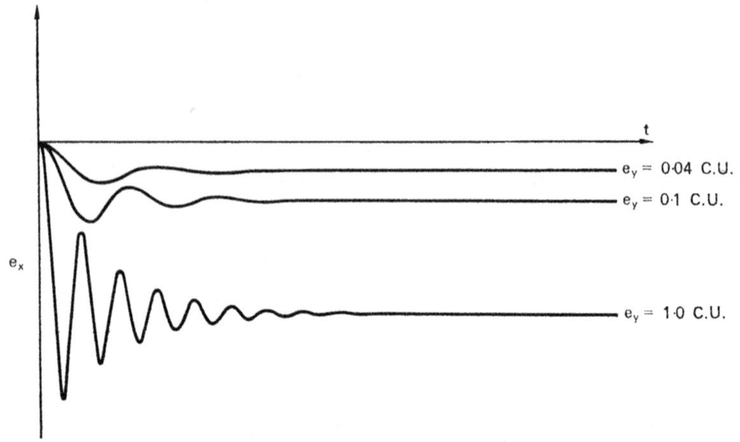

FIG. 5.10. Responses of nonlinear mass spring damper system to different amplitudes of applied force.

ship between the anode current and grid voltage were considered linear, we would get an equation of the form

$$\ddot{x}+\frac{1}{C}\left(\frac{1}{R}-K\right)\dot{x}+\frac{1}{LC}x = 0 \tag{5.44}$$

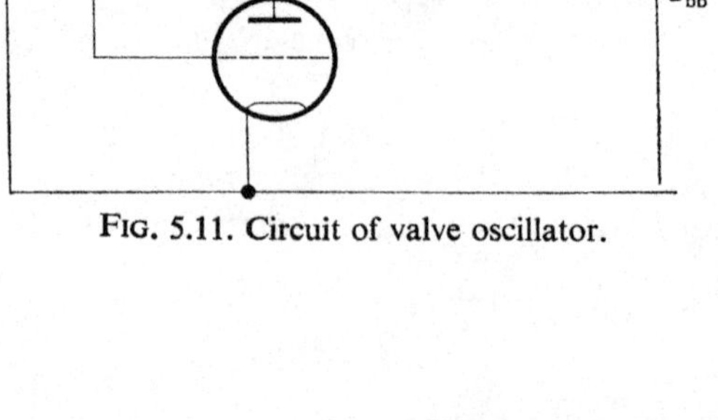

FIG. 5.11. Circuit of valve oscillator.

where K is a constant relating the rate of change of anode current to the rate of change of anode voltage. The value of K depends on the g_m and anode resistance of the valve, the value of the inductance L, and the mutual inductance M. This is a second order differential equation with a damping term, and to obtain continuous oscillation of the voltage x the damping term would have to be zero. This would happen for the case of $1/R = K$. However, even if the circuit components were selected to give this condition, it would be impossible to maintain it, as slight variations in the valve characteristics would cause the oscillations to build up or die away. Another problem, of course, would be to trigger the oscillator and get it to oscillate with a particular amplitude level. It is therefore obvious that the linear model of the oscillator is not the correct one. The relationship between the anode current and grid voltage is not linear, saturation of the anode current occurring for large values of grid voltage. The saturation effect is used in the design of the oscillator so that the damping term is negative for small values of x, causing divergent oscillations, and positive for large values of x, causing convergent oscillation. The result is that oscillations build up when the oscillator is switched on, until the amplitude reaches a level where the effect of saturation causes a balance between the negative and positive damping effect. Oscillation will then be maintained at this level. The only effect of small variations in the circuit parameters will be to change the level of oscillation so that the balance of the damping term is maintained. This effect of oscillations diverging or converging to a particular amplitude occurs frequently in non-linear systems, and is generally referred to as a limit cycle oscillation.

Including the saturation effects of the valve in the analysis of the oscillator, and normalizing the frequency of oscillation to 1 radian per second, we obtain the normal form of the Van der Pol equation,

$$\ddot{x} - \varepsilon(1 - x^2)\dot{x} + x = 0 \tag{5.45}$$

where the value of ε is a function of the gain and saturation characteristics of the valve. Considering this equation, we can see that for x less than 1 the damping term is always negative, and for x greater than 1 it is positive. The limit cycle of oscillation therefore must have an amplitude greater than 1.

To solve this equation on an analog computer it is necessary to make some assumptions about the values of the variables, and to specify a range of values for ε. By assuming a sinusoidal solution, and equating the integral of the damping term to zero over one cycle, it can be shown that the amplitude of the limit cycle is 2 units. To allow for initial values of x outside the limit cycle, we will consider x in the range 0 to 4, and investigate the effect of varying ε in the range 0 to 1. For scaling purposes consider the solution of the equation as being sinusoidal. If the maximum value of $x\,|_{t=0}$ is 4, then this will be the maximum value of x, as starting with this initial value the oscillations will converge. As the natural frequency is 1 rad/sec, the maximum values of the derivatives can therefore be taken as

$$\dot{x}_M = \ddot{x}_M = 4$$

giving scale factors

$$a_x = a_{\dot{x}} = a_{\ddot{x}} = 0{\cdot}25 \text{ C.U./unit}$$

with the resulting computer equation

$$\frac{e_{\ddot{x}}}{0{\cdot}25} = \varepsilon\left[1-\left(\frac{e_x}{0{\cdot}25}\right)^2\right]\frac{e_{\dot{x}}}{0{\cdot}25}-\frac{e_x}{0{\cdot}25} = 0$$

which becomes

$$e_{\ddot{x}} = \varepsilon[1-16e_x^2]e_{\dot{x}}-e_x \tag{5.46}$$

$$e_{\dot{x}} = \int_0^t e_{\ddot{x}}\,dt+e_{\dot{x}}\,|_{t=0} \tag{5.47}$$

$$e_x = \int_0^t e_{\dot{x}}\,dt+e_x\,|_{t=0} \tag{5.48}$$

The initial conditions are

$$e_{\dot{x}}\,|_{t=0} = 0 \text{ and } e_x\,|_{t=0} \text{ variable from 0 to 1 C.U.}$$

A suitable computer flow diagram is shown in Fig. 5.12. In order to be able to vary ε by changing only one potentiometer setting, an extra amplifier is used in the set up. In general if the scaling is optimized, multiplication of a variable by a constant greater than unity, such as in amplifier 4, would cause overloading of the amplifier. However in this case it is justified, because due to the fact that $e_{\dot{x}}$ and e_x are 90° out of phase, the product $e_{\dot{x}}(e_x)^2$ will always be less than 1 C.U. Recordings of typical computer solutions of the equation are shown in Fig. 5.13, where in addition to the usual displacement versus time graphs, phase plane plots are included. This is a very useful form of presentation of the results, and is used frequently in the study of nonlinear systems. $e_{\dot{x}}$ is

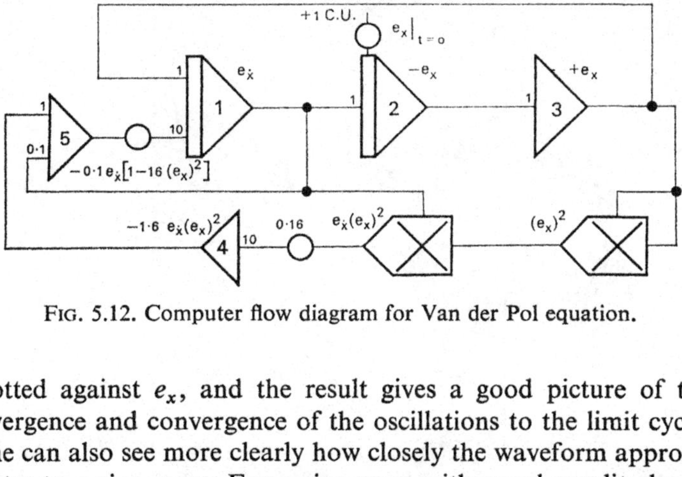

FIG. 5.12. Computer flow diagram for Van der Pol equation.

plotted against e_x, and the result gives a good picture of the divergence and convergence of the oscillations to the limit cycle. One can also see more clearly how closely the waveform approximates to a sine wave. For a sine wave with equal amplitudes of $e_{\dot{x}}$ and e_x and the same gains on the x and y axes of the recording equipment, the phase plane plot would be a circle.

Correct scaling is even more important when using nonlinear computing units than with a completely linear set up. With linear units the main errors are due to the tolerances of the computing resistors and capacitors. As a result of this, errors in the output voltage are percentages of the actual voltage level, unless the

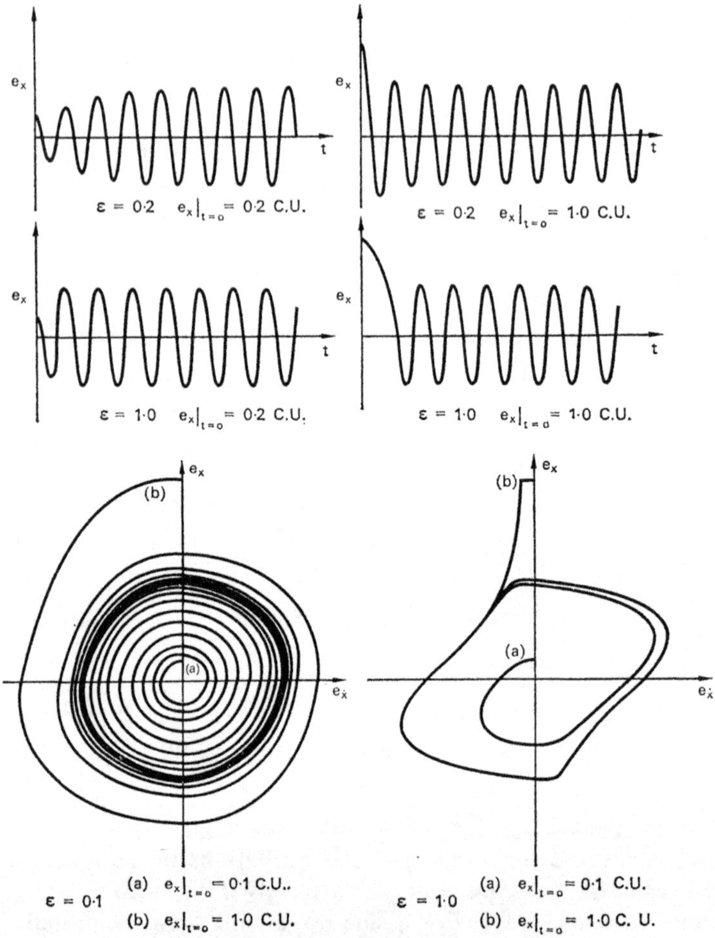

FIG. 5.13. Solutions of the Van der Pol equation.

voltage is so low that amplifier offsets and noise have to be considered. With nonlinear units the error curve is typically as shown in Fig. 5.14. From this it can be seen that as errors are quoted as a percentage of the full-scale voltage, at low levels of the output the error as a percentage of the actual voltage can be very high. If the error curve shown is that of a multiplier in a 100 V computer, for a required output of 1 V we can expect an output in the range 0·9 to 1·1 V. An added problem in squarers and multipliers is the attenuation effect in the unit. On a voltage basis the output of a multiplier, with input voltages x and y is xy/ref. voltage. For a 100 V computer this means $xy/100$. If x is say 50 V and y is 20 V, then the multiplier output is 10 V, and if both x and y drop to 20 V the output is 4 V. It is therefore important to ensure that voltages, particularly at the inputs of nonlinear units, are scaled to swing over as large a part of their dynamic range as possible.

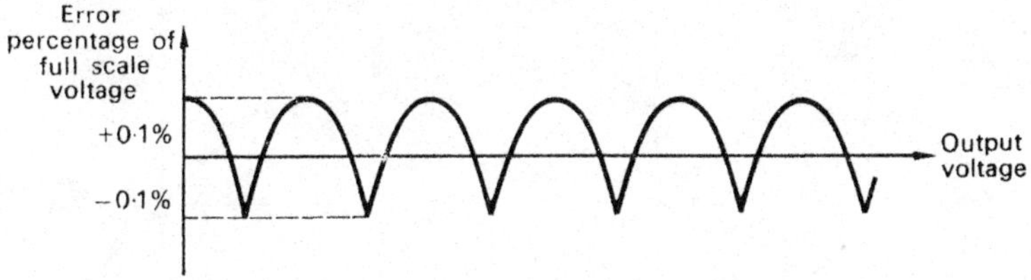

FIG. 5.14. Error curve for quarter square multiplier.

5.4. Special Nonlinear Units and Circuits

In this section we will consider some special types of nonlinear units based on the techniques described in Chapter 2 for explicit function generation. We will also consider circuits, which include nonlinear units, for implicit function generation.

Limiting. This is a very common form of nonlinearity, and most computers provide special units to generate the effect. A typical circuit for simple limiting is shown in Fig. 5.15, with a plot of the output voltage. For input voltages in the range $-e_2 < e_i < +e_1$ the operation of the unit is linear and

$$e_0 = -\frac{R_0}{R_1} e_i.$$

Where e_i is greater than $+e_1$ the voltage at the wiper of potentiometer P_2 becomes positive, diode D_2 conducts and e_0 is limited to the value $-(R_0/R_1)e_1$. However, due to the forward impedance of D_2 and the output impedance of P_2, e_0 will increase slightly with increasing e_i. Also, because of the diode characteristic, the limit curve will not have a sharp corner. For e_i less than $-e_2$, D_1 conducts and limits e_0 to $(R_0/R_1)e_2$. Variation of the potentiometer settings allows the limit voltages to be set at any point on the output range of the amplifier. More complex circuitry can be used to reduce the feedback impedance when limiting action occurs, to give a flatter characteristic and sharper corners. However, for many applications the simple limiter is adequate.

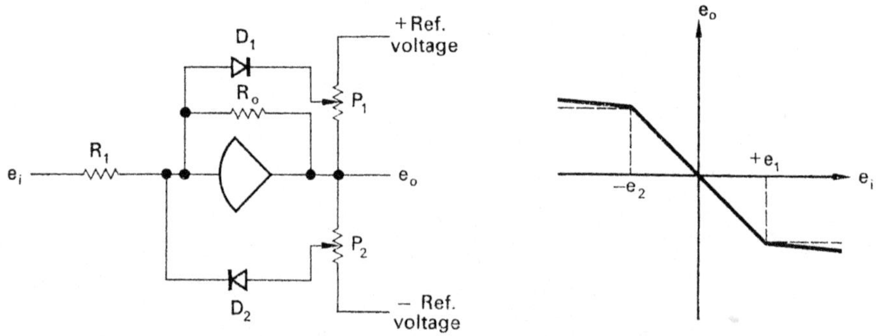

FIG. 5.15. Diode limiter circuit and output characteristic.

Dead zone. This is again generally available as a special unit in the computer. It is based on the use of two of the nonlinear diode sections described in Chapter 2 and the circuit is shown in Fig. 5.16. In this circuit the diodes D_1 and D_2 are biased off by the reference voltages when $-e_2 < e_i < +e_1$. Outside this range either D_1 or D_2 conduct, and the output voltage is given by the equations

$$e_0 = -\frac{R_0}{\text{input impedance}}(e_i - e_1) \quad \text{for } e_i \text{ positive}$$

$$= -\frac{R_0}{\text{input impedance}}(e_i + e_2) \quad \text{for } e_i \text{ negative}$$

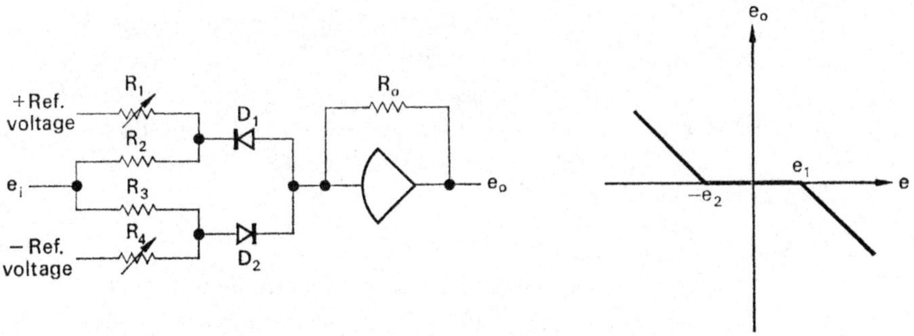

FIG. 5.16. Dead zone unit and output characteristic.

The values of e_1 and e_2 are determined by the settings of R_1 and R_4.

Idealized diode characteristic. This is a very useful circuit and is easily set up on the computer either using diode networks available in the machine, or externally patched components. The circuit is shown in Fig. 5.17, with a plot of the input output characteristic. When e_i is negative, e_0' is positive, diode D_1 conducts and $e_0 = -R_0/R_1 . e_i$. When e_i is positive, e_0' is negative, diode D_2 conducts and limits e_0' to a small negative value. As D_1 is cut off, e_0 remains at zero. Because D_1 is inside the feedback loop of the amplifier the effects of the diode character-

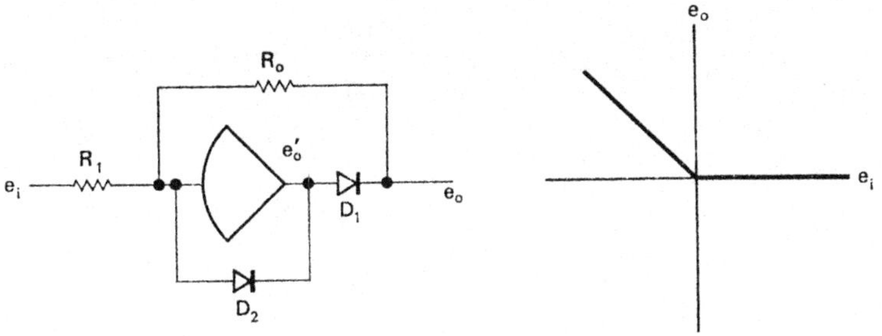

FIG. 5.17. Circuit for idealized diode characteristic.

istic are reduced by the gain of the amplifier. The resulting output curve has an accurate characteristic with a sharp corner. By changing the direction of the diodes the output voltage is obtained for positive e_i. If a bias voltage is summed into the amplifier the breakpoint on the output characteristic can be at any point along the e_i axis.

Modulus circuit. One of the most useful applications of the idealized diode characteristic is in the generation of the modulus of a voltage. The circuit for doing this is shown in Fig. 5.18 with

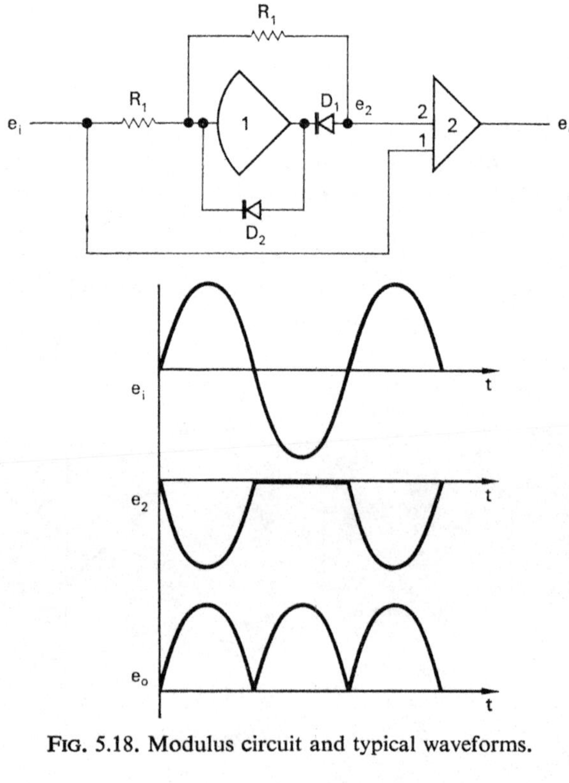

FIG. 5.18. Modulus circuit and typical waveforms.

output waveforms for the case of a sinusoidal input voltage. For positive values of e_i the idealized diode circuit output e_2 equals $-e_i$ and for negative values is zero. If e_2 is multiplied by 2 and summed with e_i in amplifier 2, the output e_0 is the modulus of e_i.

Division. No divider units are provided in an analog computer, but the division operation can be carried out implicitly. A multiplier is used in conjunction with an amplifier to solve the equation

$$yz - x = 0$$

as shown in the circuit of Fig. 5.19. For the case of an ideal

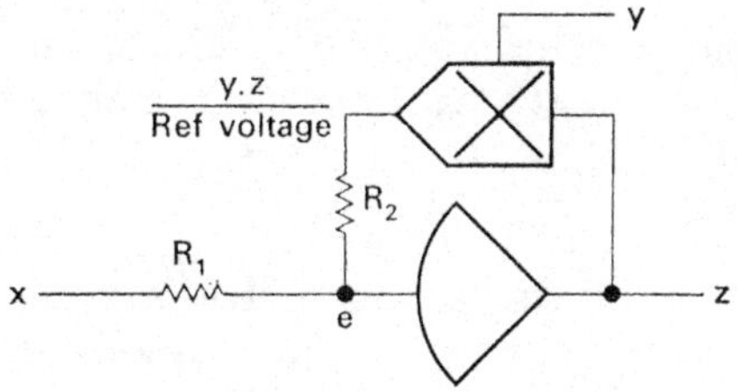

FIG. 5.19. Division circuit.

amplifier with zero input current, the currents in R_1 and R_2 are equal, i.e.

$$\frac{x-e}{R_1} = \left[\frac{e - \dfrac{y.z}{\text{ref. voltage}}}{R_2}\right]$$

As the amplifier gain is high e tends to 0.

Therefore

$$\frac{x}{R_1} \text{ tends to } -\frac{1}{R_2}\left(\frac{y.z}{\text{ref. voltage}}\right)$$

giving

$$z = -\frac{R_2}{R_1}(\text{ref. voltage})\left(\frac{x}{y}\right)$$

Normally R_1 and R_2 are equal, giving for a 100 V computer

$$z = -100\frac{x}{y}$$

where x, y and z are measured in volts not computer units. If x, y and z are measured in computer units the factor of 100 disappears and $z = -(x/y)$.

When using the division circuit, care must be exercised to ensure that y is always greater than 0 and positive. If y tends to 0, z will tend to infinity, causing the amplifier to overload and if y is negative the output of the multiplier will be the same sign as x, causing instability.

When scaling a division circuit the scale factor for the output has to be selected for the worst possible case, i.e. x_{max}/y_{min}. This will generally mean that x has to be attenuated at the input to the division circuit.

Square root. This is similar to the division case, except that if a multiplier is used to perform the squaring operation both inputs come from the output of the amplifier as shown in Fig. 5.20.

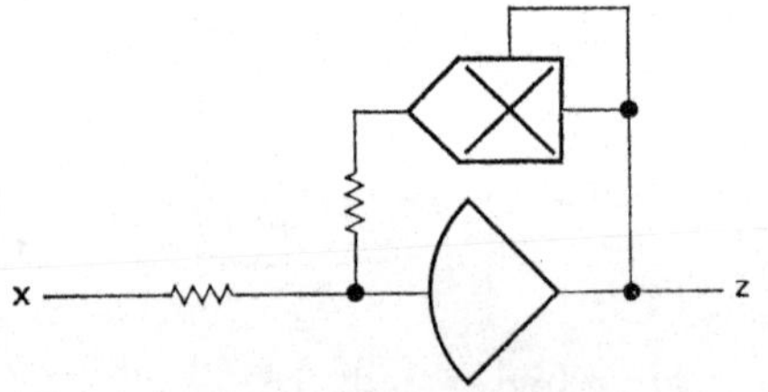

FIG. 5.20. Square root circuit.

Using the same analysis as for the division circuit we get

$$z = 10\sqrt{x} \text{ if measured in volts}$$

or

$$z = \sqrt{x} \text{ if measured in computer units.}$$

As multipliers in most modern computers are of the quarter square type, it is possible to separate them into squaring units. Some manufacturers make provision for this, with the advantage that one multiplier can be used to carry out two squaring or square root operations.

Generalized integration. In Section 5.1 we showed how easily functions of time could be generated by solving appropriate differential equations. Using the technique of generalized integration, this method of function generation can be extended to functions of any variable.

Consider the equation

$$y = f(x) \tag{5.49}$$

Differentiating this with respect to time we have

$$\frac{dy}{dt} = \frac{dy}{dx} \cdot \frac{dx}{dt} \tag{5.50}$$

Now if we make the right-hand side of equation (5.50) the input to an integrating unit, the output will be

$$-\int_0^t \frac{dy}{dx} \cdot \frac{dx}{dt}\, dt \tag{5.51}$$

which is equal to

$$-\int_{x_1}^{x_2} \frac{dy}{dx}\, dx \tag{5.52}$$

The integration period t will be the time required for the independent variable x to go from x_1 to x_2. Equation (5.51) can be implemented using the circuit of Fig. 5.21. To be able to use this circuit it is necessary to have dx/dt available in the computation.

EXAMPLE: Generation of sin x and cos x.

Let $$y = \sin x$$

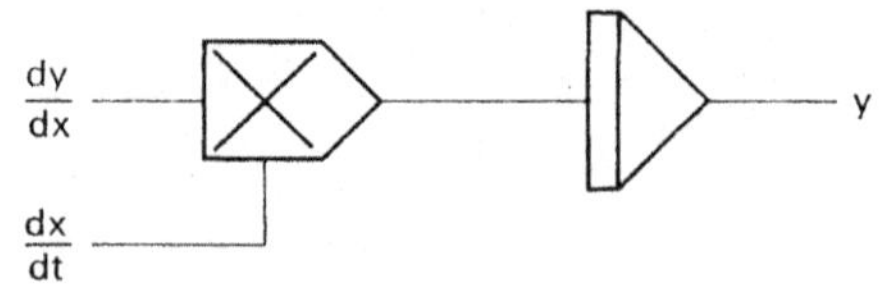

FIG. 5.21. Generalized integrator circuit.

Differentiating we get

$$\frac{dy}{dx} = \cos x$$

$$\frac{d^2y}{dx^2} = -\sin x$$

To generate sin x we therefore have to solve the equation

$$\frac{d^2y}{dx^2}+y = 0$$

Let us see how we can use generalized integrators to solve this providing we have dx/dt available.

$$\frac{dy}{dt} = (\cos x)\frac{dx}{dt}$$

$$\frac{d}{dt}\left(\frac{dy}{dx}\right) = -(\sin x)\frac{dx}{dt}$$

$$= -y.\frac{dx}{dt}$$

The equation can be solved using the circuit of Fig. 5.22.

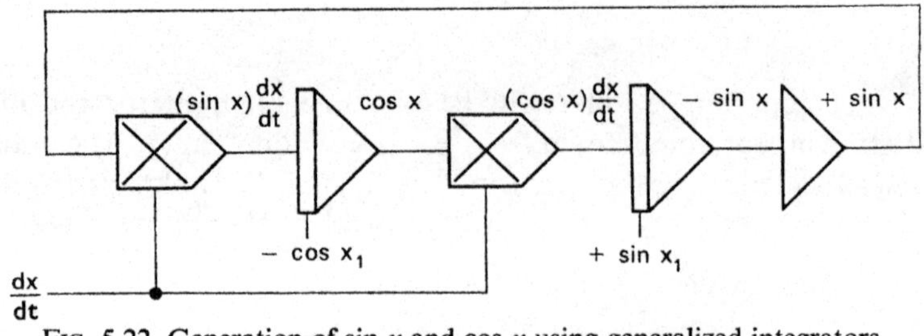

FIG. 5.22. Generation of sin x and cos x using generalized integrators.

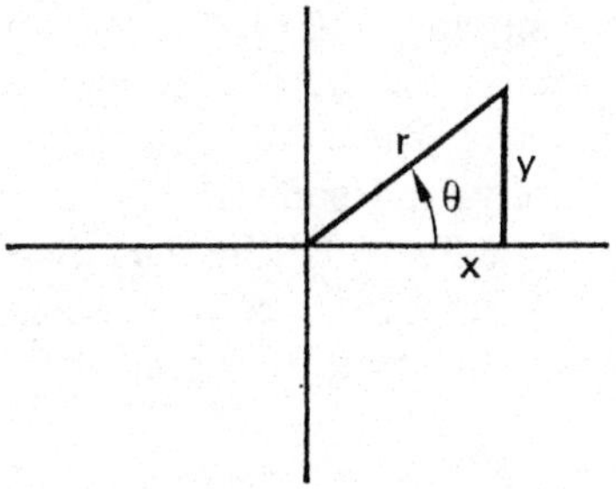

FIG. 5.23. Rectangular to polar coordinate transformation.

The integrators are set with initial conditions corresponding to the value of x_1 at which the computation is to be started.

Inverse resolution. When transforming from rectangular coordinates x, y to polar coordinates r, θ, as shown in Fig. 5.23, the following relationships are obtained

$$\frac{y}{x} = \tan\theta = \frac{\sin\theta}{\cos\theta}$$

which multiplied across gives

$$y\cos\theta - x\sin\theta = 0 \tag{5.53}$$

and

$$r = x\cos\theta + y\sin\theta \tag{5.54}$$

Equations (5.53) and (5.54) are solved as shown in the circuit of Fig. 5.24. Consider amplifier 1 with zero input current and gain $= -k$. If we equate the currents through the two input resistors to zero, we get

$$\frac{(x\sin\theta - e)}{R} + \frac{(-y\cos\theta - e)}{R} = 0$$

Now $e = -\theta/k$ and as k is large tends to 0. Therefore $y\cos\theta - x\sin\theta$ tends to 0.

This part of the circuit is therefore an implicit solution of equation (5.53), forcing the output of amplifier 1 to equal θ. Equation (5.54) is easily solved by multiplying $\sin\theta$ and $\cos\theta$ by y and x respectively, and summing in amplifier 2 to give an output r. Because of the phase shift in the function generators and multipliers, it may be necessary to connect a small capacitor across amplifier 1 to prevent the circuit from oscillating.

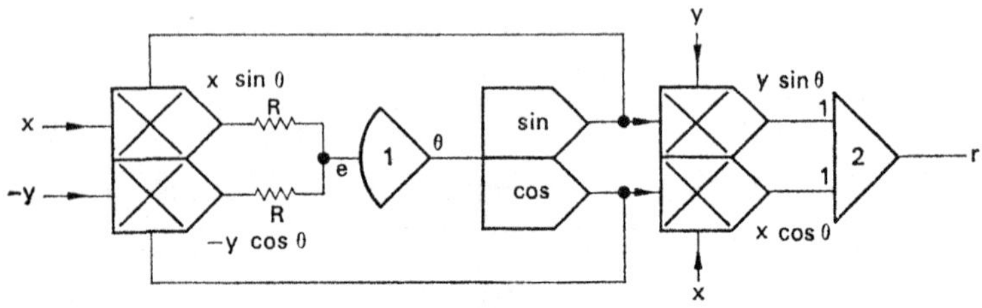

FIG. 5.24. Circuit for rectangular to polar coordinate transformation.

CHAPTER 6

Simulation of Linear Transfer Functions

In this chapter a knowledge of the Laplace transform will be assumed. This is a very useful tool, enabling us to convert differential equations into algebraic equations which can be manipulated by the ordinary rules of algebra. When the algebraic equations have been reduced to a suitable form they can be converted back, using the inverse Laplace transform, to give functions of the independent variable which are the solutions of the differential equations.

Consider a physical system with an output variable x, the behaviour of which, as a result of the variation of the input variable y, can be described by a second order linear differential equation of the form

$$a_2 \frac{d^2x}{dt^2} + a_1 \frac{dx}{dt} + a_0 x = b_0 y \qquad (6.1)$$

with

$$\left.\frac{dx}{dt}\right|_{t=0} = x|_{t=0} = 0$$

x and y are functions of time and a_0, a_1, a_2, and b_0 are constants. Taking the Laplace transform of both sides of the equation we get

$$(a_2 s^2 + a_1 s + a_0) x(s) = b_0 y(s) \qquad (6.2)$$

where s is a complex variable $\alpha + j\omega$ and $x(s)$ and $y(s)$ are the Laplace transforms of $x(t)$ and $y(t)$. As this is an algebraic equation in s, we can rearrange it to give the ratio

$$\frac{x(s)}{y(s)} = \frac{b_0}{a_2 s^2 + a_1 s + a_0} \qquad (6.3)$$

The right-hand side of equation (6.3) is generally referred to as the transfer function of the system. It is often represented in block diagram form, as shown in Fig. 6.1, with $y(s)$ as the input to the block and $x(s)$ as the output.

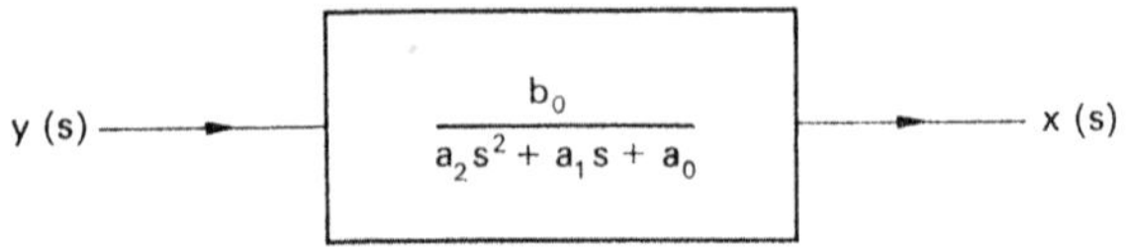

FIG. 6.1. System transfer function.

When investigating the behaviour of a physical system, it will often be found that the information about it is presented in the form of a block diagram. This will consist of a number of individual blocks, representing non-interacting parts of the system. The relationships between the outputs and inputs of the blocks will be given as transfer functions.

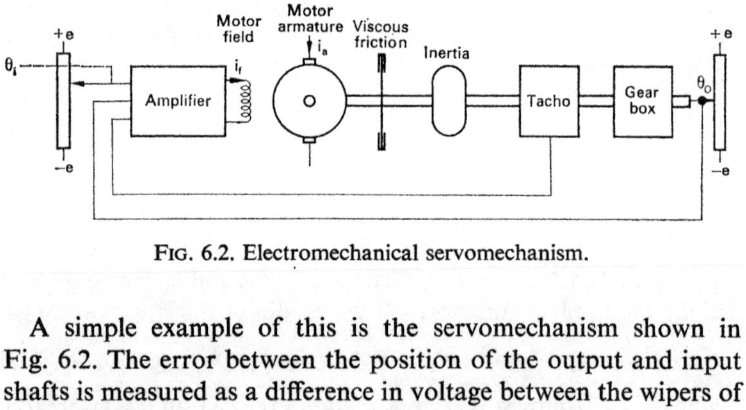

FIG. 6.2. Electromechanical servomechanism.

A simple example of this is the servomechanism shown in Fig. 6.2. The error between the position of the output and input shafts is measured as a difference in voltage between the wipers of two potentiometers connected to the shafts. This error voltage is fed to an amplifier, the output of which provides the field current for a motor fed with constant armature current. The motor drives a tachometer and through a gear-box the output potentiometer and load. If the system has the following specification:

Potentiometer constants	K_1 V/rad
Amplifier gain	K_2
Inductance of the motor field	L_f H
Resistance of the motor field	R_f Ω
Torque constant of the motor	K_3 N/amp of field current
Inertia of motor armature and load	J kg-m^2
Viscous friction constant	f N/rad/sec

we can write the equations for the various parts of the system.

If the feedback loops are disconnected, the input to the amplifier is $K_1\theta_i$ V. Let the voltage at the output of the amplifier which is connected to the motor field windings be e_f. Then we have

$$e_f = K_1 K_2 \theta_i \text{ V}$$

If the motor field current is i_f, we also have

$$e_f = R_f i_f + L_f \frac{di_f}{dt} \tag{6.4}$$

Taking the Laplace transform of both sides of equation (6.4) for the case of zero initial conditions, we get

$$e_f(s) = i_f(s)[R_f + sL_f]$$

which gives

$$\frac{i_f(s)}{e_f(s)} = \frac{1/R_f}{1+s\,L_f/R_f}$$

Putting $1/R_f = K_f$ and $L_f/R_f = T_f$, this becomes

$$\frac{i_f(s)}{e_f(s)} = \frac{K_f}{1+sT_f} \tag{6.5}$$

Let the motor torque be P.

Then $$P = K_3 i_f$$

The equation for the motor and load is

$$P = J\frac{d^2\theta}{dt^2} + f\frac{d\theta}{dt} \tag{6.6}$$

where θ is the position of the motor output shaft. Taking the Laplace transform, for the zero initial condition case we get

$$K_3 i_f(s) = \theta(s)[s^2 J + sf]$$

which gives

$$\frac{\theta(s)}{i_f(s)} = \frac{K_3/f}{s[1+s(J/f)]}$$

Putting $K_3/f = K_m$ and $J/f = T_m$, this becomes

$$\frac{\theta(s)}{i_f(s)} = \frac{K_m}{s(1+sT_m)} \tag{6.7}$$

Let the position of the servomechanism output shaft be θ_0.

Then $\theta_0 = K_4\theta.$

Let the output of the tachometer be e_T.

Then $e_T = K_5 \dfrac{d\theta}{dt}$

Taking the Laplace transform we get

$$\frac{e_T(s)}{\theta(s)} = K_5 s \tag{6.8}$$

The servomechanism can therefore be represented in block diagram form as shown in Fig. 6.3.

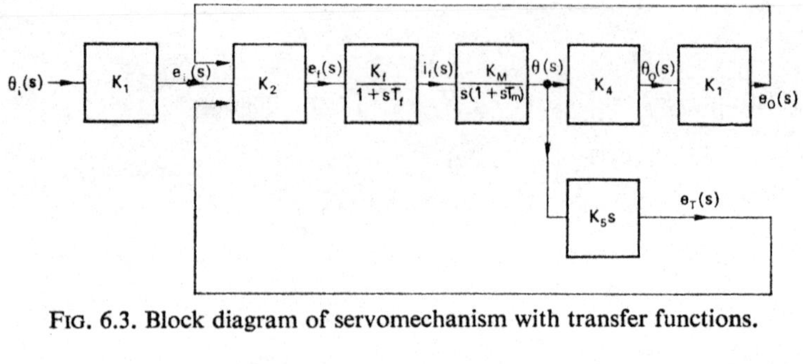

FIG. 6.3. Block diagram of servomechanism with transfer functions.

There are two general methods of setting up transfer functions on an analog computer:

1. Using only integrators, summers and potentiometers.
2. Using complex resistor capacitor networks associated with operational amplifiers.

6.1. Simulation of Linear Transfer Functions using Integrators, Summers and Potentiometers

In general the transfer functions to be simulated will be of the form

$$\frac{x(s)}{y(s)} = \frac{b_m s^m + b_{m-1} s^{m-1} + \ldots + b_0}{a_n s^n + a_{n-1} s^{n-1} + \ldots + a_0} \tag{6.9}$$

where for real systems $m \leq n$. To set them up on the computer two methods of approach are possible.

The first method for setting up transfer functions is to multiply across and obtain the Laplace transform of the corresponding differential equations with zero initial conditions.

$$(a_n s^n + a_{n-1} s^{n-1} + \ldots + a_0)x(s) = (b_m s^m + b_{m-1} s^{m-1} + \ldots + b_0)y(s) \tag{6.10}$$

To solve this on the computer in the normal way, we would take the highest derivative of x to the left-hand side of the equation and everything else to the right-hand side. We would assume the highest derivative of x available at the output of an amplifier, and integrate it the required number of times to get x. Appropriate fractions of each of the derivatives would be fed back and summed with the input functions into the amplifier whose output is the highest derivative of x. However, the problem would arise of differentiating the input function n times. To avoid this difficulty, we divide through equation (6.10) by the highest power of s operating on the right-hand side of the equation. In this case dividing by s^m we get

$$\left(a_n s^{n-m}+a_{n-1}s^{n-m-1}+\ldots+\frac{a_0}{s^m}\right)x(s)=\left(b_m+\frac{b_{m-1}}{s}+\ldots+\frac{b_0}{s^m}\right)y(s) \tag{6.11}$$

which can be rearranged in the form

$$\begin{aligned} s^{n-m}x(s) &= \frac{1}{s^m}\left[\frac{b_0}{a_n}\,y(s)-\frac{a_0}{a_n}\,x(s)\right]+\frac{1}{s^{m-1}}\left[\frac{b_1}{a_n}\,y(s)-\frac{a_1}{a_n}\,x(s)\right]+\ldots \\ &+\left[\frac{b_m}{a_n}\,y(s)-\frac{a_m}{a_n}\,x(s)\right]+\ldots \\ &-s^{n-m-2}\left[\frac{a_{n-2}}{a_n}\right]x(s)-s^{n-m-1}\left[\frac{a_{n-1}}{a_n}\right]x(s) \end{aligned} \tag{6.12}$$

To set this up on the computer we would only require integrators, summers and potentiometers.

As an example to illustrate the technique, consider a system with the transfer function

$$\frac{x(s)}{y(s)}=\frac{s^2+7s+25}{s^3+12s+29s+90} \tag{6.13}$$

where say $y(t)$ is a voltage input to the system, and the output $x(t)$ is a shaft angle measured in radians. On the computer it will be necessary to have scale factors for the input and output of the system. As t tends to infinity, s tends to zero, and we get $x(t)/y(t)$ tending to $25/90 = 1/3{\cdot}6$. If the maximum demanded value of $x(t)$ is 1 rad, then the maximum value of the input $y(t)$ is 3·6 V. The system may be lightly damped, so for scaling purposes take the maximum value of $x(t)$ as 2 rad. Let the computer variables be $e_{x(t)}$ and $e_{y(t)}$, with corresponding scale factors a_x and a_y. Using the above maximum values of $x(t)$ and $y(t)$ we get

$$a_x = \frac{1}{2} = 0{\cdot}5 \text{ C.U./rad}$$

and

$$a_y = \frac{1}{3{\cdot}6} \quad \text{say } 0{\cdot}25 \text{ C.U./V}$$

We can write the transfer function in terms of the computer variables as

$$\frac{e_{x(s)}}{a_x}\cdot\frac{a_y}{e_{y(s)}} = \frac{s^2+7s+25}{s^3+12s^2+29s+90}$$

Putting in the values of the scale factors we get

$$\frac{e_{x(s)}}{e_{y(s)}} = \frac{2s^2+14s+50}{s^3+12s^2+29s+90} \tag{6.14}$$

which multiplied across gives

$$(s^3+12s^2+29s+90)e_{x(s)} = (2s^2+14s+50)e_{y(s)}$$

As the highest power of s on the right-hand side is 2, we divide through by s^2 to get

$$\left(s+12+\frac{29}{s}+\frac{90}{s^2}\right)e_{x(s)} = \left(2+\frac{14}{s}+\frac{50}{s^2}\right)e_{y(s)}$$

which can be arranged in the form

$$se_{x(s)} = \left[2e_{y(s)}-12e_{x(s)}\right]+\frac{1}{s}\left[14e_{y(s)}-29e_{x(s)}\right] + \frac{1}{s^2}\left[50e_{y(s)}-90e_{x(s)}\right] \tag{6.15}$$

To set this up on a computer three integrators are required to compute e_x, and a suitable flow diagram is shown in Fig. 6.4.

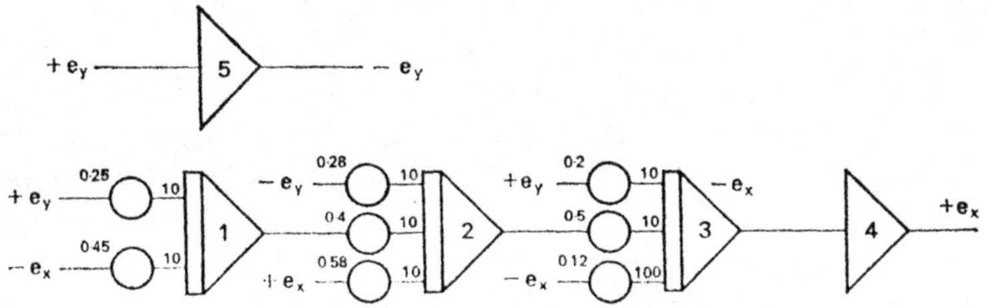

FIG. 6.4. Computer flow diagram for simulating transfer function using the first method.

This is obtained by starting with the third term on the right-hand side of equation (6.15), assuming $-e_x$ and $+e_y$ are available and summing them with appropriate gains at the input of the first integrator. Its output and minus the second term on the right-hand side of the equation are then summed into the second integrator. The minus sign is required because of the sign change through the first amplifier. The output of the second integrator plus the first term on the right-hand side of the equation are summed into the third integrator. The output of this is $-e_x$ which is inverted through amplifier 4. The gains of the integrators are obtained by considering the maximum gain required in the third term of equation (6.15). In this case it is 90, and this is the total gain needed from $-e_x$, at the input of integrator 1, to the output of integrator 3. As a first attempt to split the gain between the three integrators, arrange for them all to be approximately the same. For this example they could be 4·5, 4 and 5. Having allocated the gains in this way the gains of the other terms summed into the integrators will have to be modified. For example, the $+e_x$ term at the input to integrator 2 has a gain of 5 through integrator 3. It will therefore only need a gain of 5·8 in integrator 2 to make up the coefficient 29. The equation can be rearranged as follows to take the distribution of gains into account:

$$se_{x(s)} = \left[2e_{y(s)} - 12e_{x(s)}\right] + \frac{5}{s}\left[2{\cdot}8e_{y(s)} - 5{\cdot}8e_{x(s)}\right] + \frac{20}{s^2}\left[2{\cdot}5e_{y(s)} - 4{\cdot}5e_{x(s)}\right] \tag{6.16}$$

The coefficients inside the brackets are the gains required in the integrators at which the terms are first introduced. Distributing the gains in this way may result in large variations between the amplitudes of the voltage swings at the outputs of the three integrators. If this happens, it will be necessary to adjust the distribution so that all the integrators are operating over as much of their range as possible.

The second method for setting up transfer functions on the computer is to write

$$\frac{x(s)}{y(s)} = \frac{x(s)}{z(s)} \cdot \frac{z(s)}{y(s)} \tag{6.17}$$

where for the case of the general form of the transfer function

$$\frac{x(s)}{z(s)} = b_m s^m + b_{m-1} s^{m-1} + \ldots + b_0 \tag{6.18}$$

and

$$\frac{z(s)}{y(s)} = \frac{1}{a_n s^n + a_{n-1} s^{n-1} + \ldots + a_0} \tag{6.19}$$

Multiplying across equation (6.19) we get

$$y(s) = (a_n s^n + a_{n-1} s^{n-1} + \ldots + a_0) z(s) \tag{6.20}$$

By bringing the highest differential of $z(s)$ to the left-hand side, equation (6.20) can be rearranged as

$$a_n s^n z(s) = y(s) - [a_{n-1} s^{n-1} + a_{n-2} s^{n-2} + \ldots + a_0] z(s) \tag{6.21}$$

This can be solved in the usual way to give $z(t)$ and its derivatives. To obtain $x(t)$, we sum the derivatives of $z(t)$ multiplied by the appropriate coefficients, as specified in equation (6.18):

$$x(s) = (b_m s^m + b_{m-1} s^{m-1} + \ldots + b_0) z(s) \tag{6.22}$$

We will again illustrate the technique by considering a system with the transfer function of equation (6.13). We carry out the same scaling procedure to obtain equation (6.14). It is then convenient to divide through the numerator and denominator by the values of their constant terms to give

$$\frac{e_{x(s)}}{e_{y(s)}} = \frac{\frac{5}{9}\left[\frac{2s^2}{50} + \frac{14s}{50} + 1\right]}{\frac{s^3}{90} + \frac{12s^2}{90} + \frac{29s}{90} + 1} \tag{6.23}$$

This can be rearranged by replacing $(s)^m$ by $(sT)^m$, where T will in general be less than unity. In this example if we put $T = 1/5$ we get

$$\frac{e_{x(s)}}{e_{y(s)}} = \frac{\frac{5}{9}\left[\left(\frac{s}{5}\right)^2 + \frac{7}{5}\left(\frac{s}{5}\right) + 1\right]}{\frac{25}{18}\left(\frac{s}{5}\right)^3 + \frac{10}{3}\left(\frac{s}{5}\right)^2 + \frac{29}{18}\left(\frac{s}{5}\right) + 1} \tag{6.24}$$

We can now write

$$\frac{e_{x(s)}}{e_{z(s)}} = \frac{5}{9}\left[\left(\frac{s}{5}\right)^2 + \frac{7}{5}\left(\frac{s}{5}\right) + 1\right]$$

i.e.

$$e_{x(s)} = \frac{5}{9}\left[\left(\frac{s}{5}\right)^2 + \frac{7}{5}\left(\frac{s}{5}\right) + 1\right] z(s) \tag{6.25}$$

and

$$\frac{e_{z(s)}}{e_{y(s)}} = \frac{1}{\frac{25}{18}\left(\frac{s}{5}\right)^3 + \frac{10}{3}\left(\frac{s}{5}\right)^2 + \frac{29}{18}\left(\frac{s}{5}\right) + 1} \tag{6.26}$$

Equation (6.26) can be multiplied across and rearranged to give

$$\left(\frac{s}{5}\right)^3 e_{z(s)} = \frac{18}{25}\left[e_{z(s)} - \left\{\frac{10}{3}\left(\frac{s}{5}\right)^2 + \frac{29}{18}\left(\frac{s}{5}\right) + 1\right\} e_{z(s)}\right] \tag{6.27}$$

The transfer function can now be set up on a computer using the flow diagram of Fig. 6.5. Amplifiers 1 to 4 are used to simulate

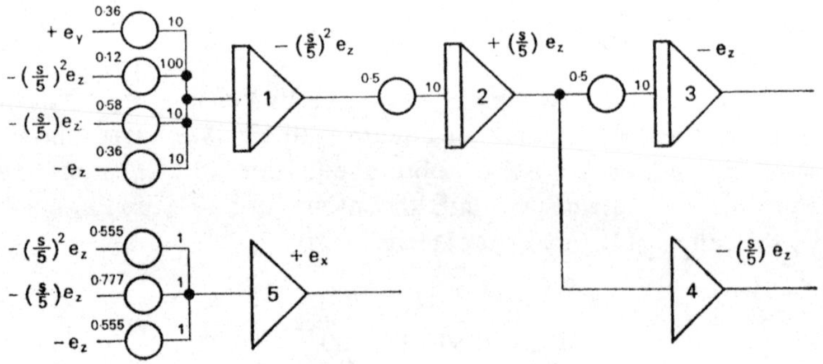

FIG. 6.5. Computer flow diagram for simulating transfer function using the second method.

equation (6.27), with each integrator having a gain of 5. As the $(s/5)^3 e_z$ term is not formed, the gains at the input of amplifier 1 are the coefficients on the right-hand side of equation (6.27) multiplied by 5. To obtain e_x the outputs of amplifiers 1, 3 and 4 multiplied by coefficients as specified in equation (6.25) are summed in amplifier 5.

Simulation of a Servomechanism

As an example of simulation, let us consider the servomechanism illustrated in Fig. 6.2 with the following values for the system constants.

$$K_1 = 5 \text{ V/rad}$$

$$K_2 = 20$$

$$K_f = 5 \text{ mA/V}$$

$$T_f = 0{\cdot}01 \text{ sec}$$

$$K_3/f = 10 \text{ rad/mA/sec}$$

$$T_m = 0{\cdot}4 \text{ sec}$$

$$K_4 = 1/20$$

$$K_4 = 0{\cdot}2 \text{ V/rad/sec}$$

Using these values, the transfer functions of the various parts of the system with the feedback loops disconnected are

$$\frac{e_i(s)}{\theta_i(s)} = 5 \tag{6.28}$$

$$\frac{i_f(s)}{e_i(s)} = \frac{100}{1+0{\cdot}01s} \tag{6.29}$$

$$\frac{\theta_0(s)}{i_f(s)} = \frac{10/20}{s(1+0{\cdot}4s)} = \frac{0{\cdot}5}{s(1+0{\cdot}4s)} \tag{6.30}$$

$$\frac{e_0(s)}{\theta_0(s)} = 5 \tag{6.31}$$

$$\frac{e_T(s)}{s\theta(s)} = 0{\cdot}2 \tag{6.32}$$

The individual transfer functions could be multiplied together, to give a single transfer function which would be simulated using either of the methods previously described. However, no information would be available about the behaviour of variables within the system, so we will simulate the individual blocks. To do this it will be necessary to make some estimate of the maximum values the variables are likely to attain. If we wish to simulate the linear region of operation of the system, it will be necessary to limit the amplitude of the input variable so that the field current and hence speed of the motor do not saturate. The maximum field current is 100 mA which gives a motor speed of 1000 rad/sec. With this maximum value of field current the maximum step input which can be applied is 0·2 rad. However, with sinusoidal inputs larger values can be accepted, so we will scale the input for a maximum value of 1 rad. As the response may be lightly damped, take the maximum value of the output as 2·0 rad. For a maximum motor speed of 1000 rad/sec, the maximum output from the tacho will be 200 V. Using these maximum values the following scale factors are obtained:

$$a_{\theta_i} = 1 \text{ C.U./rad}$$

$$a_{e_i} = 0.2 \text{ C.U./V}$$

$$a_{i_f} = 0{\cdot}01 \text{ C.U./mA}$$

$$a_{\dot{\theta}_0} = \frac{1}{50} = 0{\cdot}02 \text{ C.U./rad/sec}$$

$$a_{\theta_0} = 0{\cdot}5 \text{ C.U./rad}$$

$$a_{e_0} = 0{\cdot}1 \text{ C.U./V}$$

$$a_{e_T} = 0{\cdot}005 \text{ C.U./V}$$

Incorporating these in the transfer functions, we get in computer variables

$$\frac{e_{e_i(s)}}{e_{\theta_i(s)}} = \frac{0{\cdot}2}{1} \cdot 5 = 1 \tag{6.33}$$

$$\frac{e_{i_f(s)}}{e_{e_i(s)}} = \frac{0{\cdot}01}{0{\cdot}2} \cdot \frac{100}{1+0{\cdot}01s} = \frac{5}{1+0{\cdot}01s} \tag{6.34}$$

$$\frac{e_{\theta_0(s)}}{e_{i_f(s)}} = \frac{0{\cdot}5}{0{\cdot}01} \cdot \frac{0{\cdot}5}{s(1+0{\cdot}4s)} = \frac{25}{s(1+0{\cdot}4s)} \tag{6.35}$$

$$\frac{e_{e_0(s)}}{e_{\theta_0(s)}} = \frac{0{\cdot}1}{0{\cdot}5} \cdot 5 = 1 \tag{6.36}$$

$$\frac{e_{e_T(s)}}{20se_{\theta_0(s)}} = \frac{0{\cdot}005}{0{\cdot}02} \cdot 0{\cdot}2 = 0{\cdot}05$$

therefore

$$\frac{e_{e_T(s)}}{se_{\theta_0(s)}} = 1{\cdot}0 \tag{6.37}$$

also

$$\theta_0(s) = \frac{\dot{\theta}_0(s)}{s}$$

therefore

$$e_{\theta_0(s)} = \frac{0{\cdot}5}{0{\cdot}02} \cdot \frac{e_{\dot{\theta}_0(s)}}{s} = 25\,\frac{e_{\dot{\theta}_0(s)}}{s} \tag{6.38}$$

With the feedback loops closed, the input to the amplifier is

$$e_1(s) = e_i(s) - e_0(s) - De_T(s)$$

where D is the fraction of the tacho output fed back. Using the same scale factor for $e_1(s)$ as $e_i(s)$, we obtain the computer equation

$$e_{e_1(s)} = e_{e_i(s)} - 2e_{e_0(s)} - 40De_{e_T(s)} \tag{6.39}$$

We now have sufficient information to draw the computer flow diagram shown in Fig. 6.6. Amplifier 1 is used to set up equation (6.39), the output of which is fed to amplifier 2 to compute the

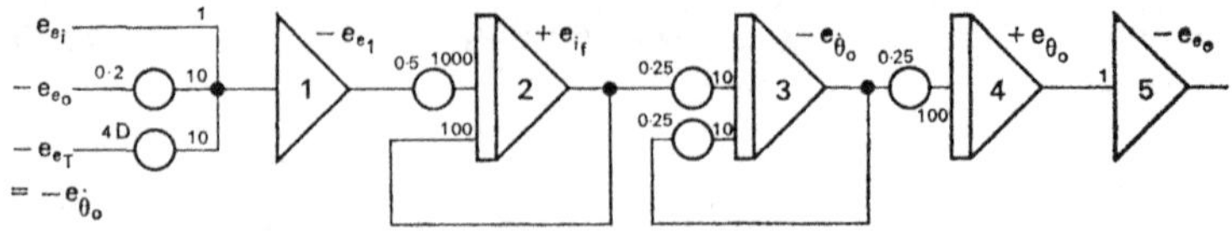

FIG. 6.6. Computer flow diagram for simulation of a servomechanism.

field current. From equation (6.34) we have

$$e_{i_f(s)}[1+0{\cdot}01s] = 5e_{e_l(s)}$$

which can be rearranged in the form

$$e_{i_f(s)} = \frac{100}{s}\left[5e_{e_l(s)} - e_{i_f(s)}\right]$$

This is the equation solved by amplifier 2. Equation (6.35) can be split into two

$$\frac{e_{\dot{\theta}_0(s)}}{e_{i_f(s)}} = \frac{1}{1+0{\cdot}4s},$$

which is solved by amplifier 3, and

$$\frac{e_{\theta_0(s)}}{e_{\dot{\theta}_0(s)}} = \frac{25}{s}$$

which is solved by amplifier 4. The output of this is fed to amplifier 5, which is an inverter, to give $-e_{e_0}$. The other feedback term $-e_{e_T}$ is from equation (6.37) equal to $-e_{\dot{\theta}_0(s)}$. The response of the system to step inputs and different values of D is recorded in Fig. 6.7.

To investigate the large signal behaviour of the system it would be necessary to simulate the nonlinearities. This would require limiter units for the field current and motor speed.

6.2. The Use of Complex CR Networks Associated with Operational Amplifiers to Simulate Transfer Functions

In the previous section we showed how transfer functions could be simulated on a general purpose analogue computer, where all the amplifiers are assigned as fixed elements. Cases arise, however, where it is necessary, either because of a shortage of amplifiers or for special purpose applications to simulate transfer functions with the minimum number of amplifiers. In such a

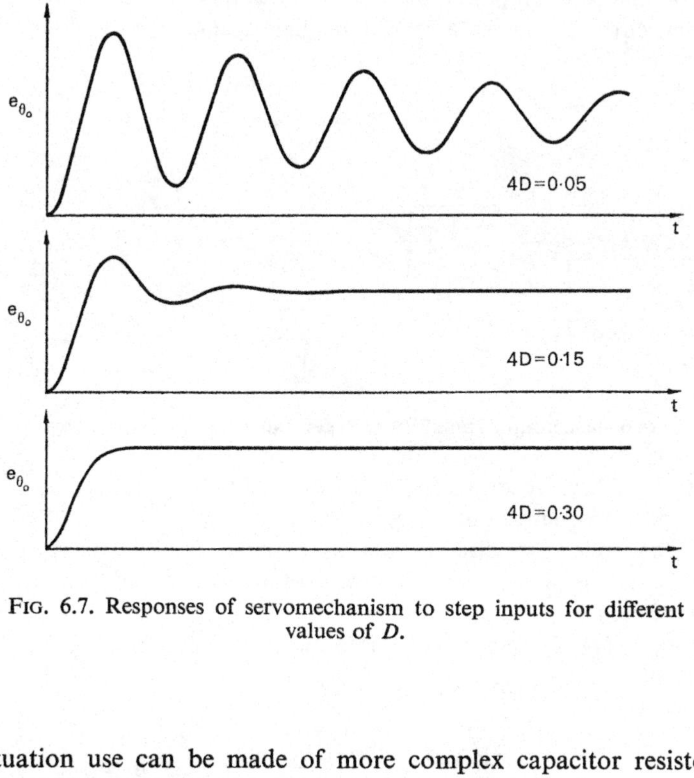

FIG. 6.7. Responses of servomechanism to step inputs for different values of *D*.

situation use can be made of more complex capacitor resistor networks than are necessary for summing and integrating units.

Appropriate networks for any transfer function can be designed using networks synthesis techniques. As a discussion of these methods is beyond the scope of this book, we will only consider some of the most useful networks for specific transfer functions.

Use of Two Terminal Networks

Consider the circuit in Fig. 6.8, where blocks *A* and *B* are two terminal networks. The transfer function is

$$\frac{e_0(s)}{e_1(s)} = -\frac{Z_B(s)}{Z_A(s)} \tag{6.40}$$

provided the amplifier satisfies the usual conditions of high gain, current into the amplifier negligible compared with current

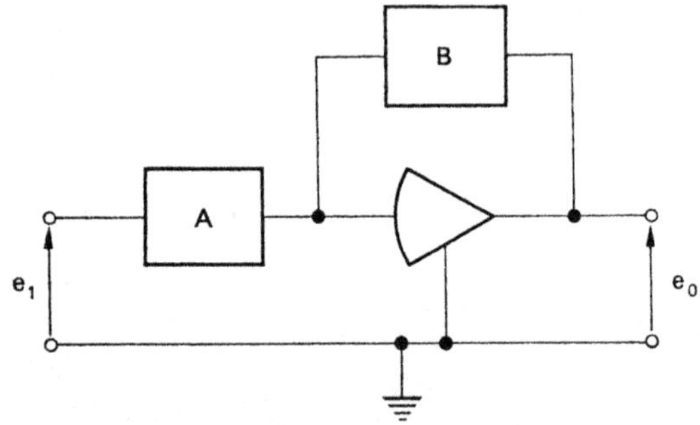

FIG. 6.8. Operational amplifier with generalized two-terminal networks.

in the *A* and *B* networks, and low output impedance, over the range of frequencies of interest.

The following circuits illustrate some of the most useful applications of two terminal networks associated with operational amplifiers.

Phase lag. The circuit for this is shown in Fig. 6.9(a).

$$Z_A(s) = R_1$$

$$Z_B(s) = \frac{R_2/sC_2}{R_2+(1/sC_2)} = \frac{R_2}{1+sC_2R_2}$$

giving

$$\frac{e_0(s)}{e_1(s)} = -\frac{R_2}{R_1}\left(\frac{1}{1+sT_2}\right)$$

where $T_2 = C_2R_2$.

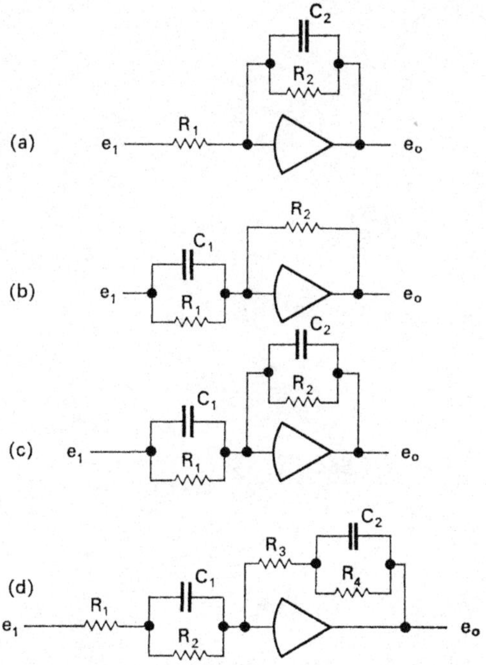

FIG. 6.9. Operational amplifier with typical two-terminal networks.

This transfer function occurs frequently in the study of feedback control systems.

Phase lead (Fig. 6.9(b)). In this case the networks of the previous example have been reversed and we get

$$\frac{e_0(s)}{e_1(s)} = -\frac{R_2}{R_1}(1+sT_1)$$

where $T_1 = C_1R_1$

Phase advance circuit (Fig. 6.9(c)).

$$Z_A(s) = \frac{R_1}{1+sT_1}$$

where $T_1 = C_1R_1$

$$Z_B(s) = \frac{R_2}{1+sT_2}$$

where $T_2 = C_2R_2$

giving
$$\frac{e_0(s)}{e_1(s)} = -\frac{R_2}{R_1}\left(\frac{1+sT_1}{1+sT_2}\right)$$

Lead lag network (Fig. 6.9(d)).

$$Z_A(s) = R_1 + \frac{R_2}{1+sC_1R_2}$$

$$= \frac{(R_1+R_2)+sC_1R_1R_2}{1+sC_1R_2}$$

$$= (R_1+R_2)\left[\frac{1+sC_1\left(\frac{R_1R_2}{R_1+R_2}\right)}{1+sC_1R_2}\right]$$

Similarly

$$Z_B(s) = (R_3+R_4)\left[\frac{1+sC_2\left(\frac{R_3R_4}{R_3+R_4}\right)}{1+sC_2R_4}\right]$$

giving

$$\frac{e_0(s)}{e_1(s)} = -\frac{R_3+R_4}{R_1+R_2}\left[\frac{1+sC_2\left(\frac{R_3R_4}{R_3+R_4}\right)}{1+sC_2R_4}\right]\left[\frac{1+sC_1R_2}{1+sC_1\left(\frac{R_1R_2}{R_1+R_2}\right)}\right]$$

The transfer function being simulated would be of the form

$$\frac{e_0(s)}{e_1(s)} = -K\left[\frac{1+saT_1}{1+sT_1}\right]\left[\frac{1+sT_2}{1+sbT_2}\right]$$

Equating terms we get

$$\frac{R_3+R_4}{R_1+R_2} = K$$

$$C_1R_2 = aT_1$$

$$C_1\left(\frac{R_1R_2}{R_1+R_2}\right) = T_1$$

$$C_2R_4 = bT_2$$

$$C_2\left(\frac{R_3R_4}{R_3+R_4}\right) = T_2$$

These relations give

$$\frac{R_1+R_2}{R_1} = a$$

or

$$R_1 = \frac{R_2}{a-1}$$

and similarly

$$R_3 = \frac{R_4}{b-1}$$

The values of the resistors and capacitors are selected using the above equations.

Approximate differentiation. In Chapter 2 we showed how differentiation could be carried out on the computer with an amplifier having resistive feedback and capacitive input. However, as was pointed out, such a circuit has fundamental difficulties associated with it. To partly overcome these and still obtain a reasonable approximation to differentiation, the circuit of Fig. 6.10 can be used. In this case

$$Z_A(s) = R_1+\frac{1}{sC_1} = \frac{1+sC_1R_1}{sC_1}$$

and

$$Z_B(s) = R_2$$

giving
$$\frac{e_0(s)}{e_1(s)} = -\frac{sC_1R_2}{1+sC_1R_1}$$

If C_1R_1 is very much less than C_1R_2, then at low frequencies

$$\frac{e_0(s)}{e_1(s)} \simeq -sC_1R_2$$

perfect differentiation, but at higher frequencies tends to R_2/R_1. Because the circuit gives a constant gain factor at high frequencies, the noise content of the output signal is much less than that of the true differentiator circuit. Also having R_1 in series with C_1 the capacitive loading effect on the previous amplifier is reduced.

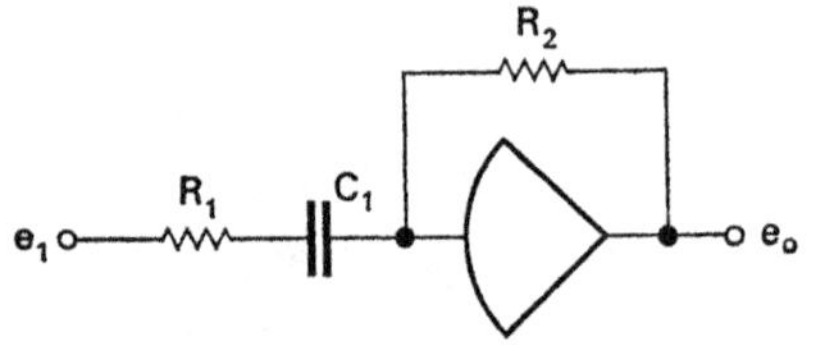

FIG. 6.10. Approximate differentiation circuit.

Use of Two-port Networks

Consider the circuit of Fig. 6.11 where blocks A and B are two-port networks. Provided the amplifier satisfies the usual specifications it can be shown that

$$\frac{e_0(s)}{e_1(s)} = \frac{y_{21}^A(s)}{y_{12}^B(s)} \tag{6.41}$$

where $y_{21}^A(s)$ is the forward short-circuit transfer admittance of block A, and $y_{12}^B(s)$ is the reverse short-circuit transfer admittance of block B. A condition that the circuit has to satisfy is that

$$y_{12}^B(s) \gg \frac{y_{11}^B(s)-y_{22}^A(s)}{k}$$

for all s. k is the amplifier gain, $y_{11}^B(s)$ is the short-circuit admittance at the input port of block B and $y_{22}^A(s)$ is minus the short-circuit admittance of the output port of block A.

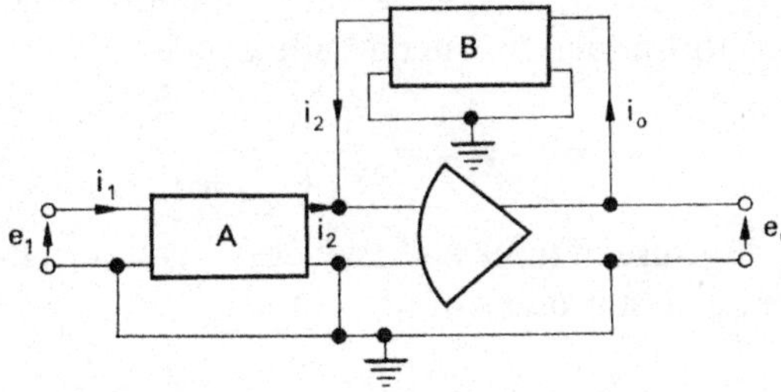

FIG. 6.11. Operational amplifier with two-port networks.

The transfer admittance of two-port *CR* networks can have zeros anywhere in the left half of the complex plane, including the $j\omega$ axis, but poles which are confined to the negative real axis. Consider the appropriate transfer admittances of blocks *A* and *B* as the ratio of polynomials so that

$$y^A_{21}(s) = \frac{A_1(s)}{A_2(s)}$$

and

$$y^B_{12}(s) = \frac{B_1(s)}{B_2(s)}$$

Then

$$\frac{e_0(s)}{e_1(s)} = \frac{A_1(s)}{A_2(s)} \cdot \frac{B_2(s)}{B_1(s)} \tag{6.42}$$

This transfer function has zeros which are the zeros of $y^A_{21}(s)$ and poles of $y^B_{12}(s)$ and poles which are poles of $y^A_{21}(s)$ and zeros of $y^B_{12}(s)$. The singularities of $e_0(s)/e_1(s)$ can therefore, in theory, be anywhere in the left-hand half of the complex plane including the $j\omega$ axis. Practical problems arise if we try to make the power of the numerator polynomial greater than that of the denominator.

An extremely useful technique for analogue computing purposes is that suggested by R. J. A. Paul in a College of Aeronautics Note No. 126, entitled *Simulation of Rational Transfer Functions with Adjustable Coefficients*, and in his book *Fundamental Analogue Techniques*. This is based on the use of generalized *T* networks as shown in Fig. 6.12. For such a network with admittances Y_1, Y_2 and Y_3, the short-circuit transfer admittances are

$$y_{21} = -y_{12} = \frac{Y_1 Y_2}{Y_1 + Y_2 + Y_3}$$

He proposed the use of three basic networks as shown in Fig. 6.13, the short-circuit admittances of which are

$$y_{21}^{(a)} = -y_{12}^{(a)} = \frac{s^2 C_A^2}{(1/R_A) + 2sC_A} = \frac{s^2(2C_A R_A)^2}{4R_A[1 + s(2C_A R_A)]}$$

$$y_{21}^{(b)} = -y_{12}^{(b)} = \frac{sC_B/R_B}{sC_B + (1/R_B)} = \frac{sC_B R_B}{R_B[1 + sC_B R_B]}$$

$$y_{21}^{(c)} = -y_{12}^{(c)} = \frac{1/R_C^2}{sC_C + (2/R_C)} = \frac{1}{2R_C[1 + s(C_C R_C/2)]}$$

Component values are selected so that

$$2C_A R_A = C_B R_B = \frac{C_C R_C}{2} = CR = T$$

The short-circuit transfer admittances therefore become

$$y_{21}^{(a)} = -y_{12}^{(a)} = \frac{1}{2R}\left(\frac{s^2 T^2}{1 + sT}\right)$$

with $R_A = R/2$ and $C_A = C$ (6.43)

$$y_{21}^{(b)} = -y_{12}^{(b)} = \frac{1}{2R}\left(\frac{sT}{1 + sT}\right)$$

with $R_B = 2R$ and $C_B = C/2$ (6.44)

and $$y_{21}^{(c)} = -y_{12}^{(c)} = \frac{1}{2R}\left(\frac{1}{1 + sT}\right)$$

with $R_C = R$ and $C_C = 2C$ (6.45)

Selecting the component values in this way results in the denominators of the three admittances being the same. When the networks are connected in parallel, in which case the admittances add, to

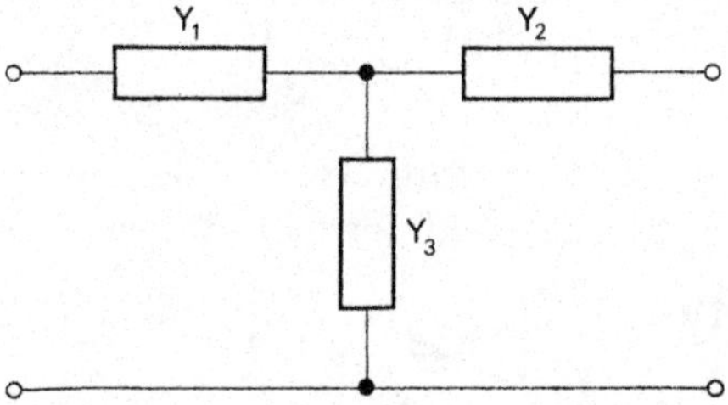

FIG. 6.12. Generalized T network.

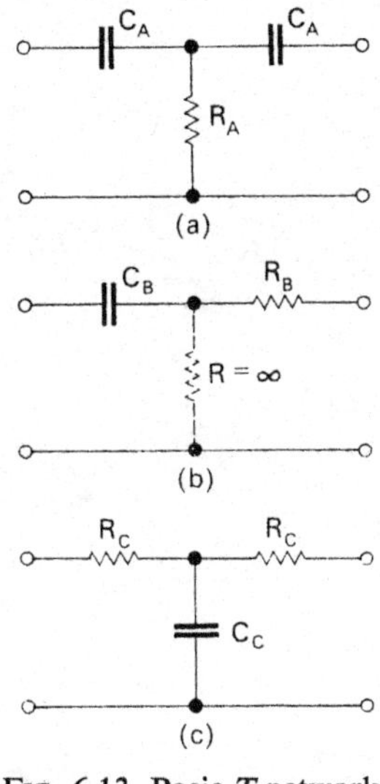

FIG. 6.13. Basic T networks.

form networks A and B of Fig. 6.11, the denominator terms cancel in the resulting transfer function.

Two typical transfer functions obtained by selecting parallel combinations of the networks are shown in Fig. 6.14. For the circuit of Fig. 6.14(a)

$$y_{21}^{A}(s) = \frac{1}{2R}\left[\frac{1}{1+sT}\right] \quad \text{and} \quad y_{12}^{B}(s) = -\frac{1}{2R}\left[\frac{s^2T^2}{1+sT}\right]$$

giving
$$\frac{e_0(s)}{e_1(s)} = -\frac{1}{s^2T^2}$$

The circuit therefore performs a double integration of $e_1(t)$, starting with zero initial conditions. For the circuit of 6.14(b)

$$y^A_{21}(s) = \frac{1}{2R}\left[\frac{1}{1+sT}\right] \quad \text{and} \quad y^B_{12}(s) = -\frac{1}{2R}\left[\frac{1+sT+s^2T^2}{1+sT}\right]$$

giving
$$\frac{e_0(s)}{e_1(s)} = -\frac{1}{1+sT+s^2T^2}$$

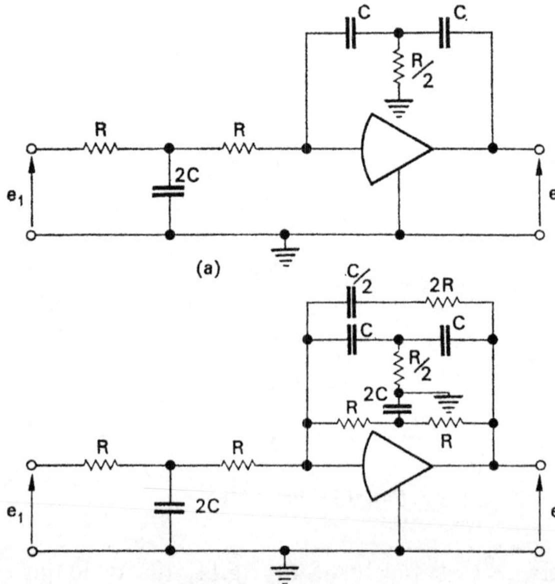

FIG. 6.14. Operational amplifier with combinations of the basic T networks.

This is the transfer function of a system the behaviour of whose output variable $e_0(t)$ as a result of the variation of its input variable $e_1(t)$ can be described by a second order differential equation with zero initial conditions. Using the networks as indicated in Fig. 6.14, it is impossible to vary the coefficients of the s and s^2 terms without changing all components, and the fact that the coefficient of s must always be the square root of the coefficient of s^2 is a severe limitation. If potentiometers are introduced into the circuits, as shown in Fig. 6.15, it is possible to vary the coefficients independently. The resistance of the potentiometers must be low so that their output impedances can be ignored. In the circuit of Fig. 6.15 one of each of the basic T networks is included in the A and B networks. When all the switches are closed, the transfer function simulated is

$$\frac{e_0(s)}{e_1(s)} = -\left[\frac{1+k_1Ts+k_2T^2s^2}{1+k_3Ts+k_4T^2s^2}\right] \tag{6.46}$$

where $T = CR$, and k_1, k_2, k_3 and k_4 are less than unity. If this is built up as a special purpose unit, a wide variety of transfer functions can be simulated by selecting the appropriate configura-

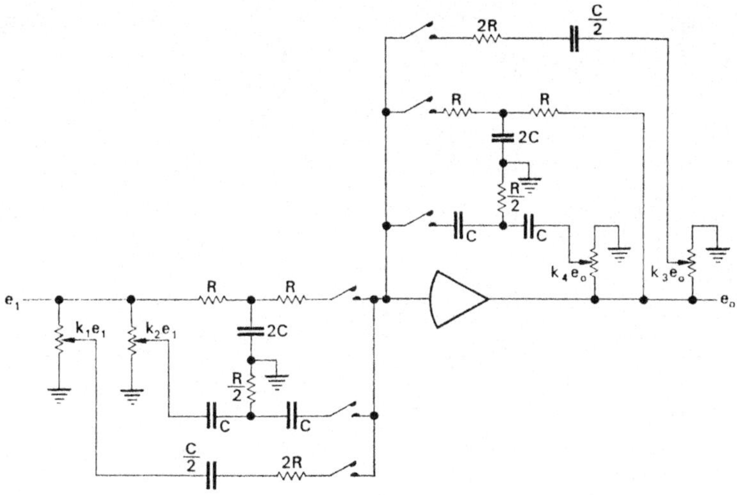

FIG. 6.15. General purpose computing unit using parallel combinations of the basic T networks.

tion of closed switches, values of T, and potentiometer settings. Initial conditions other than zero cannot be set into the network, but it is felt that this is not a severe limitation. Higher order transfer functions can be simulated by cascading a number of circuits.

In many applications it will be necessary to simulate transfer functions of the form

$$\frac{e_0(s)}{e_1(s)} = -\frac{kTs}{1+aTs+bT^2s^2} \tag{6.47}$$

or

$$\frac{e_0(s)}{e_1(s)} = -\frac{1}{1+aTs+bT^2s^2} \tag{6.48}$$

where k, a and b are fixed constants. In such cases networks with fewer components than have previously been described can be used. Consider the circuit of Fig. 6.16. If the amplifier satisfies the usual specifications we can write the following equations

$$[e_1(s)-e_2(s)]sC_1+[e_0(s)-e_2(s)](1/R_2) - [e_2(s)](1/R_1) = 0 \tag{6.49}$$

and

$$e_2(s)(1/R_1)+e_0(s)sC_2 = 0 \tag{6.50}$$

From equation (6.50) we have

$$e_2(s) = -e_0(s)sC_2R_1 \tag{6.51}$$

which can be substituted in equation (6.49) to give

$$[e_1(s)+e_0(s)sC_2R_1]sC_1+[e_0(s)+e_0(s)sC_2R_1](1/R_2) +e_0(s)sC_2 = 0 \tag{6.52}$$

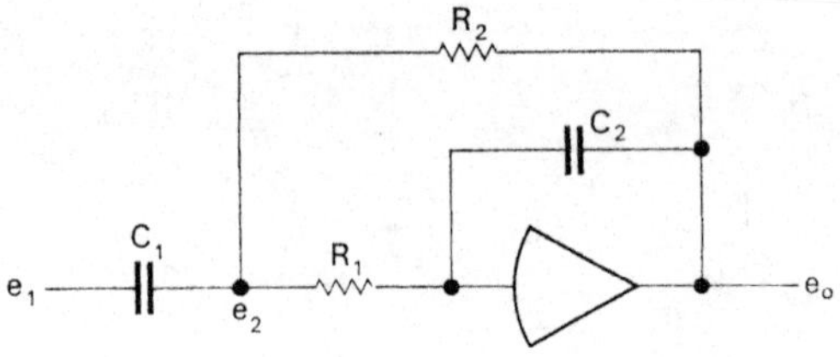

FIG. 6.16. Circuit for simulation of transfer function $kTs/(1+aTs+bT^2s^2)$.

Solving for $e_0(s)$ we get

$$e_0(s)[s^2C_1C_2R_1R_2+1+sC_2(R_1+R_2)] = -e_1(s)sC_1R_2$$

which gives

$$\frac{e_0(s)}{e_1(s)} = -\frac{C_1R_2s}{1+C_2(R_1+R_2)s+C_1C_2R_1R_2s^2} \tag{6.53}$$

Comparing equation (6.53) with equation (6.47), we have

$$kT = C_1R_2, \quad aT = C_2(R_1+R_2) \quad \text{and} \quad bT^2 = C_1C_2R_1R_2$$

These equalities have to be manipulated to obtain values for C_1, C_2, R_1 and R_2 in terms of k, b and T.

$$\frac{bT}{k} = C_2R_1$$

$$\frac{R_1+R_2}{R_1} = \frac{ka}{b}$$

from which
$$\frac{R_2}{R_1} = \frac{ka-b}{b}$$

$$\frac{C_1R_2}{C_2R_1} = \frac{k^2}{b}$$

giving
$$\frac{C_1}{C_2} = \frac{k^2}{ka-b}$$

EXAMPLE: If $k = 2$, and $a = b = 1$,

i.e.
$$\frac{e_0(s)}{e_1(s)} = -\frac{2Ts}{1+Ts+T^2s^2}$$

then $(R_2/R_1) = 1$, $(C_1/C_2) = 4$, and $C_2R_1 = 0{\cdot}5T$

Let $T = CR$ and $R_1 = 0{\cdot}5R$

then $C_2 = C$, $R_2 = 0{\cdot}5R$, and $C_1 = 4C$

Consider the circuit of Fig. 6.17, for which we can write the following equations

$$[e_1(s)-e_2(s)](1/R_1)+[e_0(s)-e_2(s)](1/R_1)-e_2(s)[sC_1+(1/R_2)] = 0 \tag{6.54}$$

and
$$e_2(s)(1/R_2)+e_0(s)sC_2 = 0 \tag{6.55}$$

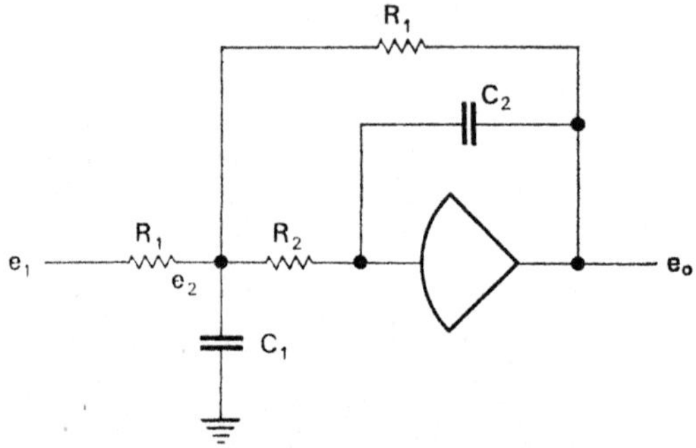

FIG. 6.17. Circuit for simulation of transfer function $1/(1+aTs+bT^2s^2)$.

From equation (6.55) we have

$$e_2(s) = -e_0(s)sC_2R_2 \tag{6.56}$$

which can be substituted in equation (6.54) to give

$$[e_1(s)+e_0(s)sC_2R_2]+[e_0(s)+e_0(s)sC_2R_2] + e_0(s)sC_2R_2R_1[sC_1+(1/R_2)] = 0 \tag{6.57}$$

Solving for $e_0(s)$ we get

$$e_0(s)[1+sC_2(R_1+2R_2)+sC_1C_2R_1R_2] = -e_1(s)$$

which gives

$$\frac{e_0(s)}{e_1(s)} = -\frac{1}{1+sC_2(R_1+2R_2)+sC_1C_2R_1R_2} \tag{6.58}$$

Comparing this with equation (6.48) we have

$$aT = C_2(R_1+2R_2), \quad \text{and} \quad bT^2 = C_1C_2R_1R_2$$

These equalities have to be manipulated to obtain values for C_1, C_2, R_1, and R_2 in terms of a, b and T.

If we put $R_1 = 2R_2$

then $$aT = 2C_2R_1 \quad \text{and} \quad bT^2 = \frac{C_1C_2R_1^2}{2}.$$

Therefore $$C_1R_1 = \frac{4bT}{a}$$

and hence $$\frac{C_1}{C_2} = \frac{8b}{a^2}$$

EXAMPLE: If $a = b = 1$,

i.e. $$\frac{e_0(s)}{e_1(s)} = -\frac{1}{1+Ts+T^2s^2}$$

$$(R_1/R_2) = 2, \quad (C_1/C_2) = 8 \quad \text{and} \quad C_2R_1 = T/2$$

If $T = CR$ and $R_2 = R$

then $R_1 = 2R$, $C_1 = 2C$ and $C_2 = C/4$.

CHAPTER 7

Iterative Operation of the Analog Computer

AN iterative analog computer, when operating in a repetitive mode, can be programmed to automatically change parameter and initial conditions values in successive COMPUTE periods. The changes are made as a result of calculations carried out using measurements taken during previous COMPUTE periods. The required solution may be the values of some parameters in the system which make the output fit a predetermined form, as in optimization problems, or it may be that the problem solution depends on updating or changing parameters at regular or irregular intervals. To be able to do this, it is necessary to have much more flexible and varied methods of controlling the operation of the computer than described in Chapter 4. It is also necessary to be able to measure voltages, make decisions as a result of the measurements, and to store voltage levels. It is therefore obvious that some other types of computing units, in addition to those described in Chapter 2, will be necessary.

7.1. Additional Hardware Required

Track-store units. Consider the integrator control circuit of Fig. 4.8 with only the initial condition input, as shown in Fig. 7.1. In the RESET mode, switch S_1 is closed and S_2, which is a single pole change-over switch, connects the capacitor C in series with a small resistor between the amplifier output and ground. The amplifier therefore operates as an inverter with a capacitor connected to its output. The output voltage e_0 follows any changes in e_{IC}, with the maximum rate of change of the amplifier output if necessary. The capacitor charges up to this voltage, but with a lag depending on the time constant resulting from the resistance in series with it. When the unit is switched to the HOLD mode, S_1 opens and S_2 disconnects the capacitor from ground and connects it to the input of the amplifier. The output voltage e_0 is now equal to the voltage stored across C at the instant the unit was switched to HOLD. Provided the charging time constant of the capacitor is small compared to the rate of change of e_0, the stored voltage will be equal to minus the value of e_{IC} at the

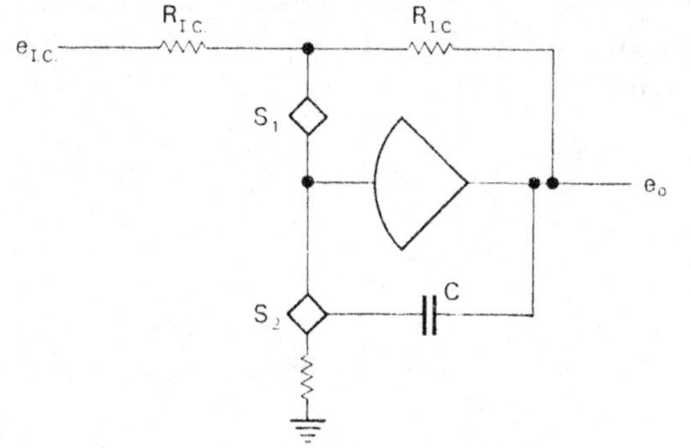

FIG. 7.1. Integrator unit with only initial condition input.

instant of switching. With an amplifier having no input current and a capacitor with infinite leakage resistance, the voltage would remain constant as long as the unit was in the HOLD mode. In practice both these effects are present and the output voltage will change slowly with time.

Integrator units operated in this way can be used for tracking and short-term storage of specified values of voltages in a computing loop. In modern computers, although the integrators can be used for this purpose, provision is generally made for converting some of the summing units to track-store units. The additional cost of providing the appropriate networks to connect across them is more than offset by the saving in the number of expensive integrators which would otherwise be necessary. Also, as the integrator has only one initial condition input resistor it is not possible to sum into it when being used for tracking purposes, whereas all the inputs of a converted summer can be used. The symbol used in flow diagrams for track-store units is shown in Fig. 7.2, where e_1 and e_2 are two input voltages, N is the number of the unit, e_0 is the output voltage and R is the logic signal controlling its operation. When R is logic 0 the unit is in the TRACK mode and e_0 is equal to minus the sum of e_1 and e_2. When R changes to logic 1 the unit goes into STORE mode and e_0 remains at the value minus the sum of e_1 and e_2 at the instant R changed from logic 0 to logic 1.

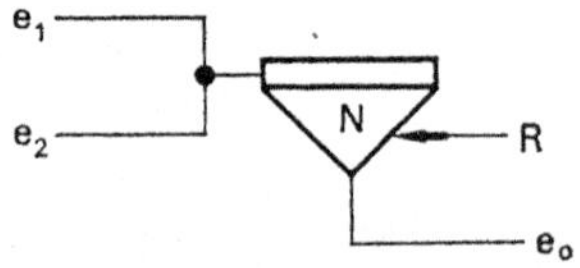

FIG. 7.2. Symbol for track-store unit.

Readers may find that in the machines they are using the modes of integrators and track-store units require different logic levels from those used in this book. There is no preferred scheme and each manufacturer has his own code.

In some computers an additional RESET circuit is provided, so that e_0 can be set to a specified initial value independent of the values of the e_1 and e_2 inputs. In such cases the additional input is drawn on the right-hand side of the unit and another logic signals is provided to control it.

Comparators. The comparator is a simple form of analog-to-digital converter. Its output is one of two logic levels, depending on the sign of the sum of the input analog signals. One of the main uses of such a unit is to detect when a voltage in a computing loop crosses a preset level. The circuit typically comprises a high gain amplifier with nonlinear feedback, driving a digital logic output stage. The basic circuit is shown in Fig. 7.3. The amplifier output voltage e_0 swings between two voltage levels set by the reference voltage values and the potential dividers formed by resistors R_1, R_2, R_3 and R_4. When (e_1+e_2) is negative, e_0 is positive and C is logic 0. When (e_1+e_2) is positive, e_0 is negative and C is logic 1. Usually the complemented logic output $\overline{C}$ is also available.

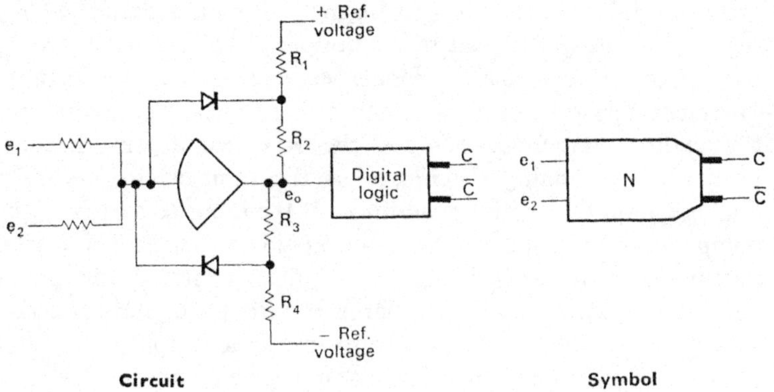

FIG. 7.3. Basic comparator circuit and symbol used to represent it.

Digital-to-analog switches. A number of free solid state and reed relay switches are provided, which can be controlled by digital logic signals. These are used for changing parameter values or voltage levels during a computation. They usually consist of a resistor in series with a switch so that when the output is connected to the summing junction of an amplifier it acts like a switched gain of 1 or 10.

Digital logic units. A complement of digital logic units such as gates, flip-flops, monostables, registers and counters are also provided. These can be interconnected by means of patch cords to provide control programs for the integrators, track-store units and digital-to-analog switches. This allows more flexible control of problems than is obtainable with only the manual switches and repetitive operation unit described in Chapter 4.

7.2. Organization of an Iterative Analog Computer

With the more flexible control of problems which is possible in an iterative analog computer, it is necessary to be able to control integrators and track-store units individually as well as in groups. Also provision has to be made for interconnecting the digital logic units. Because of the coupling problems which could arise if digital and analog signals were in too close proximity, manufacturers provide two patchpanels on their computers, one for analog interconnections and the other for digital interconnections. The analog patchpanel is the same as for ordinary analog computers, with the addition of the input terminals of the comparator units and the digital-to-analog switches. The digital patchpanel terminates digital logic units, integrator and track-store unit control lines, comparator outputs, digital-to-analog switch control lines, free push buttons, logic outputs, indicator inputs, and all clock signals. The computer configuration is shown schematically in Fig. 7.4.

7.3. Application of Track-store Units

If we want to store the value of a voltage in a computing loop at any time, it is necessary to track it using a track-store unit, and at the appropriate time switch to STORE. The voltage level which has been stored can then be used to calculate new initial conditions for the circuit, as an input voltage, or to control parameter values during the next or later COMPUTE periods. Once we have used the unit to store a particular voltage value, it cannot again be used for tracking purposes until the voltage is no longer required. When the stored voltage is being used to calculate initial conditions for the next COMPUTE period, the requirement for the voltage ends once the initial condition has been set. This is when the computing loop is switched to COMPUTE, in which case the track-store unit can be switched back to TRACK. However, in those cases where the stored voltage is required during the next or later

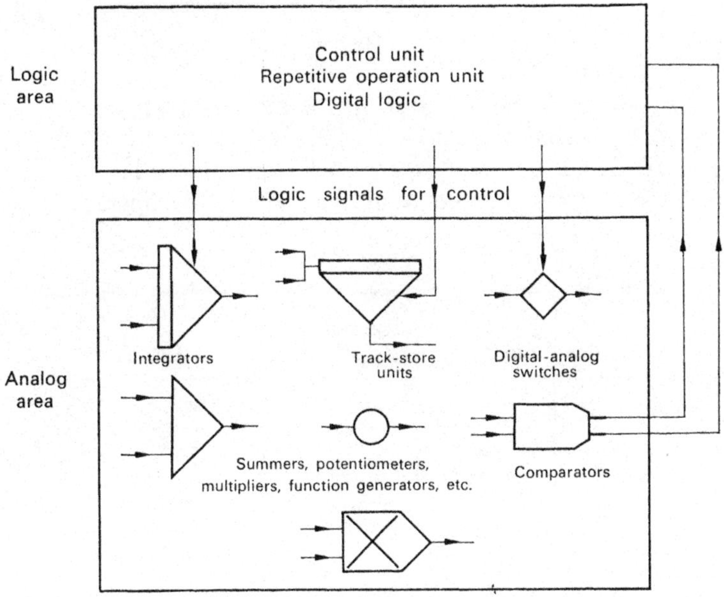

FIG. 7.4. Iterative analog computer schematic.

COMPUTE periods, it is not possible to switch the track-store unit back to TRACK for that period. It is then necessary to use two track-store units in cascade, normally referred to as a memory pair.

7.4. Memory Pair Operation

A memory pair is connected as shown in Fig. 7.5, where e_1 is the voltage being tracked, e_{IC} is used to set an initial initial condition on track-store unit 2 at the beginning of a set of repetitive operations, and e_0 is the stored output voltage.

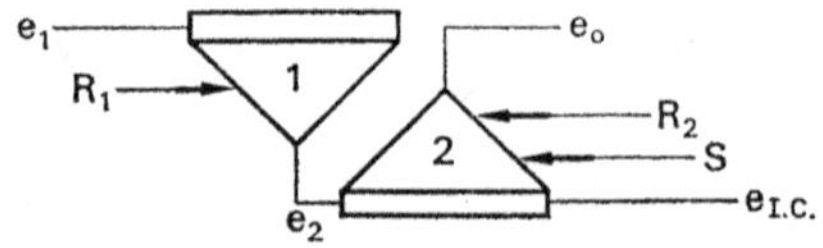

FIG. 7.5. Memory pair.

A sequence of logic control for the memory pair is set out in Table 7.1. The logic signals R_1 and R_2 will frequently be complementary signals, so that when track-store unit 1 is in TRACK, track-store unit 2 is in HOLD and vice versa. The operation of a

TABLE 7.1

Logic line	Logic level	Track-store unit number	Mode
R_1	0	1	Track e_1
R_1	1	1	Store
R_2 S	0 0	2	Set e_0 to $-e_{IC}$
R_2 S	0 1	2	Track e_2
R_2 S	1 1	2	Store

memory pair is illustrated in Figs. 7.6 and 7.7, where e_1 is some voltage generated in a computing loop. In Fig. 7.6 the memory pair is being controlled by the output of the repetitive operation unit, and in Fig. 7.7 by the output of a comparator. In Fig. 7.6, when the *RO* button is depressed, its logic 1 output starts the

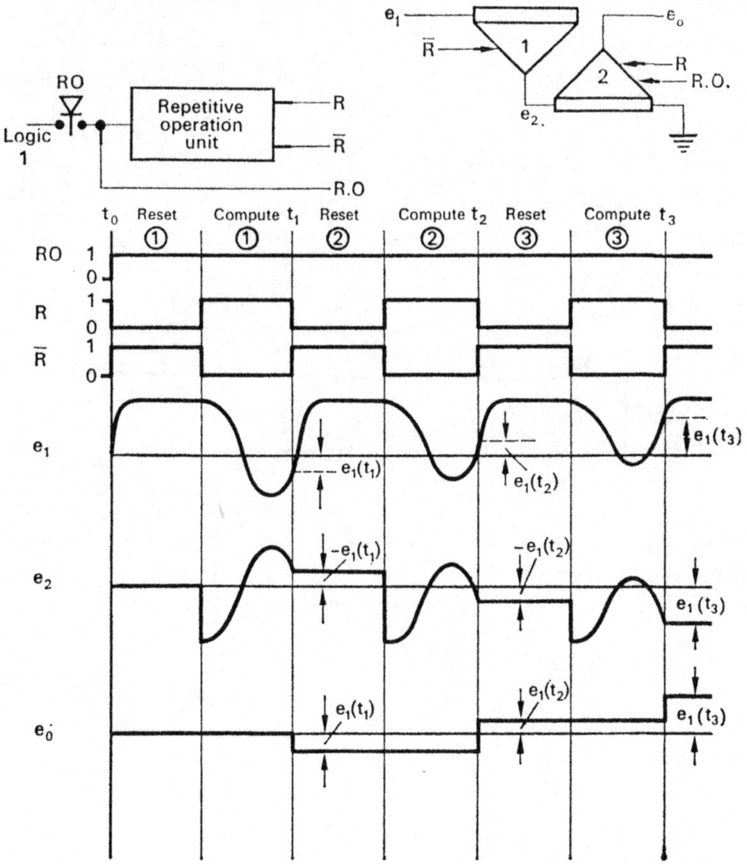

FIG. 7.6. Memory pair controlled by repetitive operation unit and typical waveforms.

repetitive operation unit. This controls the problem with RESET and COMPUTE times as selected by the operator. The *RO* logic 1 also switches the initial initial condition circuit of track-store unit 2 to HOLD, e_0 having been set by the circuit in this case to zero volts. During the first RESET period, e_1 sets to its initial condition voltage, track-store unit 1 is in STORE and unit 2 is tracking e_2, which is

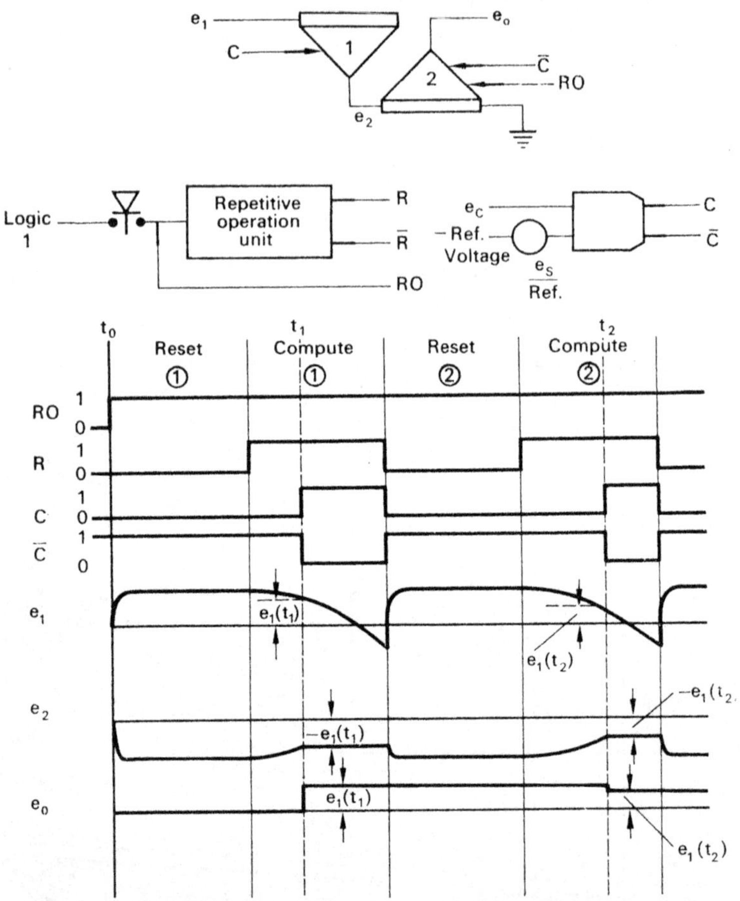

FIG. 7.7. Comparator controlled memory pair and typical waveforms.

zero volts. In the first COMPUTE period, track-store unit 1 tracks e_1 and unit 2 stores zero voltage. During the second RESET period, track-store unit 1 stores the value of $-e_1(t_1)$ at the end of COMPUTE period 1 and unit 2 tracks this value. During COMPUTE period 2 track-store unit 1 again tracks the new e_1 while unit 2 stores the voltage $e_1(t_1)$. We therefore have the value of e_1 at the end of

COMPUTE period 1 available during COMPUTE period 2, perhaps controlling a parameter value or the gain of an input voltage. The sequence repeats itself so that we have available during any COMPUTE period the value of e_1 at the end of the previous COMPUTE period.

In Fig. 7.7 where the track-store units are controlled by the comparator outputs the pattern of events is similar, except that the value of e_1 which is stored can be selected at any time during a COMPUTE period. In this case the comparator operates when a voltage e_c exceeds the value e_s. Track-store unit 1 is controlled by the comparator output C and is in TRACK during the RESET period and the part of the COMPUTE period before the comparator operates. Track-store unit 2 is controlled by $\bar{C}$, and it only tracks

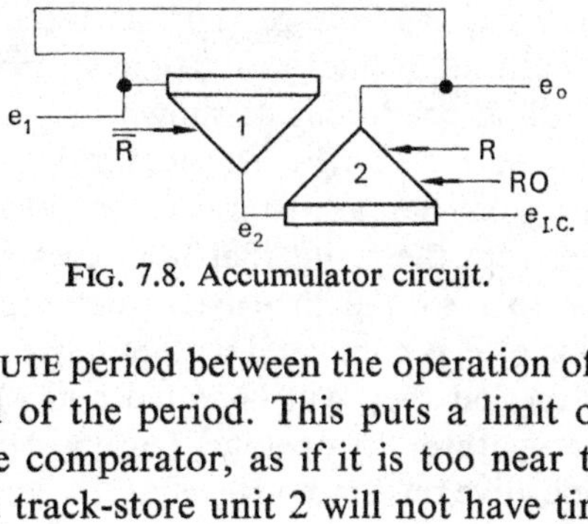

FIG. 7.8. Accumulator circuit.

during the COMPUTE period between the operation of the comparator and the end of the period. This puts a limit on the time of operation of the comparator, as if it is too near the end of the COMPUTE period track-store unit 2 will not have time to track e_2 accurately.

If a memory pair is connected as shown in Fig. 7.8, it will act as an accumulator, and if it was being used in the circuit of Fig. 7.6, the value of e_0 after n COMPUTE periods would be $e_1(t_1)+e_1(t_2)+\ldots+e_1(t_n)$. This allows us to sum voltages and if required, obtain the average over a number of COMPUTE periods. Another application would be to make e_1 a preset value, which would mean that at the end of each COMPUTE period or when a comparator operated e_0 would be incremented by the preset value. We could therefore change parameter values or initial condition values in steps, in successive COMPUTE periods.

7.5. Track-Store Units used for Function Generation

In Chapter 5 it was shown that functions of time could be generated easily, using in most cases only linear computing units, whereas functions of other variables required costly function generators. One possible application of memory pairs and comparators is to allow the generation of a function of any variable, by sampling a function of time being generated repetitively at high speed. As an example we will consider the generation of $(e_x)^2$ where e_x is a variable in a computing loop. A suitable computer flow diagram with the waveforms at different amplifier outputs is shown in Fig. 7.9. To generate a voltage proportional to t^2 requires two integrators connected in cascade, the output of the first one being a voltage e_t proportional to t and the output of the second being the voltage $(e_t)^2$. If these two integrators are cycled between RESET and COMPUTE at a very high repetition rate, with the initial conditions as shown in Fig. 7.9(a), the first two waveforms of Fig. 7.9(b) are obtained. The voltage e_t is deliberately run from the positive reference value to the negative reference value, with the result that $(e_t)^2$ goes from the positive reference value to zero and then back to the positive reference value. The value of e_t is compared with minus e_x and once during each COMPUTE period they will be equal and of opposite signs, causing the comparator to operate. During each RESET period, e_t goes to the positive reference value and the comparator is reset. At the beginning of each COMPUTE period the C output of the comparator is logic 1 and the $\overline{C}$ output is logic 0. Track-store unit 1 therefore tracks $(e_t)^2$ during the first part of the COMPUTE period until the comparator operates, when it goes to STORE. The value of $(e_t)^2$ at that instant is then transferred to track-store unit 2. The voltage at the output of track-store unit 2 is therefore the value of $(e_t)^2$ during each COMPUTE period, when e_t is equal to e_x and is a quantized version of the required function $(e_x)^2$. The reason for e_t going from positive to negative is to allow for e_x being positive or negative.

The accuracy with which $(e_x)^2$ is generated will depend on the accuracy of $(e_t)^2$ and the ratio of the frequency of repetition of $(e_t)^2$ and the frequency of e_x.

If the RESET and COMPUTE periods were each 1 msec and e_x a frequency of 1 Hz, then the $(e_x)^2$ waveform would have 500 samples per cycle of e_x giving a good approximation.

Another useful example of function generation is the case of sin x and cos x.

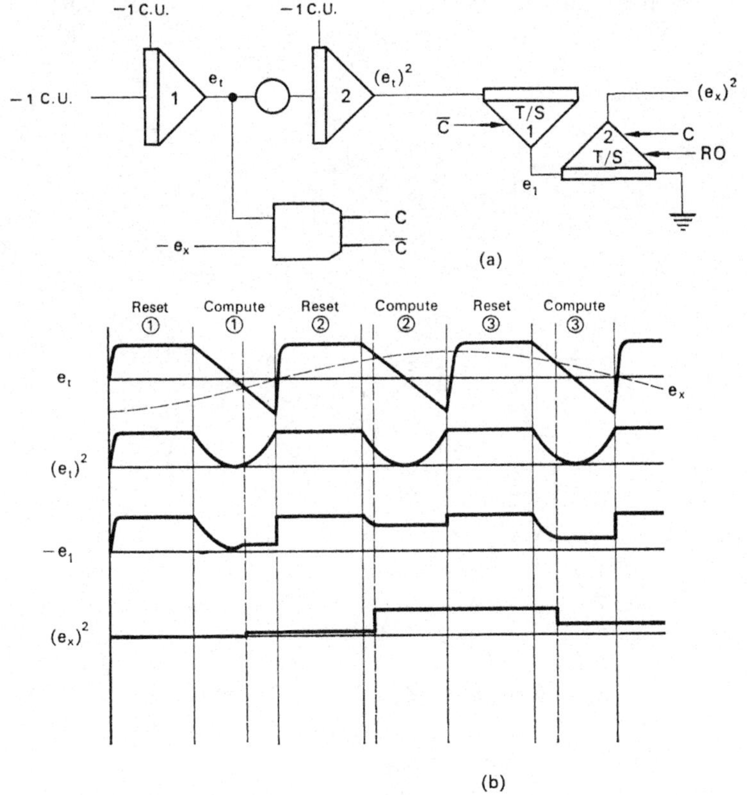

FIG. 7.9. Track-store units used for generation of $(e_x)^2$, (a) circuit, (b) waveforms.

7.6. Use of Track-Store Units to Solve a Simple Two-point Boundary Value Problem

Consider the equation $(d^2y/dx^2)+Ky = 0$, with the boundary conditions $y = 0$ at $x = 0$ and $y = y_h$ at $x = D$, where D is less than $(\pi/\sqrt{K})$, and the value of (dy/dx) at $x = 0$ is unknown. The required value of (dy/dx) can of course be easily calculated, but solving the equation on a computer serves as a good illustration of the application of iterative techniques. To solve the equation on an analog computer, x is represented by time, the

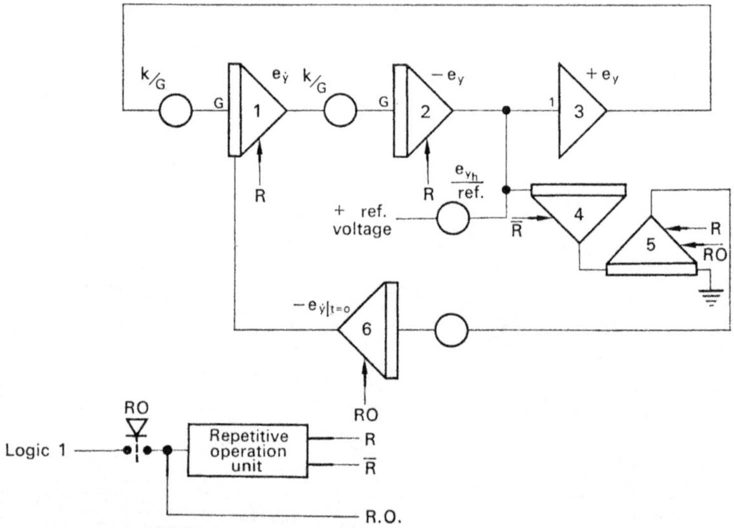

FIG. 7.10. Track-store units used to solve a simple two-point boundary value problem.

value of y at $t = 0$ being set as one initial condition and the value of (dy/dt) at $t = 0$ adjusted on successive COMPUTE runs until the other boundary condition is satisfied.

The adjustments to (dy/dt) can be made automatically using track-store units, if the equation is solved repetitively. A suitable flow diagram is shown in Fig. 7.10. The second order equation is solved by amplifiers 1 to 3 which are controlled by the repetitive operation unit. Amplifiers 4 to 6 provide the control loop for adjusting the initial value of $e_{\dot{y}}$. When the *RO* button is pressed, the logic 1 output starts the repetitive operation control unit, puts the initial initial condition circuit of amplifier 5, which is a track-store unit, to HOLD, and amplifier 6 which is an integrator into COMPUTE. During the first COMPUTE period, as the initial value of $e_{\dot{y}}$ is zero there is no output from any of the amplifiers. At the end of the period, as e_y is zero, the error voltage transferred to the output of amplifier 5 is e_{y_h}. A fraction of this, depending on the potentiometer setting, is continuously integrated by amplifier 6, the

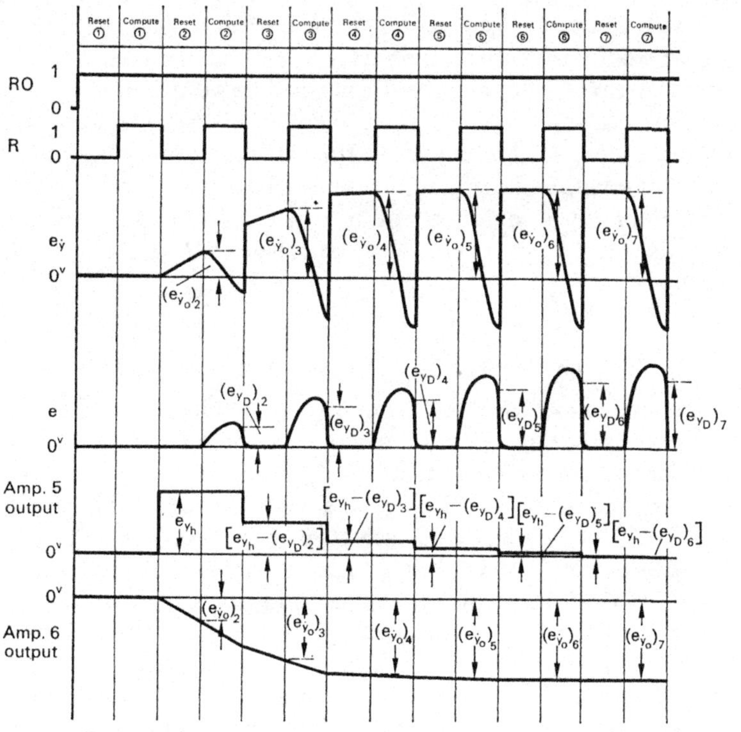

FIG. 7.11. Typical waveforms obtained at the outputs of units of Fig. 7.10.

output of which is tracked by the initial condition circuit of amplifier 1 during the RESET period. At the beginning of the second COMPUTE period, $e_{\dot{y}}$ has an initial condition voltage equal to minus the output voltage of amplifier 6. The computer solves the equation with this initial condition and at the end of the second COMPUTE period the value of e_y is again compared with the set boundary condition, and the new error stored at the output of amplifier 5. Amplifier 6 continues integrating with this new error signal input, to provide another trial initial value for $e_{\dot{y}}$. The sequence is repeated until an initial value of $e_{\dot{y}}$ is obtained which satisfies the boundary condition. The output of amplifier 5 becomes zero and the output of amplifier 6 remains constant. The rate at which $e_{\dot{y}}$ converges to the correct value is dependent on the gain in the control loop. If it is too high the system will be unstable and if too low convergence will be very slow. The loop gain can be adjusted by varying the gain of the integrator and the potentiometer preceding it. Typical waveforms obtained at different points in the solution are shown in Fig. 7.11.

If amplifier 6 could be put into HOLD during the COMPUTE periods, the memory pair could be replaced by a single track-store unit.

7.7. Simulation of the Trajectory of a Bouncing Ball

Consider a ball dropped from an initial height h_0 at time t_0, successively hitting the ground and rebounding at times t_1, t_2, etc. Ignoring the effects of drag on the ball, we can write the equation of motion as $\ddot{h} = -g$, where g is the acceleration due to gravity. If the ball has a coefficient of restitution a, which varies between 0 and 1, it rebounds after hitting the ground, with a velocity a times that which it had just prior to impact. To simulate the motion of the ball on a computer we have to be able to measure the impact velocity of the ball, stop the computation, set in the rebound velocity and start the computation again. This can be easily accomplished using a comparator, track-store unit and a few digital logic elements as shown in the flow diagram of

Fig. 7.12. Amplifiers 1 and 2 solve the equation of motion of the ball, 3 and 4 measure the impact velocity and set up the rebound velocity, the comparator detects when the ball hits the ground, and amplifier 5 provides a time base for the display. The operation of the circuit is controlled by the push button, AND gate, and monostable. Before the push button is pressed B, G and M are all logic 0, the comparator output C is logic 1 because of the initial value of e_h, amplifiers 1, 2 and 5 are in RESET and amplifier 3 which is a track-store unit is in TRACK. After the push button is

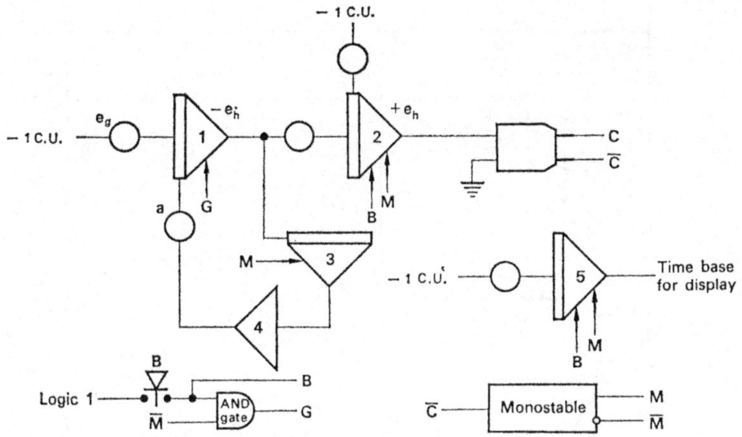

FIG. 7.12. Computer flow diagram for simulation of the trajectory of a bouncing ball.

pressed, B and G are logic 1, M is logic 0 and amplifiers 1, 2 and 5 are in COMPUTE. The voltage e_h starts from its initial value e_{h_o} and decreases to zero. This is detected by the comparator, and the logic 0 to logic 1 transition of C triggers the monostable. Because $\bar{M}$ goes to logic 0 the AND gate output G also goes to logic 0, and therefore amplifier 1 goes into RESET. The logic 0 to logic 1 transition of M puts amplifier 3 to STORE and amplifiers 2 and 5 into HOLD. Amplifier 3 which had been tracking the velocity of the ball is now storing the value at the instant the ball hit the ground.

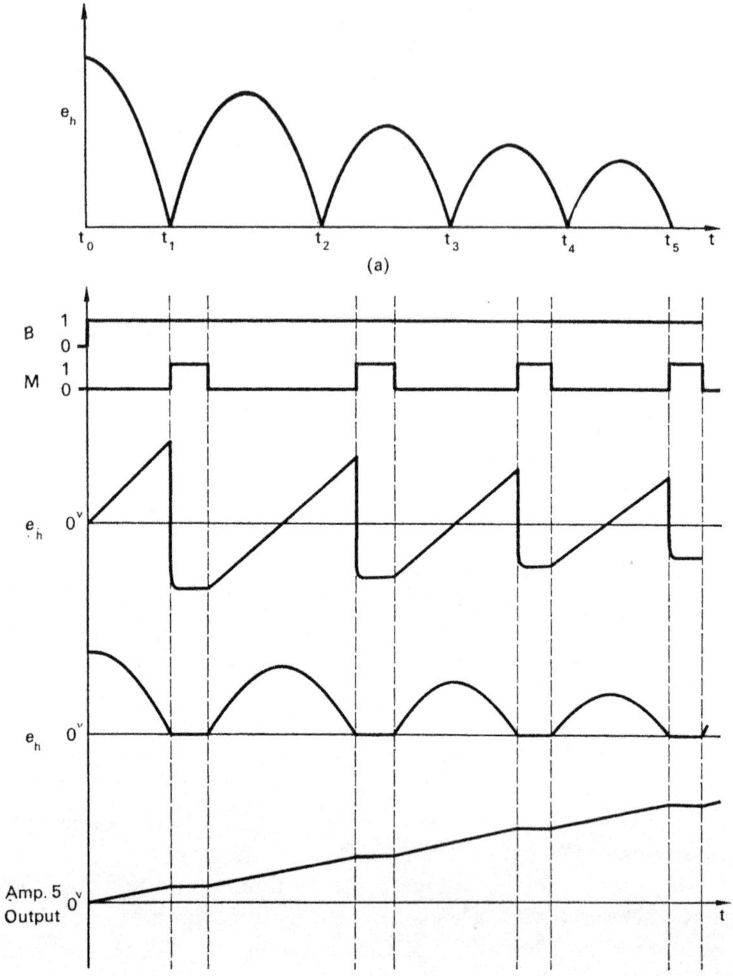

FIG. 7.13. Typical waveforms obtained at the outputs of units of Fig. 7.12.

This is inverted and multiplied by a before being tracked by the initial condition circuit of amplifier 1 to set the rebound velocity. The pulse width of the monostable is adjusted to allow time for the initial condition to set accurately. At the end of the monostable pulse, the circuit reverts to the COMPUTE condition and another bounce is computed. Each time the ball hits the ground the logic stops the problem and sets up the rebound velocity of the ball. If the output of amplifier 5 is used to drive the time base of the display, it will stop when the circuit is not computing, and the trace will rebound from the point of impact, as shown in Fig. 7.13(a). Typical waveforms at various parts of the circuit are shown in Fig. 7.13(b).

7.8. Parameter Optimization

The performance of a system is dependent on the values of the parameters in the equations describing its behaviour. In parameter optimization the basic problem is to maximize or minimize a criterion function, dependent on the solution of the system equations, by carrying out a systematic search of parameter space. The criterion function selected will be a measure of the system performance.

Parameter optimization is an important area of application for iterative analog computers. The system equations can be set up on the computer, which is programmed to control the parameters, measure the criterion function, and adjust the parameter values in order to move towards the desired maximum or minimum. For complex systems, however, the digital hardware capacity is easily exceeded, and a hybrid computer becomes necessary.

As an example of parameter optimization, consider a system described by the second order differential equation

$$\ddot{x}+2\zeta\omega_n\dot{x}+\omega_n^2 x = 0 \tag{7.1}$$

with initial conditions $\dot{x}\,|_{t=0} = 0$ and $x\,|_{t=0} = -A$. It is desired to optimize the frequency and damping ratio of the system by adjusting the values of ω_n^2 and $2\zeta\omega_n$.

The output response of the system will be of the form shown in Fig. 7.14. A measure of the frequency is given by the time T from $t=0$ until the response curve crosses the $x=0$ line, and the damping by the voltage δ which is the amplitude of the first undershoot. Both of these can be easily measured, compared with specified values, and the errors used to control the coefficients ω_n^2 and $2\zeta\omega_n$. The system is simulated on the computer

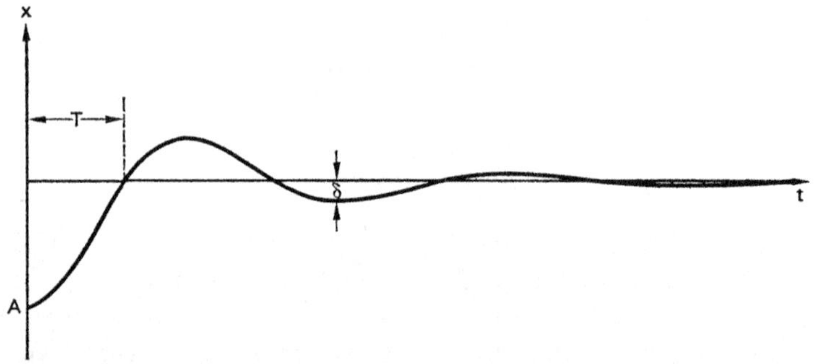

FIG. 7.14. Response of a second order system with initial condition.

using the circuit of Fig. 7.15, with the following scaling. At time $t = 0$ the system initial conditions are $\dot{x} = 0$ and $x = -A$. The initial value A will therefore be the maximum value of x, and for the worst case where ζ equals 0, it will oscillate about zero with this as peak amplitude. The maximum values are therefore

$$x = A, \quad \dot{x} = \omega_n A, \quad \text{and} \quad \ddot{x} = \omega_n^2 A$$

From these we obtain the scale factors

$$a_x = \frac{1}{A}, \quad a_{\dot{x}} = \frac{1}{\omega_n A}, \quad \text{and} \quad a_{\ddot{x}} = \frac{1}{\omega_n^2 A}$$

all with units C.U. per unit of the variable. Converting equation (7.1) into computer variables we get

$$\frac{e_{\ddot{x}}}{1/\omega_n^2 A}+2\zeta\omega_n\frac{e_{\dot{x}}}{1/\omega_n A}+\omega_n^2\frac{e_x}{1/A} = 0 \tag{7.2}$$

which can be divided through by $\omega_n^2 A$ to give

$$e_{\ddot{x}} = -e_x - 2\zeta e_{\dot{x}} \tag{7.3}$$

The relations between the derivatives are

$$e_{\dot{x}} = \omega_n \int_0^t e_{\ddot{x}}dt+0 \tag{7.4}$$

and

$$e_x = \omega_n \int_0^t e_{\dot{x}}dt + e_x|_{t=0} \quad \text{where} \quad e_x|_{t=0} = -1\,\text{C.U.} \tag{7.5}$$

Equation (7.3) is satisfied by having gains of unity at the inputs of amplifier 1, and equation (7.4) and (7.5) by making the gains of the integrators equal, and of value greater than the maximum ω_n.

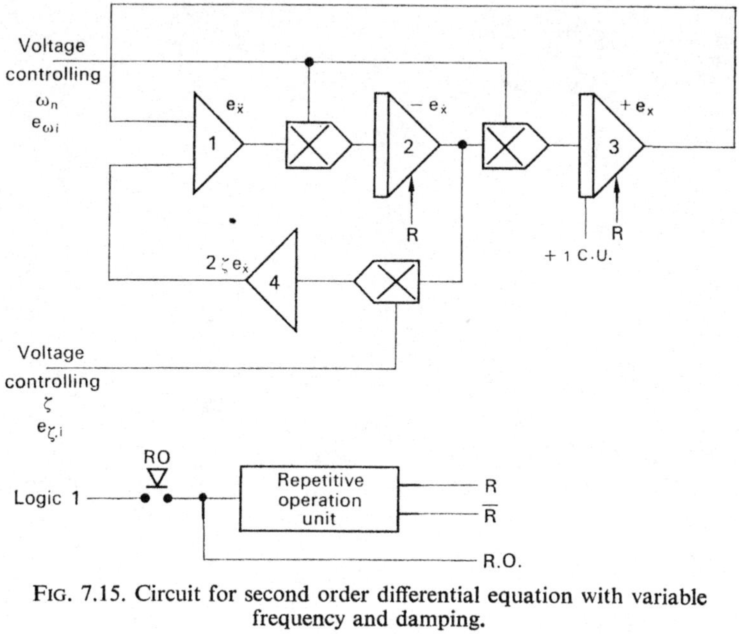

FIG. 7.15. Circuit for second order differential equation with variable frequency and damping.

Variation of ω_n is obtained by controlling the gains of the two multiplier units preceding the integrators, in the range 0 to 1. As ζ will always be less than 0·5 the gain of 2ζ is obtained using the third multiplier.

Measurement of T and control of ω_n. This can be carried out using the circuit of Fig. 7.16. To measure *T*, amplifier 5 integrates a constant voltage during the time e_x is going from its initial value to 0, and is then put into HOLD. The integrated voltage $e_{T(i-1)}$ is therefore proportional to *T*. This is compared with a voltage $e_{T,S}$ proportional to the required value of *T*, and the difference appears at the output of amplifier 6. Amplifiers 7 and 8 are connected as an accumulator circuit, and at the end of each COMPUTE period a proportion of the output of amplifier 6 is added to the output of amplifier 8. This sets the gain of the multipliers

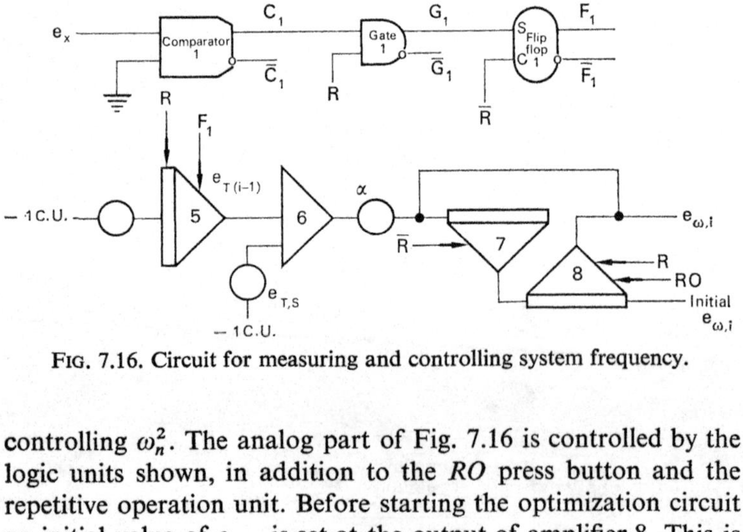

FIG. 7.16. Circuit for measuring and controlling system frequency.

controlling ω_n^2. The analog part of Fig. 7.16 is controlled by the logic units shown, in addition to the *RO* press button and the repetitive operation unit. Before starting the optimization circuit an initial value of $e_{\omega(i)}$ is set at the output of amplifier 8. This is necessary to give the circuit a value of ω_n^2 to start from. When the *RO* button is pressed, amplifier 8 goes to STORE with the initial value of $e_{\omega(i)}$ and the repetitive operation unit starts. At the beginning of each COMPUTE period amplifier 5 starts integrating from zero. When e_x crosses zero, amplifier 5 is put into HOLD and it must stay in HOLD for the rest of the COMPUTE period. The logic signal which puts it into HOLD must not therefore be affected by e_x crossing zero at later times. The zero crossing is detected by comparator 1 and the logic 0 to logic 1 transition of C_1 is used to set flip-flop 1. To ensure that the flip-flop cannot be set by spurious signals during RESET, C_1 is only gated to the flip-flop when R is logic 1. The flip-flop is cleared during the RESET period, by the signal.

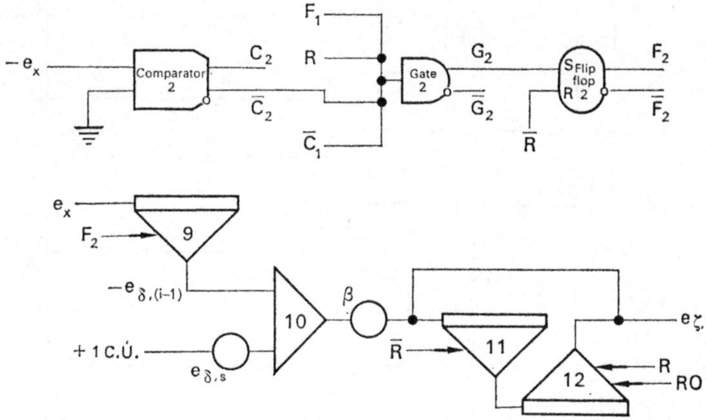

FIG. 7.17. Circuit for measuring and controlling system damping.

Measurement of δ and control of the damping ratio. One possible circuit for doing this is shown in Fig. 7.17. The system output is tracked by amplifier 9 during the first part of the COMPUTE period, and when it reaches the peak of the first undershoot the amplifier goes to STORE until the beginning of the RESET period. The peak value of the undershoot $-e_{\delta(i-1)}$ which is stored is compared with a voltage e_δ calculated for the specified value of the damping

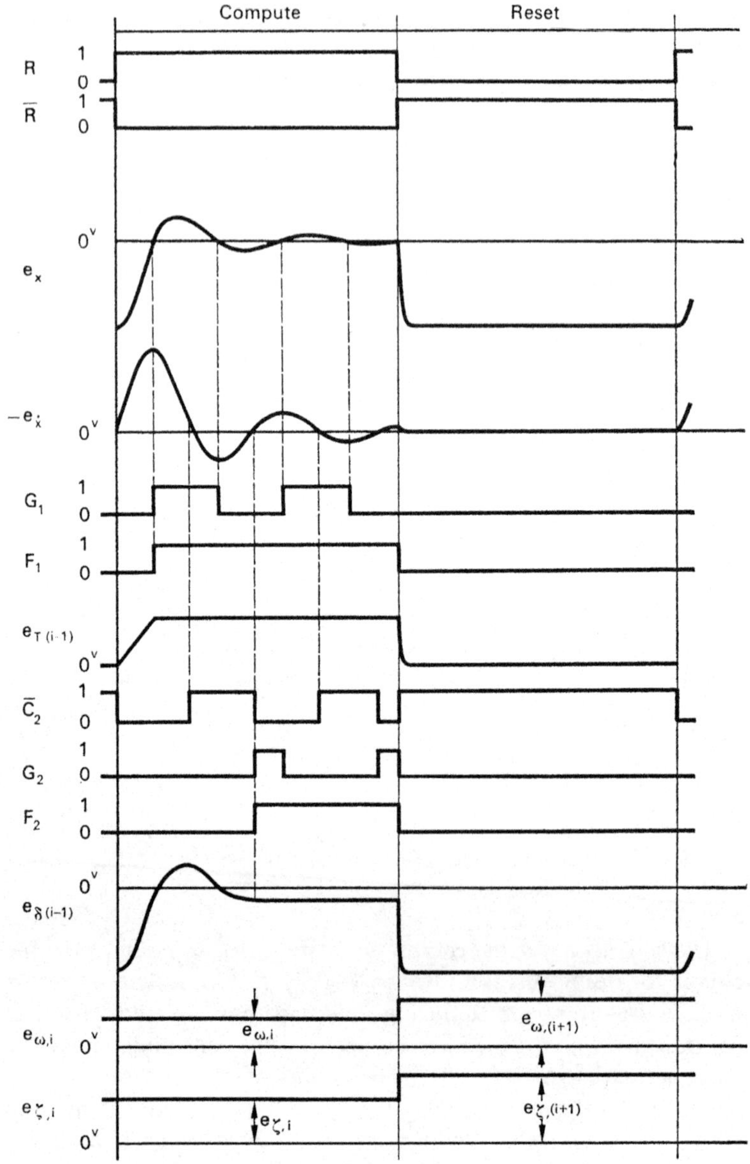

FIG. 7.18. Typical waveforms at outputs of units of Figs. 7.15, 7.16 and 7.17.

ratio. At the end of the COMPUTE period a fraction of the error is added to the output of the accumulator circuit, formed by interconnecting amplifiers 11 and 12. The output of amplifier 12 controls the gain of the multiplier which sets the value of 2ζ. This part of the circuit is controlled by the logic units shown in the figure, in addition to the *RO* push button, and the repetitive operation unit. An initial value of $e_{\zeta(i)}$, controlled by the *RO* push button, is set at the output of the accumulator circuit before the optimization is started.

As peak values of e_x occur when $e_{\dot{x}}$ passes through zero, due to the 90 degrees of phase shift between the signals, we can use the output from a comparator detecting these zero crossings to control the track-store unit tracking e_x. However, as there are a number of times that $e_{\dot{x}}$ crosses zero, we have to select the appropriate one. This can be done in a number of ways, and the method illustrated uses an AND gate, the output of which triggers a flip-flop. The $\bar{C}_1$ input to the gate ensures that the zero crossing detected is when e_x is negative, i.e. an undershoot, and the F_1 signal ensures that the zero $e_{\dot{x}}$ at the beginning of the COMPUTE period is ignored. The R input is just a precaution to make sure that the gate will only operate during the COMPUTE period. The first logic 0 to logic 1 transition at the output of gate 2 can therefore only be at the peak of the first undershoot of e_x, setting flip-flop 2, and switching amplifier 9 to STORE. Further operations of G_2 during the COMPUTE period cannot affect the flip-flop, which is cleared at the beginning of the RESET period. The accumulator circuit is controlled by the repetitive operation unit.

The gains of the control loops, which are set by the potentiometers in the inputs of the accumulator circuits, are selected to ensure convergence. As the interaction between damping ratio and frequency is small, the simple system of control works satisfactorily with the two loops operating at the same time. For a system where interaction between the variables being controlled was more severe, a more complex optimization procedure would be necessary. Waveforms obtained at various points in the circuit are illustrated in Fig. 7.18.

7.9. Use of Comparators and Digital-to-analog Switches for Function Generation

Apart from their use for interative operation of the analog computer, comparators, digital-to-analog switches and logic units can be useful for generating special functions. A particular area of application is in the generation of functions with discon-

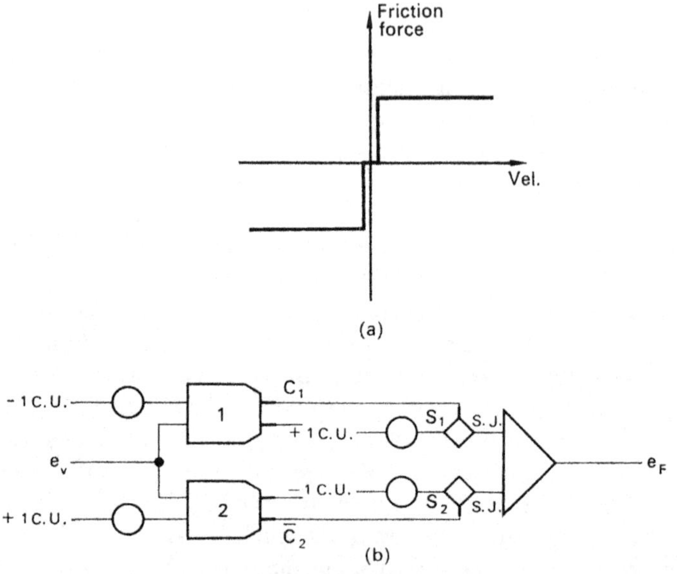

FIG. 7.19. Approximate static friction characteristic and circuit for simulating it on the computer.

tinuities. A good example is in the study of mechanical systems, where it is often necessary to simulate an approximation to static friction effects, as shown in Fig. 7.19(a). The circuit of 7.19(b) gives more satisfactory results than the pure analog simulation. When the voltage e_v, proportional to the system velocity, is zero, the comparators are biased so that the two digital-to-analog switches are open, and the voltage eF, proportional to the friction force, is zero. When e_v is positive or negative, switch 1 or switch 2 is closed and an appropriate value of e_F is switched in. The dead zone can be adjusted to very low values. Another similar example is the simulation of relay characteristics, of the form shown in Fig. 7.20(a), which exhibit both dead zone and hysteresis effects. A possible circuit for

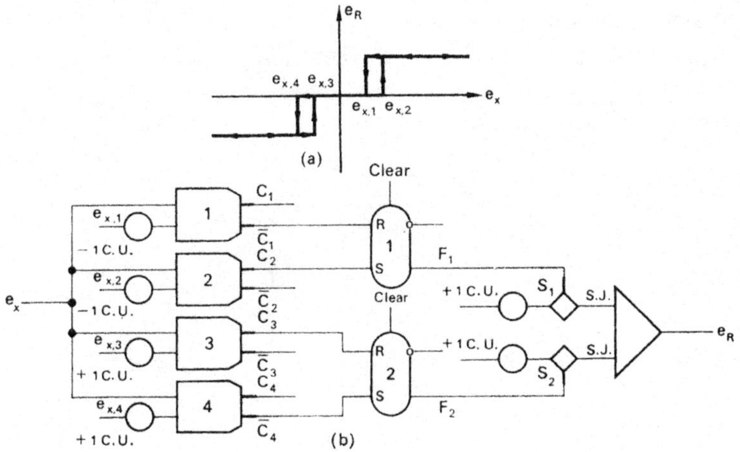

FIG. 7.20. Relay characteristic and circuit for simulating it on the computer.

simulating this is shown in Fig. 7.20(b). Comparators are used to detect each of the switching points and their outputs control set-reset flip-flops operating the two digital to analog switches. The operation of the circuit is as follows. Initially, with e_x equal to 0 the two flip-flops are cleared, the switches S_1 and S_2 are open and e_R is equal to 0.

If e_x increases in the positive direction:

at $e_{x,1}$, $\overline{C}_1$ goes from 1 to 0, F_1 stays 0, S_1 is open.

at $e_{x,2}$, C_2 goes from 0 to 1, F_1 goes from 0 to 1, S_1 closes.

When e_x reverses:

at $e_{x,2}$, C_2 goes from 1 to 0, F_1 stays 1, S_1 is closed.

at $e_{x,1}$, $\bar{C}_1$ goes from 0 to 1, F_1 goes from 1 to 0, S_1 opens.

If e_x increases in the negative direction:

at $e_{x,3}$, C_3 goes from 1 to 0, F_2 stays 0, S_2 is open.

at $e_{x,4}$, $\bar{C}_4$ goes from 0 to 1, F_2 goes from 0 to 1, S_2 closes.

When e_x reverses:

at $e_{x,4}$, $\bar{C}_4$ goes from 1 to 0, F_2 stays 1, S_2 is closed.

at $e_{x,3}$, C_3 goes from 0 to 1, F_2 goes from 1 to 0, S_2 opens.

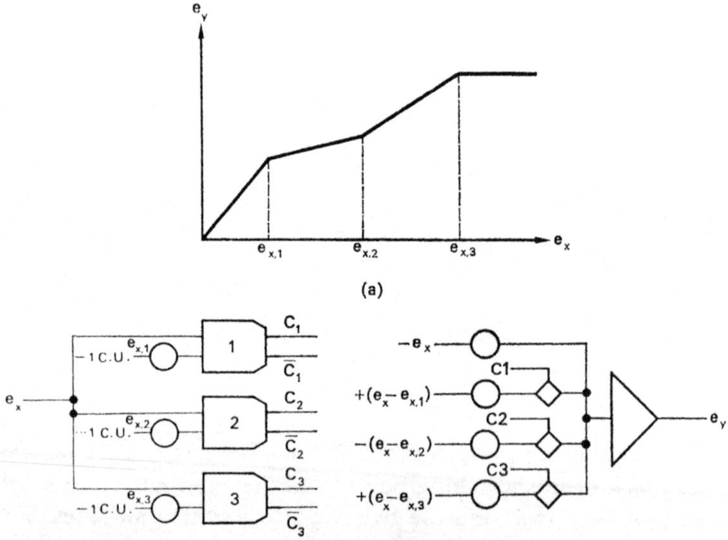

FIG. 7.21. Use of comparators and digital-to-analog switches for function generation.

Another way of implementing this simulation would be to use two comparators as in Fig. 7.19, but with the level of the bias supplies controlled by digital-to-analog switches operated from the comparator outputs. This would be arranged so that with e_x equal to 0 the comparators would be biased to $e_{x,2}$ and $e_{x,4}$. When the modulus of e_x exceeded either of these values the appropriate comparator would operate, and as well as closing the appropriate switch to give a voltage e_R, it would open a switch reducing its bias voltage to $e_{x,1}$ or $e_{x,3}$.

For generating curves where only a few breakpoints are necessary for accurate simulation, comparators operating digital-to-analog switches to control the breakpoints and slopes are convenient, easy to set up and change. Figure 7.21 illustrates the method, where the comparators are used to switch additional inputs in parallel to the amplifier, depending on the value of e_x, to give the required function.

This method of function generation is of course only possible on the larger computers, where a plentiful supply of comparators and switches are available.

CHAPTER 8

Hybrid Computing

It is difficult to obtain agreement on what the term hybrid computer really means. It is sometimes used when referring to an iterative analog computer, more generally when referring to the combination of a general purpose analog computer with a digital computer and sometimes for special purpose computers with units which are digital in operation but have analog input and output signals. As the second case is the most widely accepted this is what we will be mainly concerned with in this chapter.

The question immediately arises: Why do we want a hybrid computer? The simplest answer to this is that certain problems arise which cannot be solved satisfactorily on either analog or digital computers but which can be broken down in such a way that a combination of the two types of machine will give a more accurate solution.

8.1. Comparison of Analog and Digital Computers

If we consider the advantages and disadvantages of the two types of machine we will see some of the reasons for considering linking them together. First let us look at the analog computer. Its main advantage is of course its speed of operation. Being a parallel type of machine with all units operating at the same time, problem solutions appear in real time, and in many cases time scaling can be introduced so that they can be obtained in a much contracted time interval. The solution of linear, nonlinear and time-varying differential equations present few difficulties, the more complex problems only requiring a larger number of computing units. The machine is relatively easy to program, although the scaling of the equations and patching could be considered rather tedious. However, once the problem has been satisfactorily set up on the computer, the performance of the system described by the equations can be thoroughly and easily investigated for a wide range of conditions and parameter values. The form of presentation of the solutions is good, giving a clear insight into the behaviour of the system being studied, and the ease of operation means that the person originating the problem can run the computer himself. This is often more satisfactory than working through an intermediary.

There are of course many disadvantages. Accuracy is limited by the manufacturing tolerances of components, and the performance of the electronic elements changes with time and environment. As a result, individual linear units have a best accuracy of slightly better than 0·01% and nonlinear units between 0·1% and 0·01%. Because of noise problems and measuring difficulties, it is not possible to resolve with any confidence voltages less than 0·01% of full scale, so that the dynamic range of the variables is limited to four decades. Similarly for time scales, although a range of frequency over five decades is possible, three is a more realistic limit. Because of these limitations, scaling of equations becomes very important. Other limitations which are frequently encountered are the lack of long-term storage capability and the difficulties of simulating transport delays and functions of more than one variable.

Now let us consider the digital computer, first looking at its advantages. The accuracy with which it can handle numbers is only limited by the word length, and for a twenty-four bit word a one bit change is equivalent to a resolution of one part in 10^7. Expressed as a percentage of full scale, as in the analog computer, this is equivalent to a static accuracy of 10^{-5}%. It is good at solving algebraic equations and has large storage capacity with no limit on the storage time. Simulation of transport delays and multivariable functions present few difficulties.

The main disadvantage is of course the serial mode of operation.

As there is only one arithmetic unit, this has to be shared by all the required operations. As a result, although individual operations can be carried out very quickly, because a large number are required the time to calculate one point of a solution can be quite long. This means that in the solution of differential equations, where it is necessary to calculate a large number of points per cycle of the solution frequency, if high accuracy is to be obtained, solutions can only be in real time if the frequencies are very low. For problems of medium complexity efficiently programmed on a fast modern machine, solution accuracies better than on an analog computer can only be obtained at frequencies below 2 Hz. Another difficulty which can arise is instability of integration routines. Operated in the normal way with results presented as a table of numbers, does not give the operator the same insight into the problem as obtained when using an analog computer. Also, changing parameter values is more difficult. Some of these difficulties can be overcome by improvements in the communication terminals provided for the machines.

Comparing the advantages and disadvantages of the two types of computer, it becomes obvious that they complement each other for many functions. Some form of marriage should therefore be possible, to try and exploit a combination of the best features of each machine.

8.2. Hybrid Computing Systems

Let us consider a number of ways by which we could arrive at a form of hybrid computer. We can of course start with either a digital computer or an analog computer and see what steps we could take to improve its performance.

Starting with a basic analog computer, the first steps in the direction of a hybrid machine were the incorporation of patchable digital logic and flexible control of the analog elements. This is of course the type of machine which has been described in the previous chapter under the title of iterative analog computer. The method of incorporating digital logic into the analog computer has very limited expansion capability, as programming of large numbers of logic units by patching is too complex and too much time is wasted in getting programs to operate satisfactorily. Where a large amount of logic is required, it is much more convenient to incorporate it in the form of a digital computer which is relatively easy to program.

Starting with a digital computer, the first steps towards hybrid were to find easier and more convenient methods of programming the machine, to make using it more attractive to the engineer with a background in analog computing. To do this one has to look at the features of the analog computer which attract the engineer, who wants a model of the system he happens to be investigating. In the analog computer, once the equations have been programmed on to it the operator can identify parts of the physical system with blocks of units in it. In a sense he tends to forget that he is working with a computer, and thinks in terms of the physical system he is investigating, the variation of voltages at the amplifier outputs being looked upon as the variation of the physical quantities. Also, system parameters which are represented by potentiometer settings can be easily changed, and their effects on the system behaviour seen immediately. Using the normal method of solving differential equations on a digital computer, where the program is fed in on punched tape or cards and results come out as a mass of printed figures, is a much less attractive proposition. It becomes necessary to find some means of programming the digital computer so that it simulates the operation of an analog computer. If this can be done and the engineer is given a communication terminal with the computer which allows him to run the problem himself, have a means of displaying outputs from any part of the system, either on a cathode ray oscilloscope or a plotting table, and easily change parameter settings by typing in new values, then he will no longer be interested in what kind of hardware is being used and will be as happy with the digital computer as with the analog. There has been a lot of interest in this approach, evidenced by the large number of simulation languages which have been developed for digital computers, and are being widely used.

Quite a large number of these languages were originally developed for checking analog computer solutions, but once developed were retained for carrying out similation in their own right. The list of languages which have been developed is too long to list here, so only some of the better known ones will be mentioned. One of the most widely used was originated by the Martin Company in the United States. Originally known as DAS, standing for Digital Analog Simulator, it had a very rudimentary form of integration routine. Further work was carried out at the Wright Patterson Airforce Base developing the language, the main improvements being to the integration routine. This modified language was known as MIDAS, standing for Modified Integration DAS, and was very widely used. The most recent version of this language is known as MIMIC. A language produced by Scientific Data Systems for their computers is known as DES 1, standing for Differential Equation Solver 1. A feature of this language is the number of integration routines available. Another language rivalling MIDAS in popularity was developed by I.B.M. for their machines and known as PACTOLUS. A more recent language DSL/90, standing for Digital Simulation Language, was introduced for their 7094 computers. European work in this field that has become well known is the APACHE code, standing for Analog Programming and Checking. This was developed at Euratom to carry out all the work associated with programming and checking of an analog computer. The second version of this program was developed for running on an I.B.M. 7090 digital computer for setting up and checking Electronic Associates 231R analog computers. Later versions of the program are more general and are able to cope with any analog computer, the structure of the machine being written into the program. The program is designed so that problems can be stated in a symbolic language which is very similar to the mathematical statement of the problem. The output from the program gives:

1. Equations scaled for the analog computer.
2. A description of the patch-panel interconnections.
3. A deck of cards for input to a semi-automatic patching device.

4. A static check value for each element.
5. A deck of cards, which with outputs from units of the analog computer, read under static check, will be submitted to APACHE for checking and diagnosis of faults.
6. Output of a digital simulation of the original problem.

Recently a working party of the British Computer Society has developed a new program APSE, Analog Programming and Scaling of Equations, written in ALGOL and FORTRAN. This can be easily modified to run on any digital computer for any analog computer.

At the present time the development of hybrid computing is by the analog computer manufacturers and users, who know how useful analog computers are, but also are fully aware of their limitations. As a result, the present generation of hybrid machines cannot be considered as fully integrated systems, consisting as they do of a general purpose analog computer and digital computer linked through an interface system. The analog computing section still has to be programmed by interconnecting units on a patchboard. If hybrid computing is going to be widely accepted, it will be necessary to design a new generation of fully integrated machines, where the programming is all carried out at one console, and interconnection of the analog units is carried out automatically. The operator would then be able to use the analog computer rather like a sub-routine which could be called up by the program as required. Such a system would be much more acceptable to the present generation of digital computer users, who do not want to get involved with the hardware of the computer in the way that is necessary on analog machines. To develop a hybrid computer of this form presents many difficulties, both from the hardware and programming points of view, but if they can be overcome the result would be a very powerful computing facility. Some work is going on in this field. In the United States, Professor Karplus at the University of California has for some time been operating a hybrid system used for solving partial differential equations. The analog part of the system consists of passive electrical networks, and the digital computer is used to take measurements of voltages and currents at the output nodes and calculate new values for the voltages and currents at the input nodes. Another research project called AIDER is being carried out at the University of Berlin. AIDER stands for analog implemented differential equation solving routine. This was briefly described by Professor Giloi in a survey paper given at the fifth

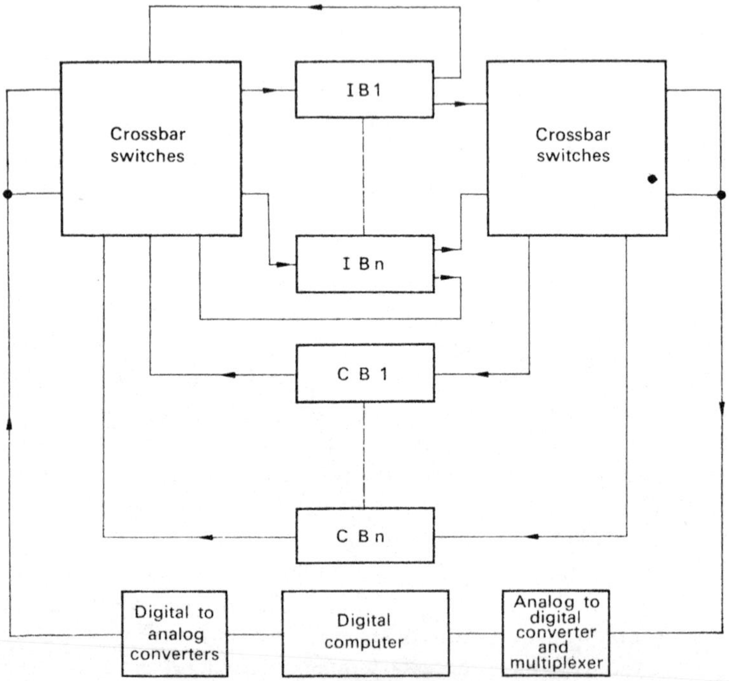

FIG. 8.1. Block diagram of AIDER system.

congress of the Association Internationale pour le Calcul Analogique at Lausanne in 1967. The object of this project is to study the possibility of having fast differential equation solving subroutines, implemented by analog hardware, in a digital computer. Their biggest problem is the automatic patching, which could involve a prohibitive amount of switching circuitry. The approach to this has been to minimize the number of switched interconnections by having groups of units connected together. It probably means having redundant units, but this can be justified if the continuing reduction in the price of hardware with the advent of more complex integrated circuits is borne in mind. They are using two types of computing blocks, integration blocks, referred to as IB's and coupling branches referred to as CB's. The integration blocks consists of two integrators, two summers and six servo set potentiometers and the coupling branches contain a number of nonlinear elements. The blocks are interconnected through two banks of crossbar switches, the interconnection being controlled by the digital computer. A schematic of the set up is shown in Fig. 8.1.

8.3. Present Generation Hybrid Computers

We will now consider in more detail the present generation of hybrid computers. As stated earlier, we are referring to the interconnection of general purpose analog and digital computers by means of suitable interface units.

A diagram of a typical hybrid computer linkage is shown in Fig. 8.2. This can be considered in two parts, the exchange of

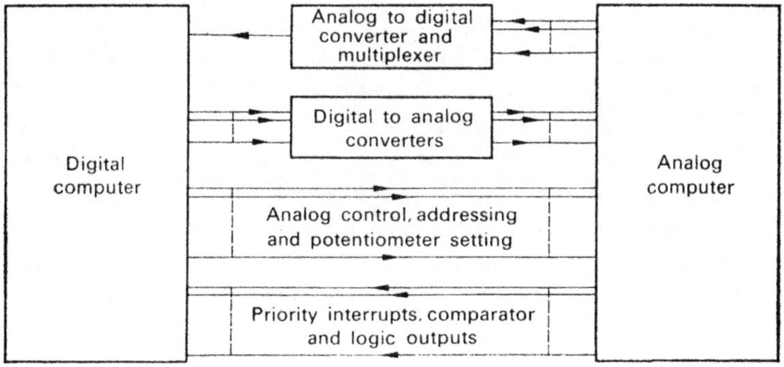

FIG. 8.2. Hybrid computer interface.

computer signals and control signals. As the analog computer operates with continuously varying voltages and the digital computer with discrete numbers, it is necessary to provide analog-to-digital and digital-to-analog conversion facilities. Depending on the type of problem which is being solved, there will be the requirement for about up to thirty of each type of conversion channel. As accurate analog to digital converters with high conversion rates are expensive, only one is normally provided, and this is shared between the channels by means of a multiplexer unit. This switches between the channels with a maximum speed depending on the speed of conversion of the converter. If n channels of analog-to-digital conversion are required, then the maximum rate each channel can be sampled is the converter conversion rate divided by n, unless provision is made for scanning some channels more frequently than others. Digital-to-analog converters are relatively inexpensive so that, although multiplexing could be used, it is more usual to have a converter for each channel. Different types of converters which can be used are described in the next section. One of the problems associated with conversion is the error which can be introduced by analog outputs not all being sampled at the same time and inputs not all being updated at the same time. The first one is because of the multiplexing and can be eliminated by having track-store units on each analog output line switched to store at the same instant and later scanned by the multiplexer. The second is due to the digital computer outputs coming in series. This can be eliminated by the digital-to-analog converters having buffer registers which are updated in series, but are transferred in parallel to the converter registers. The other main error is the time delay introduced by the conversion processes and the processing time in the digital computer. Various means of minimizing this by using phase advance networks and predictive digital extrapolation are used, but it cannot be eliminated completely. More research is necessary into methods of correcting for it.

Control signal channels are necessary in both directions. From the digital to the analog computer they are for controlling the setting of potentiometers, addressing of analog unit outputs, operation of check routines, control of integrators, track-store units, digital-to-analog switches, and the patchable digital logic. They are also used for control of the converters, so that information is fed into or out of the digital computer store on a cycle stealing basis or on command from the program. From the analog to the digital computer they are to take comparator decisions, digital logic outputs and overload signals as interrupt signals. These are programmed on a priority basis to call for servicing by the digital computer or changes in the digital computer program.

8.4. Analog-to-digital and Digital-to-analog Converters

If the maximum advantage is to be obtained from a hybrid computer, it is essential that when transferring signals between the two machines the introduction of errors should be minimized as much as possible. In order to do this it is essential that high quality conversion units are used. The best accuracy for individual units of the analog computer is 0·01%, so we should use converters with at least this accuracy. The conversion rate required will be dictated by the processing speed of the digital computer and the type of problem being solved. In some cases where the amount of digital processing is small, information could be accepted at quite high rates. In such cases a high rate of conversion will be required, particularly from the analog-to-digital converter which is multiplexed between a number of channels. Converters of the successive approximation type are available with accuracies of 0·01% and conversion rates up to 50,000 per second. The digital-to-analog converters introduce no difficulties as far as speed of conversion is concerned. Conversion rates in excess of 100,000 per second are easily obtainable.

Digital-to-analog converters. A basic arrangement is shown in Fig. 8.3 and consists of a resistor network R_1 to R_n which has one end of all the resistors connected together and to a reference voltage and the other ends connected through switches to the summing junction of an amplifier. The switches are controlled by flip-flop outputs, which are set by the digital word being converted. The resistor values are weighted according to the significance of the bits in the digital word controlling the associated switches. The amount of current in R and hence the voltage at the amplifier output are proportional to the value of the digital

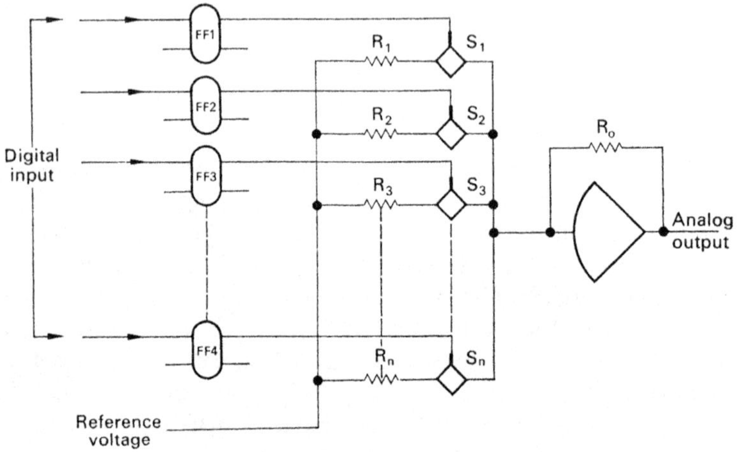

FIG. 8.3. Circuit of digital-to-analog converter.

word. The conversion time depends on the speed of operation of the switches and the settling time of the amplifier. For slow-speed converters reed relay switches with operate times of 0·5 msec are suitable, but for high-speed operation solid state switches, probably field effect transistors, would be used. These have operate times less than a μsec, so the settling time of the amplifier, which may be several μsec, is the limiting factor. In some converters, other configurations of resistor networks are used, but the basic idea is the same.

Analog-to-digital converters. The basic arrangement of a successive approximation type of converter is shown in Fig. 8.4(a) and a typical waveform appearing at the output of the digital-to-analog converter during a conversion cycle in Fig. 8.4(b). This is a feedback type of converter, the output of the digital-to-analog

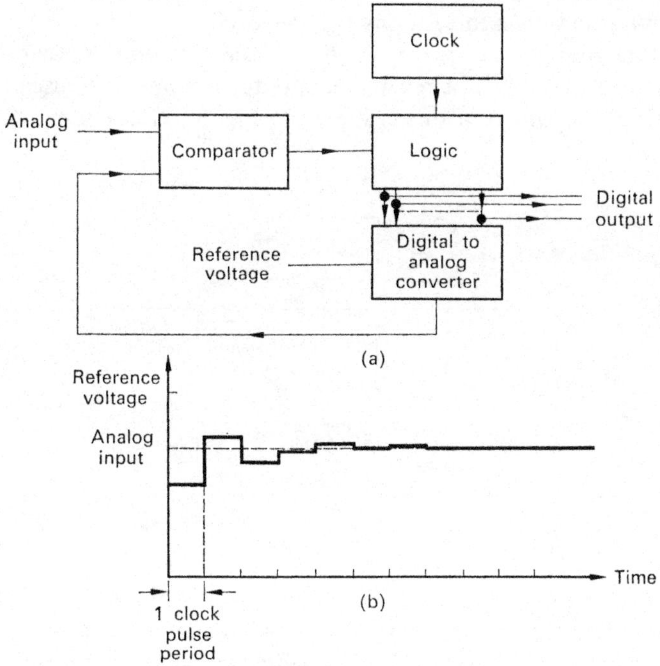

FIG. 8.4. Successive approximation analog-to-digital converter.

converter being compared with the analog input. The logic sets up the digital output by successively dividing the voltage range in half. On the first clock pulse the sign of the voltage is checked, on the second the output is set to half scale and, depending on the sign of the comparator output, to quarter or threequarter scale on the third clock pulse. On succeeding clock pulses the digital output converges on the value of the voltage level being converted. To convert to an accuracy of n bits requires only $n+1$ clock pulses. The accuracy is limited by the accuracy of the resistors and switches in the digital-to-analog converter, and the resolution of the comparator. For use with a multiplexer, this type of converter is the most commonly used. Starting from zero on each conversion, fast convergence is obtained and the time of conversion is the same for any voltage level.

If a converter is being fitted in each channel another type based on the use of a reversible counter is sometimes used. The basic arrangement of this is shown in Fig. 8.5. Depending on the

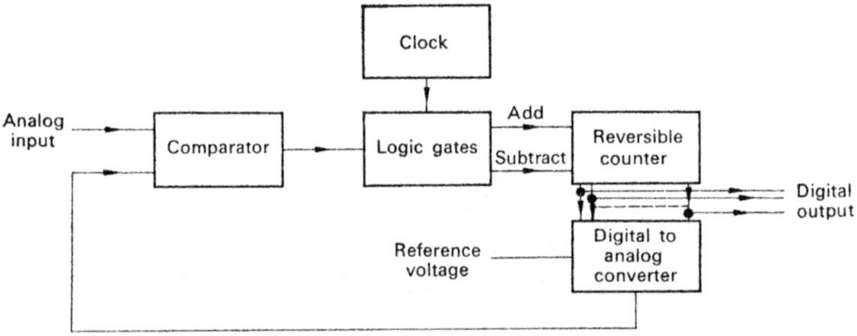

FIG. 8.5. Analog-to-digital converter using reversible counter.

sign of the comparator output, clock pulses are gated to either the add or subtract inputs of a reversible counter. As a result, the contents of the counter are incremented or decremented until the output of the digital-to-analog converter equals the analog input. The output of the counter is then a digital representation of the analog input level. An advantage of this type of converter is that it can operate continuously, and where the analog signal is varying the contents of the counter will be automatically updated to follow it. There is, however, a limitation on the rate at which the analog input can change if successful tracking is to be achieved. If the converter accuracy is 0·01%, then the maximum rate of change of the converter is 0·01% of the maximum voltage per clock period. For a 10 V converter with a 1 MHz clock rate this gives a maximum slope of 1000 V/sec. If the input is a 10 V sine wave of frequency ω rad/sec, it has a maximum slope of 10ω V/sec. Therefore the maximum value of ω the converter can follow is 100 rad/sec. Faster tracking can be achieved by increasing the clock rate or decreasing the accuracy. When tracking has been achieved, a digital read-out can be obtained in one clock period.

8.5. Applications of Hybrid Computers

Hybrid computing can be divided into two broad areas:

1. Analog computation under digital control.
2. Combined computation, where part of the problem is solved on the digital computer and part on the analog computer.

Under the first heading we have automatic setting up and running of the analog computer and control of complex iterative problems. Under the second heading we have problems, parts of which require very high accuracy, beyond the state of the art of the analog computer, and other parts requiring computing speed beyond the state of the art of digital computers.

Analog computation under digital control. For a complex simulation problem, a large number of man-hours are required for scaling, patching and checking out the analog computer set-up. The use of a digital computer linked to the analog computer, so that it can address and monitor unit output values, and control the setting of potentiometers and integrator modes, will result in a considerable reduction in the number of setting up man-hours required. If a program such as APSE is available for the digital computer, the setting up procedure can be carried out by relatively inexperienced people. The amount of time required to obtain results once the computer has been set up can be reduced by continual use of the digital computer for changing potentiometer settings and reading out results. Its use will probably result in better records being kept, as at any time when changes are made, it is easy to get the computer to print out potentiometer settings and outputs.

In some problems, once the system has been simulated on the analog computer, it is necessary to carry out a large number of runs on the simulated system, with varying parameters and inputs. A good example of this is the investigation program which could be carried out on a simulated missile system. The missile would be fired against a target aircraft whose flight path would vary from run to run. The missile would have random initial errors and in-flight disturbances and the object of the program would be to obtain an analysis of the miss distances obtained over a large number of runs. Such a program would be very tedious if each run had to be programmed and the results taken and analysed manually. With a hybrid computer, the digital computer would be programmed to control the running of the analog computer, change parameters, store, analyse, and print out the results.

The above form of control of the analog computer could be considered as open loop control, as changes in the analog set-up are made as a result of a predetermined program. There is another mode of control which could be referred to as closed loop control. In this case measurements are made on the system during each analog computer run, and these are fed into the digital computer and analysed. As a result of the analysis, values of the system parameters and initial conditions are changed for the next computer run. An application of this is the field of system optimization which we have already briefly considered in the chapter on iterative analog computers. The use of a digital computer instead of patchable logic allows more complex systems to be investigated and more complex optimization strategies to be implemented. We have previously defined what the basic optimization problem is, and Fig. 8.6 shows a block diagram of an optimizer system. The block SYSTEM EQUATIONS would be set up on the analog computer and the other three blocks programmed on the digital computer. To minimize or maximize the criterion function F, it is necessary to have some program for adjusting the values of the system parameters α_i, where i has values 1 to n. One possible method is to vary each parameter in turn by a small trial amount, measure the effect on F, and hence calculate approximate slope components $\Delta F/\Delta\alpha_i$ for each parameter direction. The values of these slopes are stored, and when they have all been evaluated they are used to determine the amounts $\Delta\alpha_i$ by which the parameters are to be adjusted for the next computer run. If an improvement in F is obtained, the parameters are again updated by the previously calculated $\Delta\alpha_i$ and another run made.

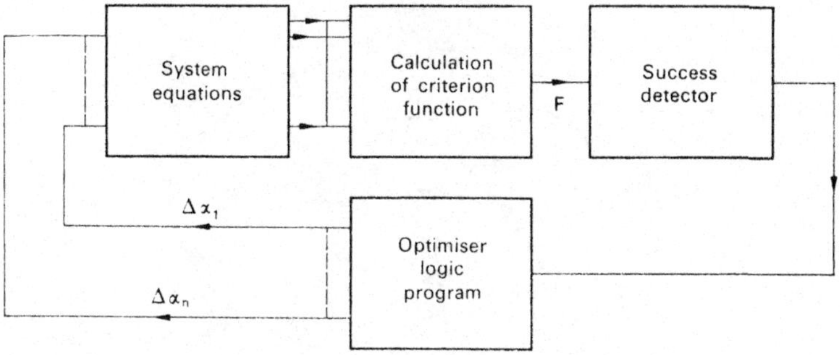

FIG. 8.6. Block diagram of optimization system.

As long as F continues to be improved the parameters are updated in the same direction. When as a result of a change in α_i, F goes in the wrong direction, the α_i are returned to the previous values and a new set of slope components are obtained. The process is continued until no further improvement in F is obtainable. Figure 8.7 shows typical paths by which a two parameter system might reach an optimum value of F. The contours are formed by joining points at which the values of F are equal. The optimization process can therefore be considered as a hill-climbing operation.

There are many problems associated with such an optimization method. It can run into difficulties if the criterion function is not well behaved but has discontinuities, ridges and narrow valleys. Another method which has been used to get over some of these difficulties, is to vary the parameters in a random manner instead of estimating a set of slope components. In this case a random set of $\Delta\alpha_i$ are selected and the α_i updated. A run is made on the analog computer and F is evaluated. If an improvement is obtained the step is confirmed, otherwise the α_i are returned to the previous state and another random set of $\Delta\alpha_i$ selected. When an improvement in F is obtained, a bias is introduced which affects future selections of $\Delta\alpha_i$. It is claimed that randomly perturbing α_i in this way can result in rapid convergence of F to an optimum value.

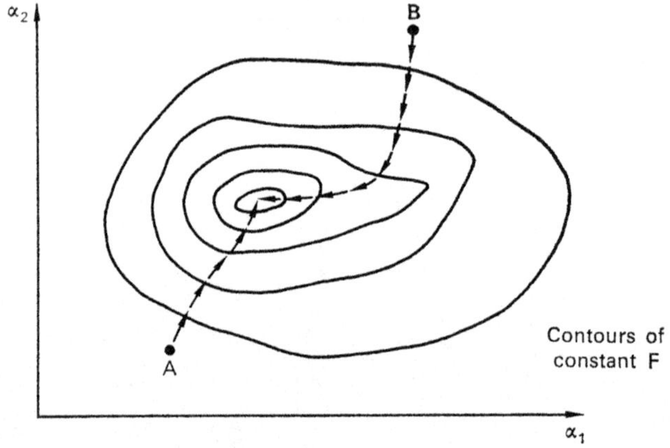

FIG. 8.7. Constant F contours for two-parameter system with typical optimization paths.

Combined computation. Operating the hybrid computer in this mode, the problem is split up in such a way that the analog computer solves those parts of the problem which involve high frequencies, but where the accuracy requirements are not high, and the digital computer solves the low-frequency high accuracy parts. A good example of this type of problem is the simulation of space vehicle missions in real or faster than real time. This naturally breaks into two sections, the dynamic response of vehicle attitude and the trajectory calculations. The calculation of the vehicle dynamics particularly for faster than real time computation involves frequencies which the digital computer cannot follow, whereas the accuracy requirements for the trajectory equations are beyond the capability of the analog computer. The vehicle dynamics equations are therefore set up on the analog computer and pose no problems either from the static or dynamic accuracy point of view. The trajectory equations are solved on the digital computer, but here even though the static accuracy is adequate, the accumulation of round off and integration truncation errors over a long period of time can build up appreciable inaccuracies.

Other examples of combined computation are optimization or adaptive control problems where the system, which can be simulated on the analog computer, is operating continuously. Because of variations in the system inputs or its environment, it is necessary to have some form of controller, which is simulated on the digital computer, to vary system parameters so as to maintain the criterion function at a maximum or minimum. Such problems arise in process control systems, where the quality of a product has to be maintained in spite of variations in the input raw materials, and in aircraft autopilots which have to adapt to changes in the aircraft responses which vary with different flight conditions.

The availability of a hybrid computer can result in considerable rethinking on ways of solving problems which previously had been tackled with limited success using a wholly analog or digital approach. Because of the difficulties which arise in generating functions of more than one variable or pure time delays on an analog computer, many problems which would best be solved on it have either to be over-simplified or else solved by purely digital means. On a hybrid computer functions of more than one variable can be obtained from the digital computer using look-up tables and time delay can be obtained by quantizing the signal, storing it in the digital computer and reading it out at the end of the required time.

It may be possible to obtain faster and perhaps better solutions of some types of partial differential equations on a hybrid computer. Quantization would be carried out in one direction only and the analog computer used to solve continuously in the other direction, if necessary iteratively. The analog solution would be stored in quantized form in the digital computer and then reconstituted into analog form again to compute the next step in the quantized direction.

APPENDIX 1

Derivation of a Generalized Form for Second Order Differential Equations

FOR the mass spring damper system of Fig. 3.1 the equation of motion for the mass is

$$M\frac{d^2x}{dt^2}+D\frac{dx}{dt}+Kx = y \qquad \text{(A1.1)}$$

The solution of this equation is in two parts:

(a) The complementary function x_1, which is the solution of equation (A1.1) when $y = 0$.

(b) The particular integral x_2, which is the steady-state solution.

The complete solution is therefore

$$x = x_1+x_2$$

For x_1, let us suggest a solution of the form

$$x_1 = Ae^{st}$$

where A and s may be complex, i.e. $A = a+jb$ and $s = \alpha+j\omega$. Differentiating, we have

$$\frac{dx_1}{dt} = sAe^{st}$$

and

$$\frac{d^2x_1}{dt^2} = s^2Ae^{st}$$

Substituting into equation (A1.1) for the case when $y = 0$, we get

$$Ms^2Ae^{st}+DsAe^{st}+KAe^{st} = 0 \tag{A1.2}$$

We can divide through by Ae^{st} as it is never zero.

Therefore

$$Ms^2+Ds+K = 0 \tag{A1.3}$$

Equation (A1.3) is the auxiliary equation for equation (A1.1) and its roots are

$$s = -\frac{D}{2M}\pm\sqrt{\left[\left(\frac{D}{2M}\right)^2-\frac{K}{M}\right]}$$

There are three possible cases:

(a) $$\frac{K}{M} > \left(\frac{D}{2M}\right)^2$$

(b) $$\frac{K}{M} = \left(\frac{D}{2M}\right)^2$$

(c) $$\frac{K}{M} < \left(\frac{D}{2M}\right)^2$$

For case (a) the roots are complex

$$s = -\frac{D}{2M}\pm\sqrt{\left[\frac{K}{M}-\left(\frac{D}{2M}\right)^2\right]}$$

Let

$$\frac{D}{2M} = \alpha \quad \text{and} \quad \sqrt{\left[\frac{K}{M}-\left(\frac{D}{2M}\right)^2\right]} = \omega$$

Therefore $s = -\alpha\pm j\omega$ and we have the complementary function

$$x_1 = A_1e^{(-\alpha+j\omega)t}+A_2e^{(-\alpha-j\omega)t}$$

where A_1 and A_2 are arbitrary constants

$$= e^{-\alpha t}(A_1e^{j\omega t}+A_2e^{-j\omega t}) \tag{A1.4}$$

Expanding the exponentials $e^{j\omega t}$ and $e^{-j\omega t}$ and combining terms, we get

$$x_1 = e^{-\alpha t}(B_1 \cos \omega t + B_2 \sin \omega t) \tag{A1.5}$$

where $B_1 = (A_1 + A_2)$ and $B_2 = j(A_1 - A_2)$.

If the right-hand side of equation (A1.1) is a step function of y units applied at time $t = 0$, the steady-state solution is the value of x as t tends to infinity. As t tends to infinity, d^2x/dt^2 and dx/dt tend to 0, and therefore x tends to y/K. The value of the particular integral x_2 is therefore y/K. We therefore have the complete solution of equation (A1.1)

$$x = x_1 + x_2$$

$$= e^{-\alpha t}(B_1 \cos \omega t + B_2 \sin \omega t) + \frac{y}{K} \tag{A1.6}$$

To evaluate B_1 and B_2 we consider the initial conditions of equation (A1.1). At $t = 0$ before y is applied

$$x = 0$$

and

$$\frac{dx}{dt} = 0$$

Differentiating equation (A1.6)

$$\frac{dx}{dt} = -\alpha e^{-\alpha t}(B_1 \cos \omega t + B_2 \sin \omega t)$$

$$+ e^{-\alpha t}(-\omega B_1 \sin \omega t + \omega B_2 \cos \omega t) \tag{A1.7}$$

Substituting for $t = 0$ in equations (A1.6) and (A1.7) we get

$$B_1 = -\frac{y}{K}$$

and

$$B_2 = \frac{\alpha B_1}{\omega}$$

$$= \frac{\alpha y}{K\omega}$$

Hence

$$x = \frac{y}{K}\left[1 - e^{-(D/2M)t}\left\{\cos\left(\sqrt{\left[\frac{K}{M} - \left(\frac{D}{2M}\right)^2\right]}\right)t - \frac{D/2M}{\sqrt{\left[\frac{K}{M} - \left(\frac{D}{2M}\right)^2\right]}}\sin\left(\sqrt{\left[\frac{K}{M} - \left(\frac{D}{2M}\right)^2\right]}\right)t\right\}\right] \quad \text{(A1.8)}$$

When the damping is zero, i.e. $D = 0$,

$$x = \frac{y}{K}\left[1 - \cos\sqrt{\left(\frac{K}{M}\right)}\,t\right] \quad \text{(A1.9)}$$

The mass therefore oscillates with constant amplitude $\pm y/K$, about a point $x = y/K$, with a natural frequency $\omega_n = \sqrt{(K/M)}$.

For the case when $K/M = (D/2M)^2$, the roots of the auxiliary equation are equal. No oscillation can occur in the system which is said to be critically damped.

Let us define a non-dimensional damping ratio denoted by ζ, where

$$\zeta = \frac{\text{actual damping coefficient in the equation}}{\text{damping coefficient which gives critical damping}}$$

The damping coefficient is D/M, and for the case of critical damping we have $(D/2M)^2 = K/M$.

The undamped natural frequency of the system $\omega_n = \sqrt{(K/M)}$. Therefore, for the critically damped case

$$\frac{D}{M} = 2\omega_n$$

Hence

$$\zeta = \frac{D/M}{2\omega_n}$$

or

$$\frac{D}{M} = 2\zeta\omega_n$$

We can therefore write equation (A1.1) in terms of ζ and ω_n:

$$\frac{d^2x}{dt^2}+2\zeta\omega_n\frac{dx}{dt}+\omega_n^2 x = \frac{y}{M} \tag{A1.10}$$

Any second order differential equation may be expressed in this generalized form. The solution of equation (A1.1) can be written in terms of ζ and ω_n as

$$x = \frac{y}{K}\left\{1-e^{-\omega_n\zeta t}\left[\cos\omega_n[\sqrt{(1-\zeta^2)}]t-\frac{\zeta}{\sqrt{(1-\zeta^2)}}\sin\omega_n[\sqrt{(1-\zeta^2)}]t\right]\right\} \tag{A1.11}$$

which becomes for the case of $\zeta = 0$

$$x = \frac{y}{K}[1-\cos\omega_n t] \tag{A1.12}$$

APPENDIX 2

Standard Symbols for use in Analog and Hybrid Computer Flow Diagrams

THE following symbols are now generally used for the preparation of analog and hybrid computer flow diagrams.

ELEMENT	SYMBOL	FUNCTION	NOTES
Signals		Analog Digital	Distinction between analog and digital signals only when both types required on one diagram
High gain amplifier	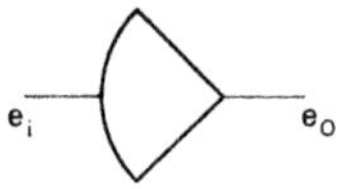	$e_O = -ke_i$	k is the amplifier gain
Summer	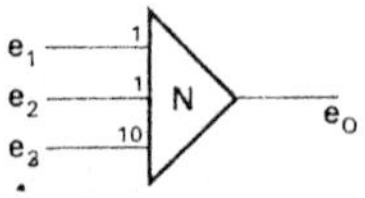	$e_O = -[e_1 + e_2 + 10e_3]$	N is amplifier number. Inputs direct to summing junction can be marked S.J.
Standard integrator	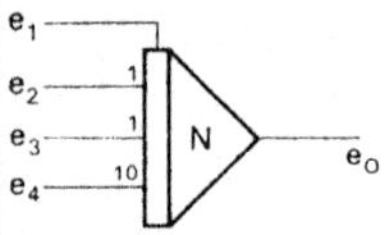	$e_O = -\int_0^t (e_2 + e_3 + 10e_4)dt - e_1$	N is amplier number. e_1 is initial condition input Standard integrator when all integrators in problem controlled from same source
Integrator with mode control indicated	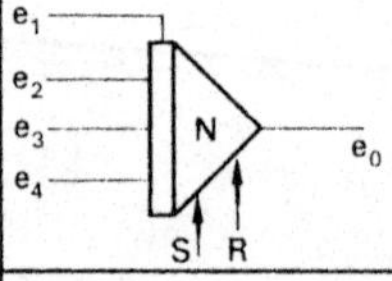	Reset when S=R=Logic 0 Compute when S= Logic 0 R= Logic 1 Hold when S=R=Logic 1	Use when integrators in problem controlled from different sources. When hold mode not used S input not shown
Track-store unit	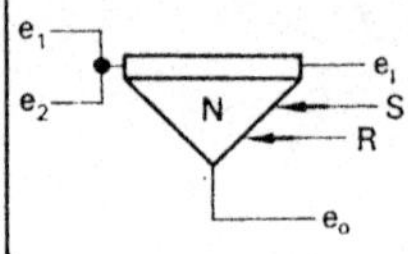	S=0 R=1 Set $e_o = -e_i$ S=1 R=0 e_o Tracks the sum $-(e_1+e_2)$ S=1 R=1 e_o stores value at time R goes from 0 to 1 or if R = 1 value at time S goes from 0 to 1	If unit has no initial Initial condition circuit S input not required

ELEMENT	SYMBOL	FUNCTON	NOTES
Potentiometer	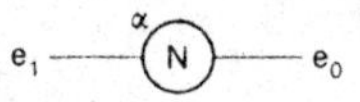	$e_0 = \alpha e_1$	Potentiometer set with load connected α is between 0 and 1
Multiplier	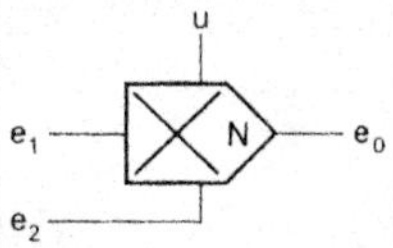	$e_0 = \frac{e_1 e_2}{u}$ u is computer reference voltage	N is multiplier number e_1 and e_2 are measured in volts u input is not generally shown
Divider	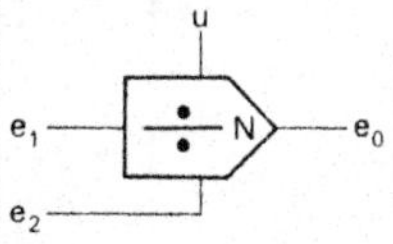	$e_0 = u \frac{e_1}{e_2}$ u is computer reference voltage	N is divider number e_1 and e_2 are measured in volts u input is not generally shown
Function generator	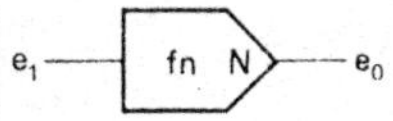	$e_0 = fn(e_1)$	N is function generator number When possible, standard mathematical symbols can be used instead of fn
Comparator	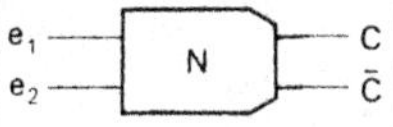	C = logic 1 if $(e_1+e_2)<0$ = logic 0 if $(e_1+e_2)<0$	N is comparator number
Digital to analog switch	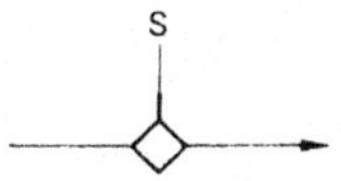	S = logic 0, switch open S=logic 1, switch closed	

ELEMENT	SYMBOL	FUNCTION	NOTES
Feedback limiter	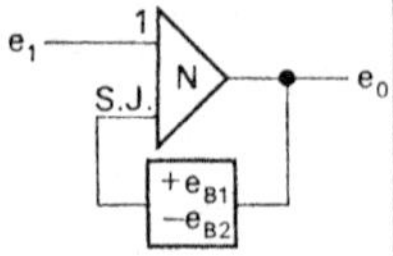	$-e_{B2} < -e_1 < e_{B1}$ $e_0 = e_1$ $-e_1 < -e_{B2}$ $e_0 = -e_{B2}$ $-e_1 > +e_{B1}$ $e_0 = +e_{B1}$	N is amplifier number
Analog to digital converter	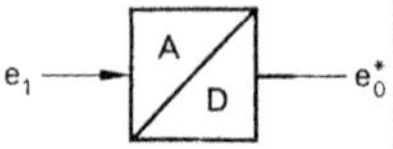	e_0^* is a digital word version of e_1	* Indicates binary number
Digital to analog converter	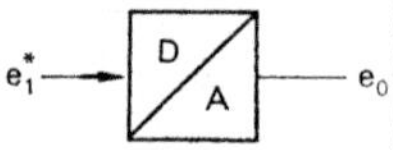	e_0 is quantized analog signal derived from successive digital words e_1^*	* Indicates binary number

Bibliography

BEKEY, G. A. and KARPLUS, W. J. *Hybrid Computation*. John Wiley & Sons, Inc., New York, 1968.

ETERMAN, I. I. *Analog Computers*. Pergamon Press, Oxford, 1960.

FIFER, S. *Analog Computation*, Vols. 1–4. McGraw-Hill, New York, 1961.

HOLLINGDALE, S. H. and TOOTILL, G. C. *Electronic Computers*. Penguin Books Ltd., England, 1965.

HUSKEY, H. D. and KORN, G. A. (editors). *Computer Handbook*. McGraw-Hill, New York, 1962.

JACKSON, A. S. *Analog Computation*. McGraw-Hill, New York, 1960.

JOHNSON, C. L. *Analog Computer Techniques* (2nd edition). McGraw-Hill, New York, 1963.

KARPLUS, W. J. and SOROKA, W. W. *Analog Methods* (2nd edition). McGraw-Hill, New York, 1959.

KORN, G. A. and KORN, T. M. *Electronic Analog and Hybrid Computers*. McGraw-Hill, New York, 1964.

LEVINE, L. *Methods for Solving Engineering Problems using Analog Computers*. McGraw-Hill, New York, 1964.

MACKAY, D. M. and FISHER, M. E. *Analog Computing at Ultra-high Speed*. Chapman & Hall Ltd., London, 1962.

PAUL, R. J. A. *Fundamental Analog Techniques*. Blackie, London, 1964.

PETERSON, G. R. *Basic Analog Computation*. The Macmillan Company, New York, 1967.

REKOFF, M. G. *Analog Computer Programming*. Charles E. Merrill Books, Inc., Columbus, Ohio, 1967.

ROGERS, A. E. and CONNOLLY, T. W. *Analog Computation in Engineering Design*. McGraw-Hill, New York, 1960.

STEWART, C. A. and ATKINSON, R. *Basic Analog Computer Techniques*. McGraw-Hill, London, 1967.

Index